Christ
and the
Patriarchs

Christ

and the

Patriarchs

New Light from
Apocryphal Literature and Tradition

ADAM

MOSES

ABRAHAM

NOAH

Marcus Von Wellnitz

International Standard Book Number
0-88290-164-8

Library of Congress Catalog Card Number
80-83035

Horizon Publishers Catalog and Order Number
2045

Printed and Distributed in the
United States of America
by

Horizon
Publishers &
Distributors

P.O. Box 490
50 South 500 West
Bountiful, Utah 84010

Introduction

Much has been written about the ancient patriarchs and about the Christ, but most all the information concerning them comes from the canonical writings in the scriptures. Yet, we know that not all they said and did was recorded in the Bible as we have it today. The Jews and the early Christians in the Near East circulated many other writings and traditions about them which were not captured in holy writ but which are, nevertheless, valuable and fascinating to read.

Many of these stories and teachings in the apocryphal literature are only marginally true or are distorted and corrupt. These were, for obvious reasons, not included in the canon of the authorized texts. Other manuscripts, however, seem true and contain much valuable historical and doctrinal data. They were deliberately excluded from canonization because they were, for one reason or another, displeasing to the compilers of scriptural material.

The purpose of this manuscript, then, is to make available to the interested reader some information about the patriarchs and Christ from apocryphal writings and traditions. This study is by no means exhaustive or complete, and makes no claim of doctrinal accuracy. The items included have been selected in view of their novel information and their interesting charm, particularly in reference to the Christian reader.

Marcus von Wellnitz

Contents

Abraham 65

Moses 105

Jesus Christ 153

Adam

Of all the ancient patriarchs, none has received more attention from the ancient writers of apocryphal literature than Adam, whom they present as the father of the human race. Their writings are filled with insights which add much to our understanding of his life and mission.

The Creation of Adam

A reference to the eternal nature of Adam before the physical creation of the body can be found in the *Clementine Recognitions*:

> But after all these things He made man, on whose account He had prepared all things, whose internal species is older, and for whose sake all things that are, were made.[1]

Kenas, an early prophet, saw the spirits of men walking in a spirit place, waiting for this world to be created to come down and live in it. (In *Pseudo-Philo*, 28:8). Enoch also talks about the souls of men which existed before the creation of the earth (II. Enoch 23:4).

There is an ancient text in which Adam himself mentions that he was involved in the creation process:

> I have created at the command of the Father. . . all things that are seen in the sky and on earth; it was I who created them all at the command of the Father.[2]

The idea that Adam could have been born like other human beings is alien to most of the apocryphal traditions. Therefore the emphasis is

---

1. Clement, *Recognitions,* I, 28. Reference to the pre-mortal life of Adam are rare, while those referring to Christ and mankind in general are quite common, for instance:
   > And I looked down from the mountain on which I stood to the sixth firmament, and there I saw a multitude of angels, of pure spirits without bodies. (*Apocalypse of Abraham,* 19)

   > I was a child of goodly kind, and had a good spirit; yea, rather because I was good, I came into a body undefiled. (*Book of Wisdom,* 8:19-20)

   > Penetrating through all bodies, illuminating the intellect of everyone, he gives them the urge to ascend towards the blessed region in which the intelligence dwelt before becoming flesh. (Pseudo-Zosimus, *Upon the Letter Omega*)
2. *The Installation of Michael,* Borgia Collection, No. 277.

placed on the creation of Adam's body from the dust of the earth. The Jews were eager to point out that God created everything by the power of his word except man, whom He created with his own hands (Gen. 2:7).[3] Some texts assert that Adam was created with two substances, namely earth and water,[4] while others support the idea of four:

> And they saw God's right hand spreading all over the world, and all his creations assembled in his hand. And then they saw how He took a speck of dust out of the earth, and a drop of water out of the waters, and a piece of wind out of the air, and out of the fire he took a bit of heat. And the angels saw how these four weak elements, cold, heat, dryness and moisture, were put into the palm of His hand, and then He created the Adam.[5]

We hear that it was necessary for man to be composed of these four elements, so that he could rule over them and, at the same time, be subject to them. Even the earth of which he was formed had to be gathered from the four corners of the globe, in order that any type of soil would take him back, wherever on the earth he might die.[6] All countries had to furnish materials for his creation.[7] His name was called Adam, perhaps because he was taken out of the earth.[8]

The place of creation was naturally assumed to have been the site of the later temple.[9] Whether this was also Eden is not quite clear. However, there are passages which mention that Adam was removed from the locality of creation to the garden of Eden.[10]

The first man was created in the image of God and was therefore very beautiful, though it was taught that he still looked like an ape compared to the divine personage.[11] Interestingly, according to Jewish writings,[12] Adam was not created as a baby but as an adult of twenty years of age. He was tall and perfect:

---

3. See Micha Josef bin Gorion, *Die Sagen der Juden,* I, 97; and also II. Enoch 44:1.
4. *Targum Yerushalmi:* Genesis 2:7
5. *The Cave of Treasures,* 2:6-9, in Riesler, *Altjüdisches Schrifttum ausserhalb der Bibel,* p. 942ff. On the four elements see also Philo, *Decalogue,* 8.
6. *Pirke de Rabbi Eliezer,* 2.
7. *Talmud: Sanhedrin,* 38a-38b.
8. There is still wide speculation as to the meaning of Adam. Adam = Adama (earth), such as also in the Latin *homo* (man) and *humus* (earth) and the Greek $\grave{\epsilon}\pi\iota\chi\vartheta\acute{o}\nu\iota os$ (man) and $\chi\vartheta\acute{\omega}\nu$ (earth). He is called Adam to honor the earth from which he was taken, or else the earth was called Adama to honor him, her first son. According to Josephus, Adam means red (*Antiquities of the Jews,* I, i, 2).
9. *Zohar,* 1, 34a: Ginzburg, *Legends of the Jews,* 1, 90, 101; *Pirke de Rabbi Eliezer,* 12.
10. *Palestinian Targum:* Genesis 2:15; *Pirke de Rabbi Eliezer,* ch. 12.
11. *Midrash Rabba: Leviticus* 20:2. It was even asserted that Adam had a tail like an animal but God removed it for the sake of man's dignity *(Midrash Rabba: Bereshith* 14:10).
12. *Midrash Rabba: Bereshith* 14:7.

> And God formed Adam with his holy hands, after his image and likeness. When the angels saw his glorious face they were moved by his beauty, for they saw his countenance, how it was engulfed like the brightness of the ball of the sun. The lustre of his eyes was like that of the sun and the light of his body like unto crystal.[13]

An interesting account of the creation depicts God as having been worried and hesitant to create man because of the troubles and pain he and his descendants would have to suffer. However, Christ offered himself as an advocate and redeemer for the cause:

> And He took the clay from the hand of the angel, and made Adam according to our image and likeness, and He left him lying for forty days and forty nights without putting breath into him. And He sighed over him every day, saying "If I put breath into him, he must suffer many pains." And I spoke to my Father, "Put breath into him, for I will be an advocate for him." And my Father said to me "If I put breath into him, my beloved son, you will have to go down into the world and suffer many afflictions for him before you will have redeemed him and will have caused him to return to his former estate." And I said to my Father: "Put breath into him, for I will be his advocate and I will go down into the world and I will fulfill your commandment." [14]

According to Jewish legends, Adam was placed in the garden forty days after his creation.[15] He was also endowed with power, authority and glory over all the works of creation.

> There he clothed himself in the robe of a king, and there he received the crown of glory upon his head. There he was also installed as prophet, priest and king and there the Lord placed him upon the throne of his glory, and there the Lord gave him dominion over all his creatures. And there all the wild beasts gathered together, and the animals and the birds appeared before Adam, and he gave them their names and they bowed their heads before him, and all their natures honored him and served him.[16]

He was also endowed with divine authority to act as God's representative or viceroy on earth:

> Everything shall be placed into your hand from now on and they [the animals] will fear you as they feared me.[17]

Adam was also instructed to give names to all the animals on the earth. For five or six days he seems to have been occupied with this task.

> And on the six days of the second week we brought, according to the word of God, to Adam all the beasts, and all the cattle, and all the birds, and everything that moves

---

13. *The Cave of Treasures*, 2:12-14.
14. *Discourse on the Abbaton*, 11b-12a, in Wallis Budge, *Coptic Martyrdoms*, pp. 474ff.
15. *Jubilees*, 3:9.
16. *The Cave of Treasures*, 2:17-21.
17. Bin Gorion, *Sagen der Juden*, I, 83.

in the water, according to their kinds, and according to their types: the beasts on the first day, the cattle on the second day, the birds on the third day, and all that which moves in the water on the fifth day. And Adam named them all by their respective names, and as he called them, so was their name.[18]

The recently found *Hypostasis of the Archons* describes the event thusly:

And the archons gathered together all the animals of the earth, and all the birds of the sky and they brought them before Adam to see what Adam would name them, and in order that he would give a name to each of the birds and all the animals.[19]

In another text this important incident is described by Christ himself:

Now it was Adam who gave names to all the cattle and to the wild beasts and to the birds, and to every living creature which moves upon the earth, and also to them which are in the water. To all of them did Adam give names in accordance with the command of my good Father.[20]

In one legend it appears that Adam himself had not received his own personal name yet, because Adam means simply 'man' or 'person.' The Lord therefore asked him, after he had named all the animals, what name he would give to himself, whereupon Adam responded that he would like to be called Adam.[21] Apparently, he also taught the animals during his stay in the garden.[22] He either had to understand their respective languages or all creations still communicated in one common tongue.[23]

The Creation of Eve

Eve was thought of as company for Adam and as a helper.[24] It seems from Jewish traditions that Eve was not created at the same time as was Adam, because he was supposed to ask specifically for her. He was evidently very lonely in the garden since the only company he had were the animals. He noticed that they were all in pairs of two, male and female, which caused him to ask the Lord for someone who would match up with

---

18. *Jubilees,* 3:1-2.
19. *Hypostasis of the Archons,* p. 136, lines 19-24.
20. *Discourse on the Abbaton,* 15a-15b; *The Conflict of Adam and Eve,* I, xxxiv, 7-8.
21. Ginzburg, *Legends of the Jews,* I, 80.
22. *Ibid.,* I, 77.
23. *Jubilees,* 3:28; See also Josephus, *Antiquities of the Jews,* I, i, 4; Clement, *Stromata,* 1:21; Philo, *Quaestiones in Genesis* 1:22-32.
24. The words "helpmeet for him" in the Bible should perhaps be better translated as "a helper matching him", see T. K. Cheyne, *Traditions and Beliefs of Ancient Israel,* p. 73.

him.[25] Another reason given was that the woman was not to be quite equal with Adam and therefore created a little later than the man.[26] Accordingly, Eve comes to be in this manner:

> God caused a sleep to come over him and he fell asleep. Then God took a rib from his diaphragm of his right side and made Eve out of it. When Adam awoke and saw her he was very pleased with her.[27]

Immediately upon awakening Adam embraced and kissed her.[28]

> And the Lord God caused a deep sleep to fall upon Adam and he slept, and He took for the woman one rib from those of him, and this rib was the origin of the woman from the ribs, and he closed up the flesh in its place and made the woman. And He woke up Adam out of his sleep and he arose on the sixth day, and He brought the woman to him and he saw her and said to her: This is bone of my bones and flesh of my flesh. She will thus be called by wife because she was taken out of her husband.[29]

The wedding between the two must have been a splendid affair. It was performed in the garden where God and angels attended amidst great jubilation and pomp.[30]

The Fall

The story of the fall is naturally treated with great interest by the ancient writers and commentators. It is quite an intriguing theme, and hardly an ancient text fails to refer to the deception of the first parents and their subsequent loss of glory.

It is Satan or Lucifer, who acts as the catalyst for the fall. It is he who was envious of the whole operation and the plan from the beginning and who lost his glory over his rebellious attitude and open claim for power and honor.

> And he, being full of pride, rose up in a shamefull manner and said: "It is right that this man Adam should come and worship me, because I existed before he came into being." And when my Father saw his great pride, and that his wicked deeds and evil doings had reached its limits, he ordered all the armies of heaven and said to them:

---

25. *Midrash Rabba Bereshith* 17:4. Thus Adam could later on not complain that God had given him Eve without that he wanted her.
26. Philo: *Quaestiones,* I, 20.
27. *The Cave of Treasures,* 3:11-13.
28. *Midrash Rabba Bereshith:* 23:5.
29. *Jubilees,* 3:5-6. According to Jewish legends Eve was made of Adam's third rib on the right side (*Targum Yerushalmi:* Genesis 2:21)
30. Ginzburg, I, 68.

"Remove the writing from the hand of the proud one, take off his armor, and throw him down to the earth for his time has now come. . . ."[31]

And one from out of the order of angels, having turned away with the order that was under him, conceived an impossible thought, to place his throne higher than the clouds above the earth, that he might become equal in rank to my power. And I threw him out from the height with his angels and he was flying in the air continuously above the bottomless.[32]

That Satan knew exactly what he was doing is attested to in the documents:

The devil sinneth from the beginning. None did before he did . . . Being good he turned devil because of his own free choice.[33]

He became different from the angels but his nature did not change, his intelligence as far as his understanding of righteous and sinful things.[34]

Satan is very eager to bring about the fall and thus have dominion on the earth. He wants to make it extremely difficult for the Father and his own brother, Jesus Christ, to find triumph and success in their plan to save the multitude of men on the earth. Satan desperately wants to be a god, even if it is only for a short period of time until the millennium. To accomplish his ambition he first had to manage the fall of his great adversary in the pre-existence, who was then Michael and now on the earth as Adam. Satan had been given the right to test men and he was determined to fully use this privilege, as Christ is claimed to have said:

I am a fisherman of men . . . the devil is also a fisherman, who catches many in his nets . . . If I have come to take for my kingdom those who are mine, why should he not do the same?[35]

Whether Satan appeared to the innocent Adam and Eve as Satan, that is, in his true nature, or whether he appeared in disguise as someone else or whether he used the serpent to speak for him, is not quite clear even in

---

31. *Discourse on the Abbaton,* 13b. That Satan was jealous of Adam, who is Michael, is also set forth in the Koran:

I will not adore Adam, for he is made of earth, and I of fire, therefore I am better than he. (Koran 7:11).

It was Michael who was in charge of evicting Satan from on high; therefore his great hate for Jehovah and Adam (Jude 1:9; Revelations 12:7) but not necessarily for the Father.
32. *II. Enoch* 29:3-4. See also Satan's attempt to set up his throne near to God's in the *Gospel of Batholemew,* 2:55.
33. Cyril of Jerusalem, *Catechetical Lectures,* I, 4. Interesting is also the account of the expulsion of Satan and his followers in the *Book of John the Evangelist* in M. R. James, *The Apocryphal New Testament,* pp. 188-189.
34. *II. Enoch* 31:4.
35. *Gospel of the Twelve Apostles,* in *Patrogia Orientalis,* 2:126-129.

the ancient traditions. In Hebrew writings Satan is usually associated with the serpent. It seems that Satan had to use the serpent since he had no body of his own and the snake was willing to let him use its tabernacle for the deception.[36] An interesting text shows how Satan deceived the serpent to join him in the conspiracy by promising him greatness and power:

> And the devil spoke to the serpent, saying, Arise, come to me, and I shall teach you a thing in which thou mayst be of service. Then the serpent came to him, and the devil said to him: I hear that thou art more sagacious than all the wild beasts, and I have come to make thy acquaintance, and I have found thee greater than all the wild beasts, and they associate with thee; notwithstanding thou doest reverence to one far inferior. Why eatest thou of the tares of Adam and his wife and not of the fruit of paradise? Arise and come hither and we shall make him be cast out of paradise through his wife, as we were also cast out through him. The serpent said to him: I am afraid lest the Lord be angry with me. The devil said to him: Be not afraid, only become my instrument and I will speak through thy mouth a word by which thou shalt be able to deceive him. . . .[37]

His objective, then, was to get man to eat of the fruit in the garden, of which the Lord had told the first couple not to partake. This so-called "forbidden fruit" is described in early Jewish and early Christian literature as either having been the fig, the nut, the wheat, the date or, most commonly, the grape out of which alcohol could be made.[38] However, we are also told that it is not revealed which fruit it was, lest men become prejudiced and look down upon the tree and its fruit which brought about our present condition.[39] One text refers to the fruit having had a wonderful fragrance which was very appealing and enticed Eve to partake.[40] The fruit of the tree of life is almost exclusively rendered as the olive, of which the oil becomes a symbol of health and vigor and healing.[41]

Of course, only Adam had been commanded not to partake of the fruit of the tree of knowledge of good and evil (Gen. 2:16-17), therefore Satan had to attempt to convince Eve that she should eat since she had not

---

36. "God hath given him power over those who do answer him," *Apocalypse of Abraham,* 14.

37. *Apocalypse of Moses,* in *Ante-Nicene Fathers,* VIII, p. 566.

38. For the fig, nut and wheat see Ginzburg, *op. cit.,* V, 98 (For the wheat there is probably the explanation that the words for wheat (חטה) and sin (חטא) resemble each other). For the date (date wine?) see *Enoch* 24:4, 25:5.

For the grape (alcohol) see *Enoch* 32:4; *Talmud Sanhedrin:* 99a; *Midrash Rabba Bereshith:* 15:7; bin Gorion, *op. cit.,* I, 87. Wine is therefore the fruit of the fall of mankind but also the fruit of the redemption (sacrament ordinance). As so often, the same substance brings about two different conditions, dependent on how it is used.

39. See *Midrash Rabba Bereshith:* 15:7.

40. *Zohar,* Bereshith, 36a.

41. For instance, *II Enoch* 8:7, 22:8, 66:2; 5. Ezra 2:12; *Gospel of Nicodemus,* 18; Clement, *Recognitions,* I, 45; Origin, *Contra Celsum* 6:27; *Vitae Adae,* 24-39; *Apocalypse of Moses,* 9-12.

expressively been forbidden to use the fruit.[42] According to the apocryphal traditions, Satan enticed Eve to eat and become as God lest the Lord would perhaps create another woman to do it.[43] He also persuaded her to partake by telling her that even God himself had become God by means of the fruit:

> God ate of the tree and so built the world. Therefore eat you of it and also build a world.[44]

In one account he even partakes of the fruit himself to show Eve that nothing harmful would follow: "As I do not die of eating the fruit, so you will not die." [45] With so much encouragement from him, Eve finally consents and eats. Immediately she saw the angel of death approaching and she knew the implication. But she assumed that she would have to die immediately and so she ran quickly to give part of the fruit to Adam lest she would die and he would be left alone in the garden.[46] In the famous *Apocalypse of Moses* the story is told by Eve to her children and grandchildren:[47]

> Then Satan came in the form of an angel, and praised God as did the angels, and looking out from the wall, I saw him like an angel. And he said to me: Art thou Eve? And I said to him: I am. And he said to me: What dost thou in paradise? And I said to him: God has set us to keep it, and to eat of it. The devil answered me through the mouth of the serpent: Ye do well, but you do not eat of every plant.

Here then follows the familiar story of Eve's explanation that they had been forbidden to eat of the one fruit, whereupon Satan answers:

> As God liveth, I am grieved for you, because you are like cattle. For I do not wish you to be ignorant of this; but rise, come hither, listen to me, and eat, and perceive the value of the tree. . . .

Eve was naturally hesitant, but Satan made the whole affair very appealing and desirable, and finally Eve consented:

> And I opened to him and he came inside into paradise and went through it before me. And having walked a little, he turned, and said to me: I have changed my mind, and I will not give thee to eat. And this he did wishing at last to entice and destroy me.

---

42. Ginzburg, *op. cit.*, III, 85.
43. *Midrash Rabba Bereshith:*19:4.
44. *Zohar: Bereshith*, 36a. Bin Gorion, *op. cit.*, I, 88, mentions a legend in which God himself drank of the fruit (wine?) and thus became wise and consequently a God.
45. Ginzburg, *op. cit.*, I, 73.
46. bin Gorion, *op. cit.*, I, 94.
47. The following quotes in the text are from the *Apocalypse of Moses*, in *Ante-Nicene Fathers*, VIII, 566-567 (hereafter cited as *ANF*)

And he said to me: Swear to me that thou wilt also give to thy husband. And I said to him: I know not by what oath I shall swear to thee, but what I know I say to thee; By the throne of the Lord, and the cherubim, and the tree of life, I will give also to my husband to eat. And when he had taken the oath from me, then he went and ascended upon the tree.[48]

Another version also worth quoting can be found in a discourse by bishop Timothy of Alexandria:[49]

And the serpent himself came at the hour of evening to receive his food according to his wont, for the serpent was like unto all the beasts, and he walked upon his feet just as did they. And the devil lived nigh unto paradise, and he lay in wait for Adam and Eve by day and by night, and when he saw Eve by herself he went into the serpent, and said within himself: Behold, I have found my opportunity; I will speak into her ear, and I will make her eat of the tree, and I will cause them to be expelled from Paradise, for I myself was expelled from Paradise for their sakes.[50]

The familiar story progressed here which culminated into the actual partaking of the forbidden fruit:

And the serpent said to her: Ye shall not surely die, but ye shall be like unto these gods, ye shall know the good and the evil, and ye shall be able to separate the sweet from the bitter. God spake unto you in this manner because when ye have eaten thereof ye shall become as gods. And the devil ceased not to speak into her ear until he had beguiled her and she ate of the tree.

After Adam had seen what had happened, the following dialogue ensued:

And he said unto her: Wherefore hast thou acted in this wise? Behold from this day forward we shall die, and God will be wroth with us, and He will cast us forth from Paradise. And Eve said unto him: Come thou and eat. If God shall blame thee, I will take everything upon myself before God. And in this way Adam took, ate, and he became naked, and he knew immediately that he was naked.

As they realized that they were naked both tried to cover themselves with leaves. Jewish legends report that none of the trees in the garden was willing to let Adam and Eve have leaves from their branches, except the fig

---

48. Interesting in this story is the point that Satan was outside of the paradise and evidently could not enter unless someone opened it up for him and let him in. This correlates with the belief that Satan has no power except that which we give him when he entices us.

49. *Discourse on the Abbaton,* 16a-17b.

50. Interesting again is the idea that Satan lived outside of the paradise, that the serpent had arms and legs like any other animal, and that he waited for revenge on account of his being expelled from paradise (the pre-existent realm).

tree which approved of their search for knowledge and realized the importance of their decision.[51]

All the other animals also had to experience a fall. According to Jewish tradition, then, the rest of the creatures did not automatically fall into mortality with the fall of Adam and Eve but had to partake of the fruit in like manner. Therefore, Eve is found in some of the ancient stories as going about in the garden, giving all the animals of the fruit.[52] The fall of the animal world is thusly described:

> And on that day was closed the mouth of all the beasts, and of cattle, and of birds, and whatever walks, and of whatever moves, so that they could no longer speak: for they had all spoken one with another with one lip and with one tongue. And he sent out of the garden of Eden all flesh that was in the garden of Eden, and all flesh was scattered according to its kinds, and according to its types unto the places which had been created for them. And to Adam alone did He give to cover his shame, of all the beasts and cattle.[53]

Josephus reports that the Lord was quite angry over what had happened:

> God said: I had before determined about you both, how you might lead a happy life, without any afflictions and care and vexation of the soul; and that all things which might contribute to your enjoyment and pleasure should grow up by my providence, of their own accord, without your own labor and pain, which labor and pain would soon bring on old age, and death would not be at any remote distance; but now thou hast abused my good will, and hast disobeyed my commands; for thy silence is not the sign of virtue, but of evil conscience.[54]

All three actors in the episode of the fall were cursed with some kind of punishment. Adam is first:

> God said to Adam: Since thou hast disobeyed my commandment, and obeyed thy wife, cursed is the ground in thy labors. For wherever thou laborest, it will not give its strength, thorns and thistles shall raise for thee, and in the sweat of thy face shalt thou eat thy bread. and thou shalt be in distress of many kinds. Thou shalt weary thyself, and rest not, thou shalt be afflicted by bitterness, and shalt not taste of sweetness, thou shalt be afflicted by heat, and oppressed by cold, and thou shalt toil much, and not grow

---

51. R. Graves and R. Patai, *op. cit.*, p. 77. See also the *Apocalypse of Moses*, in *ANF*, VIII, 567.

52. *Midrash Rabba Bereshith:* 19:5; *Pirke de Rabbi Eliezer*, ch. 14; *Apocalypse of Moses*, in *ANF*, VIII, 566. Only the bird Malham refused to partake and was therefore the only creature which retained its immortality (the basis of the legend of the Phoenix bird?).

53. *Jubilees*, 3:28-30. That the speech of animals was taken is also found in the *Conflict of Adam and Eve*, I, 18, and in Philo, *Quaestiones in Genesis*, 1:32.

54. Josephus, *Antiquities of the Jews*, I, i, 4.

rich; and thou shalt make haste, and not attain thy end; and the wild beasts, of which thou wast lord, shall rise up against thee in rebellion, because thou hast not kept my commandment.[55]

That Adam became mortal and thereby subject to the slow decay and eventual loss of most of the body functions, such as seeing, hearing, etc., had been made clear to him:

> And He said: Since thou hast forsaken my covenant, I have brought upon thy body seventy plagues. The trouble of the first plague is the injury of the eyes; the trouble of the second plague, of hearing, and so, in succession, all the plagues shall overtake thee.[56]

Another text agrees:

> Behold, I will bring upon thy body seventy blows; with divers griefs shalt thou be tormented, beginning with thy head and thine eyes, and thine ears, down to thy toenails and in every limb.[57]

Eve was also cursed by the Lord following her decision to disobey:

> Since thou hast obeyed the serpent, and disobeyed my commandment, thou shalt be in distress and unbearable pains, thou shalt bring forth children with great tremblings, and in one hour shalt thou come to bring them forth, and loose thy life in consequence of thy great straits and pangs . . . And thou shalt turn again unto thy husband and he shall be thy lord.[58]

In addition, in another story, Eve was to cover her head whenever she is near a holy place. This is to serve as a reminder of the disobedience and as a symbol of mourning, pain and distress.[59] Finally it is the serpent's turn to receive punishment:

> Since thou hast done this and hast become an ungracious instrument . . . cursed art thou of all the beasts. Thou shalt be deprived of food which thou eatest; and dust shalt thou eat all the days of thy life; upon thy breast and belly shalt thou go, and thou shalt be deprived of thy hands and feet; there shall not be granted thee an ear, nor wing, nor one limb. . . .[60]

---

55. *Apocalypse of Moses*, in *ANF*, VIII, 567-568. That Adam did not do well by obeying Eve is also mentioned in *Pirke de Rabbi Eliezer*, ch. 14:

> Thou shouldst not have obeyed her, for thou art the head, not she.

56. *Ibid.*, p. 565.

57. *Vita Adae*, 34:1.

58. *Apocalypse of Moses*, in *ANF*, VIII, 568. Both Adam and Eve receive the exact same punishment: labor (עצבון), either physical toil or the bearing of children. The same Hebrew word is used for both punishments.

59. bin Gorion, *op. cit.*, I, 96.

60. *Apocalypse of Moses*, in *ANF*, VIII, 568.

That the serpent walked on two legs, that he was as tall as a camel and also very beautiful and smart, is a common Jewish teaching.[61] However, all this was lost and his legs and his language were gone.[62] Because it told lies, even its tongue was split into two parts.[63] Another interesting speech by the Lord to the serpent is this one:

> I created you to be king over all animals, cattle and the beasts of the field, but you were not satisfied. Therefore you shall be cursed above all cattle and above every beast of the field. I created you of upright posture, but you were not satisfied. Therefore you shall go on your belly. I created you to eat the same food as man, but you were not satisfied. Therefore you shall eat dust all the days of your life. You wanted to cause the death of Adam in order to espouse his wife. Therefore I will put emnity between you and the woman.[64]

Satan, of course, is quite happy with the way his plan turned out. For a short time on earth he becomes ruler of the earth and can reign as he pleases. In an old text he tells Adam after the fateful incident:

> O Adam, I was cast forth from my glory because of thee, and behold, I have caused thee to be expelled from paradise . . . because thou didst cause me to become a stranger to my home in heaven. Know thou that I shall never cease to contend against thee and all those who shall come after thee until I have taken them down into Amente with me.[65]

There are varying statements as to the duration of time which Adam and Eve spent in the garden of Eden. They range from five and a half hours to seven years.[66] One story mentions that they did not have to leave the garden until forty-five days after the fall.[67] Upon the command of the Lord the angel were to see to it that Adam and Eve had to leave the garden, but Adam pleaded with them to let him stay for just a moment in order that he might ask the Lord for mercy. Immediately the cherubim felt sorry for the two and permitted them to remain while they prayed for forgiveness. However, the Lord appeared and questioned the cherubim about their neglect of duty:

---

61. Ginzburg, *op. city.*, I, 71-72.

62. *Ibid.*, I, 73.

63. *Ibid.*, V, 101.

64. *Midrash Rabba Bereshith*: 20:4-5. The serpent aspired to more than he was supposed to. He gambled, and lost and did not receive what he had coveted but he also lost what he already possessed. See also the *Conflict of Adam and Eve*, I, iv, 3.

65. *Discourse on the Abbaton*, 21a.

66. Five and a half hours: *II. Enoch* 32:2. Six hours: *Midrash Rabba Bereshith:* 18 and *Talmud: Sanhedrin*, 38b, and *Cave of Treasures*, 5:1. One day: bin Gorion, *op. cit.*, I, 105-106. Seven years: *Jubilees* 3:15.

67. *Jubilees* 3:32.

Then said the Lord to his angels: Why have you stopped to drive Adam and Eve out of paradise? It is not that I have sinned or that I have made a wrong judgment? Then the angels fell on the ground and worshipped the Lord and said: Thou art just, Lord, and thou judgest in righteousness. And, while turning to Adam, the Lord said: I will not permit thee to be in paradise from henceforth . . .

When Adam pleaded to be able to partake of the fruit of the tree of life, the Lord could not permit him but promised that one day he would be in paradise again:

When thou hast left paradise, if thou shalt keep thyself from all evil, because thou art destined to die, I will raise thee up when the resurrection comes, and thou mayest partake of the tree of life, and thou shalt be free from death forever.[68]

When the Lord had left, Adam made one more attempt at persuading the angels for a favor. He asked them whether they would allow him to take from the garden some of the herbs and spices and let them grow in the lone and dreary world outside. This time the cherubim were more careful and consulted with the Lord first, who gave his permission that Adam could take with him some of the plants.[69] He was also given a special rod or staff by the Lord which he could use in the new world. This was, According to tradition, the staff which was handed down by the patriarchs until it was given to Moses.[70] The Lord also made for them some garments to wear. Some of the Jewish writings associate the garment of skin with the garment of light and maintain that Adam and Eve lost their glory (light) and received an ordinary dress of (animal?) skin.[71] Other legends attribute the garment to the skin which the serpent shed when he became mortal.[72] That their nature had changed upon eating the fruit and leaving paradise became immediately apparent to both of them for they were no longer as glorious as they had previously been:

And, indeed, when Adam looked at his flesh, that was changed, he wept bitterly . . . And Adam said to Eve: Look at thine eyes, and at mine, which used to see angels before . . . our eyes have become flesh, they cannot see in the same way as they saw

68. *Apocalypse of Moses,* in *ANF,* VIII, 566.

69. *Ibid.,* also in Ginzburg, *op. cit.,* I, 81-82.

70. Ginzburg, *op. cit.,* II, 293.

71. *Zohar; Bereshith,* I, 36b for example, mentions that both had a garment of light before the fall but it became skin after the move from paradise. This notion is probably due to the closeness of the Hebrew words for light (אור) and skin (עור).

72. bin Gorion, *op. cit.,* I, 96, 100. Snakes shed their skins at almost regular intervals and this occurrence was attributed back to the fall in the garden.

before. And Adam said to Eve: What is our body today, compared to what it was like in previous days when we lived in the garden?[73]

When they complained to the Lord about it he explained:

> When you were under my care, you had a bright nature within you, and therefore you could see things, even those far away. However, after your transgression your bright nature was taken from you, and now you cannot see things far away but only those close by; this is after the capability of the flesh.[74]

Adam and Eve Made a Home in the Mortal World

In their new world outside the garden, Adam and Eve settle at Elda, "in the land of their creation." [75] Here they lived in a cave, according to most of the legends and traditions. Since they do not know very much about the harsh world, angels have to come and teach them many things pertaining to making a living.[76]

> And when they came to the gate of the garden and saw the wide earth before them, covered with large and small stones and with sand, they were much afraid and trembled . . . They saw themselves now in a strange land which they had never seen and were not familiar with.[77]

Everything was a brand new experience for the two, and even the most ordinary occurrences were novel and frightening to them. It began with the first night in the cave. Evidently, they had never experienced darkness, and this event brought great fear to them. They thought that it was the end of all things and that now the predictions about their death would be fulfilled and that the hour of their death had come. It was so frightening that Adam even passed out. But the rising sun in the morning brought some relief for them, even though they were at first also afraid of the glow and the brightness and heat emanating from the heavenly body.[78] The Lord proceeded to tell them the reason for having darkness on the earth:

> O Adam, as long as the angels were obedient to me, a bright light was upon them. But when one transgressed my commandment, I deprived him of that brightness and he then became dark . . . I made him fall from heaven down onto the earth, and that was the darkness which came upon him. And on you, O Adam, the light rested while you were in the garden and while you were obedient to me. But when I heard about your

---

73. *The Conflict of Adam and Eve,* I, iv, 2 and 8-10; See also *Pirke de Rabbi Eliezer, 14; Targum Yerushalmi; Genesis* 3: 7, 21; *Apocalypse of Adam,* p. 64, lines 6-11, 14-15, 24-25.
74. *Ibid.,* I viii, 2.
75. *Jubilees* 3:32.
76. R. Graves and R. Patai, *op. cit., p. 78.*
77. *The Conflict of Adam and Eve,* I, ii, 2-3.
78. *Ibid.,* I, xi, xvi.

transgression, I deprived you of that bright light. But, in my mercy, I did not turn you into darkness, but I made for you a body of flesh. . . . Had I turned you into darkness, it would have been as if I had killed you.[79]

The Lord then gave them some means of making fire and light in the cave during the dark hours so that the two would no longer have to be afraid and helpless. In the book of *The Conflict of Adam and Eve* it is golden rod, in another text they are given two stones.[80]

At first the two experienced some trouble with the burning coals and the fire when they touched it because they got burned by the heat and ended up scorched and singed.[81] We must keep in mind that both were like children and unacquainted with much of their environment and therefore an easy prey for Satan and his schemes.

Adam and Eve also became very hungry and thirsty. It seems that they were not used to this condition and had to be told by the Lord how to behave in this situation. They went to God with their problem:

O God, since we transgressed your commandment and broke your law, you have brought us into a strange land and you have made us to suffer and faint and be hungry and thirsty. Now, therefore, O God, we ask you to give us something to eat from the garden to satisfy our hunger, and something by which we can satisfy our thirst. Behold, O God, for many days we have eaten nothing and have drunken nothing, and our flesh is dried up and our strength is gone and sleep has left our eyes from fainting and from weeping.[82]

At first, God gave them something to eat, either from the garden or from the parts of the earth where something was growing, particularly figs.[83]

Then they sat down to eat the figs, but they did not know how to eat them, because they had not been used to eating earthly food. They were also afraid that their stomachs would become heavy and their flesh thick and that earthly food would become a pleasure for them. But God, out of pity, sent an angel to them so they would not suffer too much for food and drink. And the angel said to Adam and Eve: God says to you that you do not have enough strength to fast too long, therefore eat, and strengthen your bodies, for you are now animal flesh which cannot live without food and drink.[84]

---

79. *Ibid.*, I, xiii, 2-8, and li, 5-7.
80. *Ibid.*, I xxix, 7 and bin Gorion, *op. cit.*, I, 109. The word "window" in the Bible (Genesis 6:16) actually refers to an apparatus for light (צהר) which is closely related to the word for flint stone (צר).
81. *Conflict of Adam and Eve*, I, xlvi, 1-2.
82. *Ibid.*, I, xxxiv, 17-19.
83. *Ibid.*, I, xxxviii-xli.
84. *Ibid.*, I, lxiv, 4-6.

Soon, however, the Lord insisted that they prepare their own food and make their own living on their daily work and from the plants available.[85] Also water from the streams and springs was being used by them to quench their thirst. Eating and drinking was equated to a symbolic foreshadowing of the Savior's mission and this concept was taught them by the Lord:

> And when you say: Give me of the water of life that I may drink and live, so can that not be done this day, but only on the day in which I will go down into the spirit world and break down the gates of steel . . . As to the water which you would like now, it cannot be done this day, but only in the day in which I shall shed my blood . . . My blood will be the water of life for you.[86]

Adam and Eve Knew of the Coming Messiah

From some of these books it is quite evident that the early Christians did teach that Adam and Eve were exactly aware of the plan of redemption and the coming of the savior in the meridian of time, even though this is overlooked and not very readily accepted and taught in conventional Christianity. In the stories and legends connected with Adam and Eve the Lord gives dramatic prophecies about what is to become of the two and their posterity:

> I will send the Word which created you . . . And the Word will save you when the five and a half days are fulfilled . . .[87]

> I will bring you into the kingdom of heaven . . . When I will come down from heaven and will become flesh of your seed, and take upon myself the problems of body of which you are suffering, then the darkness, which came upon you in the cave will come upon me in the grave . . . I shall be counted as one of the sons of men in order to save them.[88]

God made also a covenant with Adam and Eve:

> But God had previously made a covenant with our father Adam before he came out of the garden when he was by the tree of which Eve had partaken and given also to him to eat.[89]

> O Adam, I have made my covenant with you and I will not turn away from it, but neither will I let you return to the garden until my covenant of the great five and a half days is fulfilled.[90]

---

85. *Ibid.,* I, lxvi.
86. *Ibid.,* I, xlii, 5-8.
87. *Ibid.,* I, iii, 1-2. The five and a half days mentioned here refer to the 5,500 years from Adam to Christ. See also *Le Combat d'Adam et Eve,* in Migne, *Encyclopedie Theologique,* XXIII, Apocraphie, I, col. 298.
88. *Ibid., I,* iv, 2, 4.
89. *Ibid.,* I, iii, 7.
90. *Ibid.,* I, vii, 2.

Adam and Eve Worshipped God and Were Baptized

Adam and Eve built an altar of stones on which to offer sacrifices in the similitude of the coming Messiah, which is likewise overlooked and not taught in the Christian churches:

> The Adam and Eve stood on their feet and Adam said to Eve: Robe yourself and I will also put on my robe. And she robed herself as Adam had told her. Then Adam and Eve took stones and stacked them in the shape of an altar . . . And Adam and Eve stood below the altar and wept. Then they pleaded with God: Forgive us our transgression and our sins.[91]

Then they dropped some of their blood on the altar and the voice of the Lord came and acknowledged this sacrifice and taught them more about the symbolism in the activity:

> O Adam, as you have shed your blood, so I will shed my own blood when I will become flesh of your seed . . . And as you have built an altar, so will I make an altar on the earth, and as you have offered your blood on it, so will also I offer my blood on an altar. And as you asked for forgiveness through that blood, so will I make my blood for the forgiveness of sins, and blot out any transgression by it.[92]

> God said further to Adam: So it will also happen to me on the earth, when I will be pierced and blood will flow from my side and run over my body, which is the true offering, and which will be offered on an altar as a perfect offering.[93]

Even the ordinance of baptism is contained in the old texts, which show therefore that at least some of the early Christians did believe that these things happened, quite in contrast to general Christian thinking of today.

> And to the North of the garden there is a sea of water . . . And when a man washes himself in it, he becomes clean of the cleanness in it, and also white of its whiteness, even if he were dark . . . And God created the sea, for he knew what would happen to the man . . . and when they should return to flesh, they should go down into the water of the sea and all of them would repent of their sins . . . and Adam and Eve would wash themselves in it and be cleansed from their sins.[94]

> And Eve went down into the water, as Adam had commanded her. And Adam also went down into the water, and they stood there praying, and they pleaded with the Lord to forgive them of their offense.[95]

---

91. *Ibid.,* I, xxiii, 3-6; *II Enoch* 68:5 mentions an altar Adam had built at Ahuzah. This place is usually interpreted as Jerusalem by the Jews.

92. *Ibid.,* I, xxiv, 4-5.

93. *Ibid.,* I, lxix, 6. According to *Jubilees* 3:27 he also offered frankencense, galbanum, stacte and other spices on the altar.

94. *Ibid.,* I, i, 2-5.

95. *Ibid.,* I, xxxii, 7. See also bin Gorion, *op. cit.,* I, 102.

Since Adam and Eve are rather helpless in this new environment and always in need of aid and council, Satan again senses his opportunity for deception and for accomplishing his aim to lead the first parents astray and thus frustrate the divine plan. He appears to them as an angel of light.[96] Since they are only familiar with angels and have not yet seen any other being they are easily taken in by the deception, thinking that Satan is a messenger from the Lord. The whole book of *The Conflict of Adam and Eve* is filled with amazing stories of how Satan attempts by various methods and means to deceive the two, kill them, or make them abandon their belief and allegiance to God. However, all attempts fail because true angels and messengers usually come to the rescue and thwart the schemes of Satan, no matter how cunningly he tried to accomplish them. He even leads Adam to the swearing of an oath to him:

> And Satan said to him: Hold out your hand and put it inside my hand. And Adam held out his hand and put it inside Satan's hand, when Satan said to him: Speak now, so true as God living, rational and speaking, who raised the heavens in space, and established the earth upon the waters, and has created me out of the four elements, and out of the dust of the earth, I will not break my promise, nor renounce my word. And Adam swore thus.[97]

Adam Instructed By Angels

In order to help Adam when he prayed for more knowledge and wisdom in making decisions here on earth, particularly later on, when his posterity lived with him and looked to him for council and guidance, a book was sent to Adam which contained all the information he sought and needed.

> God indeed sent down a book to Adam from which he became acquainted with the supernal wisdom . . . This book was brought down to Adam by the "master of mysteries" preceded by three messengers.[98]

Adam was then instructed by the angel:

> Adam, Adam, do not reveal the glory of the Master, for to you alone and to the angels is the privilege given to know the glory of the Master. Therefore he kept the book with him secretly . . .[99]

The angel who delivered the book, according to legend, was the famous Raziel and the book was later on called the Book of Raziel.[100] It contained items which related to human existence on earth:

---

96. *Ibid.,* I, xxvii. See also note 35.
97. *Ibid.,* I, lxx, 15.
98. *Zohar: Bereshith,* 37b.
99. *Ibid.,* 55b.
100. Raziel (= Secret of God?)

... whether a calamity will come, a famine or wild beasts, floods, and drought, whether there will be an abundance of grain or death, whether the wicked will rule the world, whether locusts will devastate the land, whether the fruits will drop from the tree unripe, whether boils will afflict men, whether wars will prevail or diseases or plagues among men and cattle ... [101]

Even the names of all men who were destined to live on this earth were included in this register. [102]

Adam is also credited with composing verses and prose after his leaving the garden. Particularly one piece was very beautiful and handed down, until it reached King David, himself a renowned composer. He included one of Adam's writings into his collection of poetic songs, known now as the 92nd Psalm. [103]

A couple of interesting little items about Adam among the Jews were that Adam was originally an uncultured and unpolished person, and it was only because of the example and encouragement of Eve that he became a spiritual giant and gentleman. [104] Adam also had a beard of which he was somewhat ashamed because he did not know why he had it and what to do with it. The Lord told him one day that it was an ornament which would distinguish him from the woman. [105]

Other Children of Adam and Eve

Finally Adam and Eve are also having offspring, as all the other creatures around him had. According to some legends it was by observing the world around him that the ancient of days received the idea to do likewise. In another story he has to be told especially what kind of phenomenon he was beholding:

> Then Adam said to them: But how do you multiply? And they answered him: We have husbands who wedded us, and we bear them children, who grow up, and who in their turn marry and are married, and also bear children, and thus we increase. And if it be so, Adam, that you do not believe us, we will show you our husbands and our children . . . And when Adam and Eve saw them, they stood dumbfounded and wondered at them. [106]

While in most texts they have at first only two children, namely Cain and Abel, there are other ancient stories which mention differing numbers:

---

101. Ginzburg, *op. cit.,* I, 91-92.
102. *Shemoth Rabba,* 39.
103. *Pirke de Rabbi Eliezer,* 19; *Midrash Rabba Bereshith:* 22:13.
104. Clement: *Recognitions,* 100:4.
105. S. Baring-Gould, *Legends of the Patriarchs and Prophets,* p. 51.
106. *Conflict of Adam and Eve,* I, lxxii, 5-8. That Adam and Eve lived in the garden without having had sexual relations was taught anciently. See *Vita Adae,* 18; Jerome, *Adversus Jovinianum,* I, 16.

And in the third week in the second jubilee she gave birth to Cain, and in the fourth she gave birth to Abel, and in the fifth she gave birth to her daughter Awan.[107]

And God looked upon his maid-servant Eve and delivered her, and she brought forth her first-born son and with him a daughter . . . And Adam ministered unto Eve in the cave until the end of eight days, when they named the son Cain and the daughter Luluwa. When the days of nursing the children had ended, Eve conceived again and when her days were come she brought forth another son and another daughter, and they named the son Abel and the daughter Aklia.[108]

And Adam knew his wife and she bore two sons and three daughters.[109]

Adam fathered three sons and three daughters: Cain and his twin, Qalmana, his wife; and Abel and his twin, Deborah, his wife; and Seth and his twin, Noba, his wife.[110]

Other sons and daughters after Cain and Abel and Seth are at times mentioned, such as nine sons in the *Book of Jubilees,* thirty-three sons and twenty-seven daughters by Syncellus, and eleven sons and eight daughters by Philo:

And these are the names of his sons: Eli, Se'el, Suri, Elmi'el, Berok, Ke'el, Nahat, Zarhamah, Sisha, Machtal, and Anat. And the names of the daughters: Hawwah, Gitash, Harebika, Zipat, Heki'ah, Shaba, Azin.[111]

The Conflict of Cain and Abel

There are some Hebrew legends which assert that Cain was not actually Adam's son but conceived by Eve from evil spirits or even Satan himself (Samael). This was probably construed to explain the emergence of evil in the world.[112] The names of the first two sons lead to a wide range of interpretation and speculation. The word Cain is predominently associated with either a stalk of straw,[113] possession,[114] or hate,[115] while Abel came to mean

---

107. *Jubilees* 4:1.
108. *Conflict of Adam and Eve,* I, lxxiv, 5-6; lxxv, 11.
109. *Jasher* 1:12. The sons are Cain and Abel but the names of the daughters are not given.
110. *Pseudo-Philo,* 1:1.
111. *Jubilees* 4:40; *Synchellus,* 1, 18; *Pseudo-Philo,* 1:2-4. Other children always follow the birth of Cain and Abel but never precede it.
112. *Zohar, Bereshith,* 36b.
    The right kind was not produced until Seth came, who is the first ancestor of all the generations of the righteous, and from whom the world was propagated.
    See also *Zohar, Bereshith,* 55a, and the *Hypostasis of the Archons,* p. 137, lines 19ff. The jealousy between Cain and Abel originated from Cain's assertion that he was better than Abel because of the former's heritage, which was from Samael (Satan?) while Abel was merely from Adam (bin Gorion, *op. cit.,* I, 134).
113. Cain supposedly stood up immediately after birth and walked to pick a stalk of straw from a field (*Vita Adae,* 21). The real association comes probably from the closeness of the Hebrew words for "received" (קין) and for "stalk" (קנה).
114. Josephus, *Antiquities,* I, ii, 1. See also Philo, *Cain,* 20 ("the one who wanted to seize everything").
115. Ginzburg, *op. cit.,* V, 135.

sorrow,[116] death,[117] or emptiness.[118] The *Apocalypse of Moses* foreshadows their future occupations by assigning to Cain the name Diaphotus and to Abel Amilabes.[119]

That trouble between the two brothers would eventually come about and even end in a great tragedy was evidently already made known to the parents by means of a dream which Eve had one night:

> Eve said to Adam, her master: My lord, I have seen in a dream this night the blood of my son Amilabes who is called Abel, thrown into the mouth of Cain his brother, and he drank it without pity. And he entreated him to grant him a little of it, but he did not listen to him, but drank it all up, and it did not remain in his stomach but it came forth out of his mouth . . .[120]

Alarmed by this dream and its logical interpretation, Adam separated the two boys and made them dwell in different locations and also taught them each a different occupation. Cain became a tiller of the ground and Abel a sheep herder.[121] It did not help much because it was Satan again who meddled in the affairs of the brothers. He saw another opportunity for deception and misery and a change for revenge and interference with the great plan of God. He therefore chose Cain for his associate and tool to bring about trouble in the world.

> And the children began to wax stronger and to grow in stature, but Cain was hard-hearted and ruled over his younger brother. And often when his father made an offering, he would remain behind and not go with them to offer up also. But as to Abel, he had a meek heart and was obedient to his father and his mother, whom he often moved to make an offering, because he loved it and he prayed and fasted much.[122]

Cain was the type of person Satan needed for his schemes and he persuaded him to join in with him in a plot to obtain what he wanted at the expense of others. A great opportunity for it came when Adam made decisions as to whom of the daughters the two brothers should marry:

> And when the children had grown up, Adam said to Eve: Cain shall marry Kelimat, who was born with Abel, and Abel shall marry Lebuda, who was born with Cain. But Cain said to his mother Eve: I will marry my sister and Abel can marry his. He said this

---

116. Josephur *Antiquities,* I, ii, 1, because of the association between Hebel (הבל) and "sorrow" (אבר).

117. *Jashar Bereshith,* 9a.

118. See Psalm 144:4, and Job 7:16.

119. *Apocalypse of Moses, ANF,* VIII, 565. For Cain from the Greek Διαφύτωρ = planter, and for Abel Μηλοτός = herder.

120. *Ibid.*

121 *Vita Adae,* 22.

122. *Conflict of Adam and Eve,* I, lxxvi, 1-3.

because Lebuda was very beautiful. When Adam heard these words he was very angry
and said: It is a transgression if you marry your sister who was born with you.[123]

In another version it is Satan who comes to Cain one day and tells him
of his parents' decision and instills in him the idea that he must kill his
brother Abel if he wants the more beautiful sister for his wife:

Satan came to him by night, showed himself and said: Since Adam and Eve love
your brother Abel much more than they love you, they wish to join him in marriage to
your beautiful sister, because they love him, but they wish to join you in marriage with
your·less favored sister, because they hate you. Now therefore, I advise you, when
they do that, to kill your brother, then your sister will be left for you, and his sister
will be cast out.[124]

These and other passages from apocryphal literature center on the idea
that Cain's quarrel with his brother was to a great extent based on his
desire to have the best and receive gain by asserting his dominion on the
rest of the family. In this undertaking he had the assistance and encouragement from Satan, who loves contention and incites people to do evil for
their own personal advantage.

After much pleading from Adam, Cain consents one day to make an
offering to God on the altar together with his brother Abel. And here the
well-known story happened in which God accepted Abel's offering but not
Cain's:

Then God looked upon Abel and accepted his offering. And God was more pleased
with Abel than with his offering, because of his good heart and pure body. There was no
trace of guile in him . . . But as to Cain, he was not happy about making offerings, but
after much anger on his father's part, he offered up his gift once, and when he did it his
eyes were greedy about the item he offered, and he took the smallest of the sheep for an
offering, and he set his eyes on it. Therefore did God not accept his offering, because his
heart was full of murderous thoughts.[125]

It was not that God arbitrarily decides whose offering to accept and
whose not to, but he looks at the heart of the person making the offering
and with what kind of spirit and attitude the gift is presented. Knowing
Cain, the Lord decided against him on the basis of his reasons for making

---

123. *Cave of Treasures,* 5:21-24.
124. *Conflict of Adam and Eve,* I, lxxvi, 10-11. That jealousy of Cain toward his brother
Abel was at least partially related to a quarrel over the sisters is also mentioned in the *Midrash
Rabba Bereshith:* 22:7; and in *Pirke de Rabbi Eliezer,* 21; as well as in the Christian text of
Clement, *Homilies,* 3:25.
125. *Ibid.,* I, lxxvii, 5-8.

the sacrifice. He knew that Cain was after gain and did not cheerfully offer up some of his possessions on the altar. Some Jewish commentators even wrote that Cain took the leftovers from one of his meals to be offered to God, because he was too greedy to give something of value, while Abel had selected the best animal from his herd as a gift to the Lord.[126] In addition, Cain evidently selected an offering from the ground, which had been cursed by the Lord, instead of an animal which could shed blood in similitude of Christ. Thereby he was perhaps deliberately mocking the sacrifice. That he was greedy is also shown in an incident where the two brothers debated whether there really is a punishment of the wicked in the hereafter. When Abel maintained that there was, Cain suggested that they should divide up the land and all earthly possessions: "I take everything on the earth in this world, and you can have everything in the next world." [127] Another time he tells Abel:

> We want to divide up the world. I am the first-born therefore I will take a double portion for myself.[128]

The whole quarrel, therefore, is a continuing urge in Cain to gain possession of his sister and material gain, even for the price of hate and eventual murder. Satan knew Cain's desires and promises him enrichment if he would only follow Satan's advise:

> Yet if you will take my advice and listen to me I will bring to you on your wedding day beautiful robes, and gold and silver in plenty . . .[129]

Cain takes heed and soon he finds himself becoming a law unto himself, when he is abusive toward his mother:

> He went to Eve, his mother, and beat her, and cursed her, and said to her: Why are you about to take my sister and marry her to my brother? Am I dead?[130]

All this was being observed by God and He took occasion to warn Cain and to let him recognize what would happen. It was not that Cain did not realize what he was doing. All his acts were committed in full knowledge of the law and the circumstances. The Lord told him:

> Know, that sin has a desire after you, but you have power over it and if you do not listen to it, it cannot entice you. Therefore it shall be your guilt into all eternity![131]

---

126. *Midrash Rabba Bereshith:* 22:5; *Pirke de Rabbi Eliezer,* 21; Philo, *Quaestiones in Genesis,* 1:62.
127. bin Gorion, *op. cit.,* I, 140.
128. *Ibid.,* I, 143.
129. *Conflict of Adam and Eve,* I, lxxviii, 7.
130. *Ibid.,* I, lxxviii, 12.
131. bin Gorion, *op. cit.,* I, 140.

Adam remained reconciliatory and made one last attempt at getting his son to repent of the evil and selfish inclinations. He succeeded in talking Cain into making another offering to the Lord. But the attempt turned out to be disasterous:

> Cain behaved with pride towards his brother, and pushed him away from the altar . . . and he offered up his own offering on the altar, with a heart full of pride and guile and fraud. But Abel set up stones nearby, and upon them did he offer up his gift with a humble heart and free of guile . . . Cain cried unto the Lord to accept his offer, but God did not accept it from him, neither did a divine fire descend to consume his offering. But he remained standing at the altar, and he looked out of humor and wrath over to his brother to see if God would accept his offering or not. And Abel prayed to God to accept his gift and a divine fire came down and consumed his offering . . . And Cain was looking on as all that was taking place and he was angry because of it. And he opened his mouth and blasphemed God because He had not accepted his offering. But God said to Cain: Wherefore are you angry? Be righteous that I may accept your gift. Not against me have you murmured but against yourself. . . . And Cain was so sullen and so angry that he went into the field where Satan came to him and said: Since your brother has gone to your father Adam because you have pushed him away from the altar, they have kissed his face and they rejoice over him far more than over you.[132]

At that time Cain made up his mind to actually go ahead and kill his brother and so be rid of him and gain by doing it. According to *Conflict of Adam and Eve* Cain invited Abel for a walk into the countryside and at an opportune moment he hit his brother with the rod he was carrying. Abel was stunned, fell on the ground and pleaded with Cain to make it quickly and not let him suffer so much pain, if he indeed wanted to murder him. So Cain looked around, found a stone and with it he hit his brother until the brains came out of the head and blood was scattered all over the area.[133] Another legend mentions that the two were fighting and it was Abel who had overpowered Cain and was on top of him. Then Cain pleaded with Abel not to hurt him, whereupon Abel set him free. But as soon as Cain was free, he took advantage of the situation and killed his brother when he was unattentive.[134] Different accounts attribute a different kind of death to Abel. It was either with a stone, a cane, a knife,[135] or even by means of flogging or biting with his teeth.[136] It was a cruel death, however, since Cain did not know how to kill another being and therefore he used different methods, as preserved in the legends.

---

132. *Conflict of Adam and Eve,* I, lxxviii, 18-26, 32.
133. *Ibid.,* I, lxxix.
134. bin Gorion, *op. cit.,* I, 137, 143.
135. *Midrash Rabba Bereshith:* 22:8.
136. Flogging: *Jubilees* 4:31; biting: *Zohar,* Bereshith, 54b.

The *Book of Jasher* tells the story this way: One day the brothers met in the field and Cain proceeded to complain that Abel's flocks continually invaded his own fields:

> What is there between me and you that you come with your flock and graze on my land? And Abel answered his brother and said to him: Why is it that you eat the flesh of my flock and clothe yourself with their wool? Now, take off the wool of my sheep with which you have dressed yourself, and pay me for the fruit and meat which you have eaten and when you have done that I will move from your land as you have ordered . . .[137]

Again it shows that the quarrel was about material goods. However, in this story Abel was not about to give in but he challenged his brother openly. The result of the argument was the murder action by Cain:

> And Cain hurried and got up and took the iron part of his instrument for ploughing and with it suddenly hit his brother and killed him, and Cain spilled the blood of his brother Abel on the earth, and the blood of his brother Abel ran on the earth before the flock.[138]

In some of the texts Cain is depicted as trying to bury the body of Abel, the evidence of his crime. In some stories he succeeds in his task, in others he does not:

> He then threw his brother into a pit which he made and covered him with soil. However, the earth did not receive the body and threw it out immediately.[139]
>
> For the wicked Cain, having taken great pains to hide it, had not been able to, for the earth did not receive it, saying: I will not receive a body into companionship until that dust that was taken up and fashioned upon me, come to me. And then the angels took it up, and laid it on a rock until his father died.[140]
>
> And Cain rose up and dug a pit in the field in which he placed his brother's body and then he put soil on top of it.[141]

Upon questioning by the Lord as to the whereabouts of Abel, Cain lies and pretends not to know what has happened. Thereupon the Lord answered according to Josephus:

> I wonder at thee, that thou knowest not what is become of a man whom thou thyself hast destroyed.[142]

---

137. *Jasher*, 1:18-20.
138. *Ibid.*, 1:25.
139. *Conflict of Adam and Eve*, I, lxxix, 12-14. Three times Cain tried to bury the remains but each time the earth refused to accept the body.
140. *Apocalypse of Moses*, in *ANF*, Viii, 570. Adam was supposed to be the first person buried in the earth and therefore Abel had to wait. See *Jubilees* 4:29.
141. *Jasher*, 1:27.
142. Josephus, *Antiquities*, I, ii, l.

When the Lord calls Cain to account for the crime he finds an unrepentant murderer who is not at all sorry or worried about the deed. As a matter of fact, Cain tries to justify the action and makes it appear as an accident. He explains that he had never seen a person killed and therefore he could not possibly have known that one can kill someone by hitting him with an instrument.[143] In another version he places the blame for his action on the Lord:

> I killed my brother but you were the one who put this evil drive in me. You are the guardian of all creatures and you let me kill Abel, so you are the one who killed.[144]

When the family discovered what had happened to Abel they were stricken with grief and disbelief:

> Then they all cried and lifted up their voices and slapped their faces and threw dust upon their heads and ripped their garments and came out to the place where Abel had been killed. And they found him lying on the ground, killed, with animals around him and they cried and wept because of this righteous man . . . And Adam carried him with tears running down his face, and he went to the cave of treasure where he placed the body and wrapped him up with sweet spices.[145]

The mark which was put on Cain by the Lord has given rise to a great amount of speculation as to what this could have been since the scriptures, as we have them, do not specify what it was. It is variously cited as a letter of the alphabet, leprosy, or even a horn.[146] In at least one text Cain obtained a black face after the offering on the altar when the wind blew the smoke in his direction.[147]

The Disobedience of the Animals and Plants

The murder of Abel also brought some changes to the land and its inhabitants as Adam and Eve and their posterity found out and often had to cope with. For the first time the mountains appear on the earth, so the Jewish legends report. The earth was level before but as a witness of the crime committed it folded and exhibited creases on its outer layer.[148] Also plants went without fruit and much yield for a long time until the birth of Seth.[149] In addition, the animals became disrespectful to men in accordance with the warning in the *Midrash:*

---

143. Ginzburg, *op. cit.,* I, 110.
144. bin Gorion, *op. cit.,* I, 145.
145. *Conflict of Adam and Eve,* II, i, 2-4.
146. Ginzburg, *op. cit.,* I, 141, note 28.
147. *Midrash Rabba: Bereshith,* 22:6.
148. Ginzburg, *op. cit.,* V, 142.
149. *Midrash Agada:* Genesis, 4:16.

> Man is entitled to pre-eminence only as long as he cultivates his God-like qualities; when he voluntarily abandons them he is even lower than the brute creation.[150]

Since man was created in the image of God, he had superiority over all the rest of the creation because he represented God to the lower creatures. However, when man acted contrary to the divine spirit, the animal and plant world denied him reverence and obedience and even openly challenged man or followed his corrupt and evil example.[151] A story in the old texts reports that an animal once attacked Seth while he was walking along with his mother Eve. When they complained about it, the animal refered back to the disobedience of Eve herself while she was in the garden, and Cain who killed his brother. Why should an animal be more obedient than man, who is in the image of God? However, Seth was able to dissuade the beast by reminding it that he was still in authority:

> And Seth said to the wild beast: Shut your mouth and be silent and stay away from the image of God until the judgment day. Then the wild beast said to Seth: Behold, I will stay away, Seth, from the image of God. And then the wild beast fled and left him wounded.[152]

The Lord explained to Adam:

> When you were under my control, all creatures were obedient to you, but after you transgressed my commandment, they all rise up against you.[153]

It must have been a traumatic experience for Adam and Eve to witness the first killing on the earth and to have lost both of their sons, whom they had probably expected to carry on.

As time went by, Adam noticed that the earth was becoming more wicked. The community of the righteous was decreasing in their relationship to the bad people on the earth, the descendants of Cain. He knew that God did not look favorably upon the transgressions and he received a revalation to tell the inhabitants of the earth about their wickedness and the coming tribulations and punishment if they did not cease from their wrongdoings. He saw all the future generations and their rulers and their learned and famous personalities, [154] but also the destruction which was to happen. Adam predicted:

---

150. *Midrash Rabba,* H. Freedman and Maurice Simon, eds.; I, 62, note 4.

151. See *Zohar,* I, i and 191ff; III, 107a. *Jubilees* 5:2 reports that man as well as the animals became corrupt, evidently because everyone is following the bad examples of the others.

152. *Apocalypse of Moses,* ANF, VIII; *Vita Adae,* 37-39.

153. *Conflict of Adam and Eve,* I, xlv, 4.

154. See *Zohar, Bereshith,* 55a; *Midrash: Jalkut,* 12.

... that the world was to be destroyed at one time by the force of fire, and at another time by the violence and quantity of water.[155]

And the total (number) of flesh will pass-away in the (water). Then God will calm down in his wrath and he will place his power on the water and he will preserve (Noah) and his sons and their wives by the means of the ark, and the animals which were pleasing to him, and the birds of the sky which he had called. He put them on the land and God will tell Noah, who will be called Deucalion by the generations: Behold, I have preserved you in the ark, and your wife and your sons and their wives and their animals and the birds of the sky, which you have called. Therefore I will give to you and your sons the earth. Like kings will you and your sons rule over it.[156]

And God revealed to Adam the whole future, also that the son will suffer for his sake (in his place).[157]

O my son, hereafter will come a flood and destroy all creatures and leave only eight souls alive.[158]

What will happen after the flood was also prophecied at that time:

He . . . will bring them into their land which will be suitable, and he will build for them a holy place and they will be called by that name . . . Then Noah will divide the earth among his sons Ham, Japeth, and Shem. He will tell them: My sons, hearken to my words. Behold, I have divided the earth among you: well, now, work on it in fear and servitude all the days of our lives.[159]

Adam was the patriarch and leader of the human race upon the earth during his time. As such he was also the prophet for his dispensation and had been anointed to this position, as related by Peter to his inquisitive investigator Clement:

I remember, Peter, that you told me of the first man that he was a prophet, but you did not say that he was anointed. If then there be no prophet without anointing, how could the first man be a prophet, since he was not anointed? Then Peter, smiling, said: If the first man prophesied, it is certain that he was also anointed. For although he who has recorded the law in his pages is silent as to this anointing, yet he has evidently left us to understand these things . . . Since it is certain that he was also anointed, because without anointing he could not be a prophet.[160]

The Death of Adam

Finally the great patriarch felt his end approaching. In a vision, where he saw all the inhabitants and rulers of the earth, he had noticed David, who would live only one minute in mortality and then die as a baby according to Jewish legend. Adam felt bad that this should be and voluntarily gave seventy years of his life to David.[161] Adam, who was supposed to

---

155. Josephus, *Antiquities,* I, ii, 3.
156. *Apocalypse of Adam,* p. 70, lines 4-24 to p. 71, lines 1-4.
157. *Cave of Treasures,* 5:13.
158. *Conflict of Adam and Eve,* II, viii, 10.
159. *Apocalypse of Adam,* p. 72, lines 3-7, 15-23.
160. Clement, *Recognitions,* I, 47.
161. *Pirke de Rabbi Eliezer,* 19.

live one celestial day, or one thousand years of our time, therefore had to die when he was only 930 years old.[162]

Over a period of time he realized that his body was getting old and he was subject to the troubles and diseases which mortality brings and which the Lord had told him would happen.[163]

> And weakness pursued us. Therefore the days of our life became short; for I recognized that I had come under the power of death.[164]

He remembered the tree of life in the garden and the idea occurred to him that, if he were to use the fruit of that tree, he would be freed from the pains and difficulties of his body, which was now almost a millenium old:

> And Adam said to Eve: Arise and go with our son Seth to paradise, and put earth upon your heads and weep, beseeching the Lord that He may have compassion upon me, and send his angel to paradise and give me of the tree in which the oil flows, that thou mayest bring it to me, and I shall anoint myself and have rest . . . And Seth went with his mother near paradise and they wept there, beseeching God to send his angel to give them of the oil of compassion. And God sent to them the archangel Michael and he said to them these words: Seth, man of God, do not weary thyself praying in this supplication about the tree in which flows the oil to anoint thy father Adam, for it will not happen to thee now, but at the last times. Then shall arise all flesh from Adam even to that great day, as many as shall be a holy people, then shall be given to them all the delight of paradise. . . .[165]

The same story is told in early Christian sources, known as the *Acts of Pilate* or the *Gospel of Nicodemus* or *Christ's Descent into Hell.* Here the scene is the spirit world where all the inhabitants of the earth wait for the coming of the Son of God. Adam knows that the arrival of Christ is imminent and therefore he tells Seth to tell all the patriarchs and prophets assembled about the oil from paradise which he wanted when he was still in mortality, but which he could not receive then but which he was promised at the time of the coming of Christ:

> And Seth said: Prophets and patriarchs, listen. My father, the first created, when he became sick unto death, sent me to the gate of paradise to ask God to have an angel lead me to the tree of compassion, that I might take of the oil and anoint my father, so that he might arise from his illness. This I did. And after my request an angel of the Lord came and asked me: What do you desire, Seth? Do you desire the oil which raises the

---

162. God had told him in paradise that he would die the same day that he partook of the fruit (Genesis 2:17). The seventy years given to David, leave him with a maximum of 930 years (*Jubilees* 4:30). One legend tells us that Adam lived 60,000 years (S. Baring-Gould, *op. cit.,* p. 37).

163. See above and notes 53-55.

164. *Apocalypse of Adam,* p. 67, lines 8-14.

165. *Apocalypse of Moses, ANF,* VIII, 566. The olive tree with its oil has always been regarded as the tree of life or tree of mercy and compassion.

sick which comes from the tree of which the oil flows, because of the illness of your father Adam? This he cannot have now. Go, therefore, and tell your father, that after 5500 years from the creation of the world, the only-begotten Son of God will become mortal and will descend below the earth and he will anoint him with that oil.[166]

Since Adam was not able to receive the life-giving oil from the tree, he knew that he had to die soon. He therefore called one last meeting:

Let all my sons come to me that I may see them before I die. And they were all brought together, for the earth was inhabited in three parts, and they all came to the door of the house into which he had entered to pray to God.[167]

Adam then asks Eve to once more tell the story of life in paradise and the fall to all the assembled. She does so, and then she begins to cry and worry about living alone without her husband:

Why is it that thou diest and I live? How long a time do I have to spend after thou diest? Tell me. Then said Adam to Eve: Do not trouble thyself about matters, for thou wilt not be long after me, but we shall both die alike, and thou wilt be laid into my place.[168]

Then the old patriarch gave up the spirit:

When Adam had ended his commandment to Seth, his limbs became loose and his hands and feet lost all their power, and his mouth became speechless, and his tongue ceased to speak. He closed his eyes and gave up the ghost. But when his children saw that he was dead, they threw themselves over him, weeping, men and women, old and young . . . Then his children stood before him, weeping and wailing the whole night until the beginning of the new day.[169]

And at the close of the nineteenth jubilee, in the seventh week, in the sixth year thereof, Adam died, and all his sons buried him in the land of his creation.[170]

And they prepared his body for burial. And the Lord said: Let also the body of Abel be brought. And, having brought other clothes, they prepared it also for burial, for it had not been prepared for burial since the day in which his brother Cain slew him. . . . And both were buried, according to the commandment of God, in the region of paradise, in the place in which God found the dust.[171]

---

166. *Acts of Pilate* or Gospel of Nicodemus, 19. When Christ appeared in the spirit world he remembered Adam and the promise made to him:

The king of glory stretched out his right hand and grasped our father Adam and raised him up . . . And holding our father Adam by his right hand, he went into paradise. . . (24).

167. *Apocalypse of Moses, ANF*, VIII, 565.
168. *Ibid.*, 566.
169. *Conflict of Adam and Eve*, II, xix, 1,2,6.
170. *Jubilees* 4:29. In another writing it is only Seth who buries Adam (*Zohar; Hadash*, 97b) or Seth, Methusalem and Enoch collectively do it (*Jashar; Bereshith*, 11b).
171. *Apocalypse of Moses, ANF*, VIII, 570. That Adam was the first person to be buried is also mentioned in *Jubilees* 4:29 (See also notes 135-137). According to another text Adam was buried at the site of the future temple (*Zohar, Bereshith*, 56b). According to the *Conflict of Adam and Eve*, II, viii, 11, the body was supposed to have been taken into the ark, so that it would not be lost during the flood.

After only six days also Eve felt that she was about to die. She asked for the privilege to be buried near her husband in these words:

> My Lord, Lord and God of all virtue, do not separate me, Thy servant, from the body of Adam, for of his members Thou hast made me; but grant me, even me, the unworthy and the sinner, to be buried by his body. And as I was along with him in paradise, and not separated from him after the transgression, so also let no one separate us now.[172]

And so it was done. Seth even received the instruction from an angel:

> Thus bury every man that dies, until the day of the resurrection. And after having given this law, he said to him: Do not mourn beyond six days. And on the seventh day, rest, and rejoice in it, because in it God, and we angels, rejoice in the righteous soul that has departed from earth.[173]

One story tell us, that the sun, the moon, and the stars did not shine for seven days after Adam's death, because they, too, were mourning his departure.[174] And we also read that Cain died in the same year as did his father:

> For his house fell on him and he died in the midst of his house, and he was killed by its stones, for with a stone had he killed Abel, and by a stone was he killed in righteous judgment. For this reason it was ordained on the heavenly tables: With the instrument with which a man kills his neighbor, with the same instrument shall he be killed. . . .[175]

In the *Book of Jasher,* Cain is killed accidentally while hunting by one of his own descendants, Lamech, who was old and could not see very well any more.[176]

There are some interesting comments about the guilt Adam shares in every man's death. Adam is often accused of being the person who brought sin and death into the world. In Hebrew tradition it is made clear that people are not being blamed for Adam's transgression but for their own sins. Accordingly, Adam even appears to every man at the moment of his departure from mortal life, to assure him that he, Adam, is not to be blamed for anything.[177]

If Adam is accused by someone, his answer is:

> I committed but one trespass. Is there any one among you, and be he even the most pious, who has not been guilty of more than one?[178]

---

172. *Ibid.*
173. *Ibid.*
174. *Vita Adae*, 26.
175. *Jubilees* 4:31-32.
176. *Jasher* 2: 26-28.
177. *Zohar, Bereshith,* 57b. This in spite of the fact that Jewish traditions often do not consider Adam very favorably, but refer to him as a blasphemer, a heretic, and a slanderer (See *Talmud,* Sanhedrin, 38b; *Midrash Rabba Bereshith:* 19:12; *Pirke de Rabbi Eliezer,* 7:24). We are told that three or four angels are always present at the death of every person (*Zohar,* II, 25a, III, 88a).
178. Ginzbur, *op. cit.,* I, 102.

Noah

Wickedness Prior to The Days of Noah

The generation of Noah was one of the most wicked to ever inhabit the earth, probably the most wicked of all time. Idolatry, evil deeds and crime seem to have reached an all-time apex in the period before the great flood. While the scriptures are not very specific as to the acts committed by the antediluvians, the apocryphal commentaries and non-canonized writings supply a more explicit and direct insight into the pre-catastrophic time.

Even while Adam was still alive the descendants of Cain degenerated into an idolatrous and wicked group of people who practiced all manner of perversion and enticed the children and young men and women from the lineage of Seth to partake also in their deeds. It was Satan who taught the people the evil ways:

> Satan came to Genun and showed him how to make trumpets and horns, and string instruments, cymbals, lyres, harps and flutes, and he played them at all hours of the day and the night. . . . There were heard beautiful and sweet sounds which excited the heart. . . . And it pleased the children of Cain and they inflamed themselves with sin. . . . And Satan taught Genun to make a strong drink out of grain and he brought together groups of people in drinking-houses and they drank together. . . . And they blew their horns and beat their drums.
>
> And Satan taught him to make dyes for their clothes and different patterns and colors, like crimson and purple . . . And all the sons of Cain appeared in beauty and in colorful dresses and with their horns, doing all kinds of wickedness . . . And they looked at the daughters of Cain and their beautiful figures and at their dyed hands and feet and their tattooed ornaments on their bodies and the fire of sin was kindled within them.[1]

It is said that Naamah, the Sister of Tubal Cain, was a particularly apt seducer of men. People followed her example, no matter how wicked. She was responsible for the first outbreak of epilepsy among men.[2]

Idolatry became fashionable among the ancients. A religion was needed and, since they did not believe in the testimonies of the patriarchs, they fashioned their own gods and images.

---

1. *Conflict of Adam and Eve,* II, xx-xxi. For the musical instruments and their singing see also bin Gorion, I, 159-160.
2. *Zohar: Bereshith* 55a.

And the sons of men went and they served other gods and they forgot the Lord who had created them on the earth. And in those days the sons of men made statues of brass and iron and wood and stone and they knelt down in front of them and worshipped them. And everyone made his own god and bowed down before him and he forgot the Lord.[3]

With the idols came also the use of witchcraft and magic. They began to observe the heaven and the stars and started to teach astrology and other kinds of divinations.[4] According to one writing, Adam had brought with him from the Garden of Eden the tea leaves and they were later turned into magic games as the idol worshippers attempted to predict and even alter the future by what they read in the leaves.[5]

The people robbed and plundered each other's property and the rich and powerful abducted the poor and helpless and forced their will upon them. It became common to kill for fun and gain.

And they stole from one another and each man robbed his neighbor and his relatives and they corrupted the land and the earth was full of violence. And their rulers and judges went to the people and took their wives and daughters by force from their husbands and fathers.[6]

Wife swapping was the order of the day and many people seem to have been walking about naked in the streets and conducted their orgies unashamedly in public.[7] To rid themselves of unwanted offspring, the women were given special drinks which rendered them infertile but enabled them to continue their sexual excesses:

And some of the sons of men caused their wives to drink a mixture that would make them barren so that they could retain their figures and their beautiful appearance would not be lost. . . . And the women who bore children looked abominable in the sight of their husbands for they were attracted to the barren ones.[8]

Even the animals were included in the wickedness and perversion. It became fashionable to marry animals and have illicit relations with them. Actual wedding ceremonies were performed and it was apparently legal to have an animal for a spouse.[9] Thus the animals were drawn into the cycle of

---

3. *Jasher* 2:4-5. According to the *Midrash Rabba Bereshith:* 23 the first idols were made in the days of Enos.
4. Bin Gorion, I, 119, 154.
5. *Zohar: Bereshith* 56a.
6. *Jasher* 4:17-18; also *Jubilees* 7:23. *The Midrash Rabba:Noah* 34:14 explains that killing is abhored by God so much because man is created in the image of God and murder therefore violates that image and is, in effect, an attempt at killing God.
7. Bin Gorion, I, 191,193; *Rike de Rabbi Eliezer* 22; *Midrash Rabba: Bereshith* 31:6; 2. *Enoch* 34.
8. *Jasher* 2:20-22.
9. *Midrash Rabba:Bereshith* 16:5.

perversion, and they, in turn, did violence to their own species and inter-mixed so that "the wolf lay with the sheep and the dog with the peacock."[10] Genesis 6:12 records that *all* flesh was corrupted at this time, apparently including men, animals, birds, and reptiles. With a few exceptions the whole of creation had forsaken its purpose and made a mockery out of righteousness.[11]

According to some early Jewish writings, even the angels in heaven became involved in the evil practices on the earth. Seeing the wickedness of God's creation, they accused them before the Lord and demanded that He should punish them for their deeds. However, the Lord responded by saying: "If you were on the earth you would sin worse." The angels then challenged God to try them out and were consequently sent down to earth to help and instruct men to repent or act as witnesses to their evil activities. Yet when these "sons of God" arrived on earth they fell for the temptations and became part of the wickedness. With their superior knowledge they became even worse than men and the height of the transgression was reached under these former angel who married the "daughters of men." [12] The offspring of this unusual union were the giants who were among the masters of corruption on the earth.[13]

Other writings deny the interpretation of these "sons of God" as real angels but claim that this title refers simply to the righteous descendants of Adam through Seth who remained true to the covenant and kept the commandments.[14] However, fewer and fewer of the posterity of the patriarchs remained with the Lord. Most of them apparently deserted their heritage and joined the wicked when they married outside the covenant and found themselves wives from the "daughters of men" who were the descendants of Cain. Thus the number of the unrighteous people on earth kept growing while the Sethites diminished.[15]

---

10. *Ibid.*, 28:8; *Jasher* 4:18; *Jubilees* 5:2, 7:14.

11. *Zohar:Noah* 60b.

12. Genesis 6:1-4 and Isaiah 14:21 refer to these stories in a rather elusive form, but the apocryphal writings contain much of the material in relation to the "fall of the angels": See *Zohar:Bereshith* 25a, b, 48a; *Jubilees* 4:15; and particularly *I. Enoch,* ch. 6-15, 69 where the names of the fallen angels are indicated.

13. *Midrash Rabba:Bereshith* 26:7; *Zohar:Bereshith* 25b, *Pirke de Rabbi Eliezer,* 22; *I. Enoch* 69:6. The number of the angels are variously given as 200, 400 or even as 409,000 (*Greek Baruch* 4:10). They are also referred to by different names such as Nephilim (Genesis 6:4) or Gibborim, Anakim, Emim, Raphaim, Irvim, Zamzummim, etc.

14. The later Jewish and the early Christian writings prefer this interpreation. See Justin Martyr, *Dialogue with Trypho,* 79; Chrysotom, *Homilies in Genesis* 6:1; Augustine, *Civitas Dei,* 25 xxiii, 4. This seems to be the prevalent opinion among modern scholars of the exegese.

15. For a good description see the *Book of Adam and Eve,* II, ch. 12-21 and the *Cave of Treasures,* 15:1-4.

The Birth of Noah

Into this world of reduced virtues and low morals Noah was born as a son to Lamech and his mother Benetos.[16] Immediately upon seeing Noah, his father is disturbed about the appearance of the child for there was something different about him:

> I have begotten a son, a changed son. He is not human, but resembles the offspring of the angels of heaven. He is of a different nature from us, being entirely unlike us. His eyes are bright like the rays of the sun, and his face is glorious and he does not look as if he belongs to me but to the angels. I am afraid that something miraculous should take place on earth in his life.[17]

Lamech is suspicious that his wife might have had relations with the fallen angels, like so many other women. However, Benetos denies this and Lamech is confused. So he goes to his father, Methuselah, and asks his advice. The old patriarch sends his son to Enoch who is still alive and here Lamech is told that everything is in order with the baby; it is not an offspring of the angels but something great will happen on the earth during the life of the newborn. Methuselah is the one who calls the little boy Noah, while Lamech and Benetos would have preferred naming him Menachim.[18]

Very little is known about Noah's youth, but it would appear that the lad was probably subject to the temptations at the time of such great wickedness and perversion. In fact, one Jewish text asserts that Noah was quite a rascal when he was young and that he did partake of the transgressions of his day but that he repented and was converted to the truth when he was about forty-eight years old.[19] Another source reports that Noah had to withdraw from the general society in order not to be affected by the conditions:

> When Noah grew up and saw how mankind was sinning before the Lord, he withdrew himself from their association and sought to serve his master in order that he would not be led astray. He was especially diligent in the study of the Book of Adam and the Book of Enoch.[20]

Most all writings refer to Noah as a very righteous man, such as "just, perfect in his generation, well-pleasing to God," in the Bible (Genesis 6:9).

---

16. *Genesis Apocryphon,* II, 3.

17. *1. Enoch* 106, 3-5. The same story appears in the *Genesis Apocryphon* II, 3 of the *Dead Sea Scrolls.*

18. *Jasher* 4:14. There are various interpretations of the meaning of the word Noah. The Bible prefers "comfort" (Genesis 5:29), also *1. Enoch* 107,3. "To be left" is another translation in *1. Enoch* 106,18; *Jubilees* 4:28; *2. Enoch* 35:1; *Book of Adam and Eve,* II, 21; "Rest" is given in the *Midrash Rabba:Bereshith* 15:2; *Jasher* 4:14.

19. *Midrash Rabba:Noah* 30:8.

20. *Zohar:Bereshith* 58b.

Philo wrote that Noah acquired all virtues,[21] was the best of his contemporaries,[22] and had committed no deliberate wrong.[23] In a world without care and love for one's fellow man, he was one of the few who took care of his ageing father and grandfather.[24]

Seeing the wickedness of their contemporaries, the patriarchs actually pleaded with the Lord to do something so that the adverse conditions would end:

> And when Enoch, Methuselah, Lamech, and Noah saw them, their hearts ached because of their doubt and unbelief; and they implored the God of mercy to preserve themselves and to bring them out of that wicked generation.[25]

To warn the inhabitants of the earth that they should repent of their evil ways, the Lord sent some minor calamities among the people before the great flood would ultimately destroy everything. The Lord, for example, withheld the bounties of the earth, for up to this time the people had lived in relative abundance of food for the earth gave plenty with each harvest.[26] It was spring all year long and the people were even said to have eaten manna.[27] But now the Lord withheld the power of the earth and also those of the rain:

> And the Lord continued to destroy the seed in those days so that there was neither sowing nor harvesting on the earth. For when they sowed the ground in order to obtain food for their support, thorns and thistles came forth which they did not sow.[28]

So far the people had lived in affluence, but now they were required to suffer and work much harder for their daily subsistence. Supposedly it was Noah again who became famous for his inovative help at this time. According to Jewish folklore it was he who invented the plough and other tools for working the ground.[29] At other times the Lord turned the events around and sent too much rain so that crops spoiled. At one such time the river Gihons went over the banks and spilled over the land and thus created the first flood when one third of the earth was supposedly under water.[30]

Yet, all these warnings did not meet with any result on the part of the population and God had to take more drastic measures. Billions of his

---

21. Philo: *De Abrahamo,* 34.
22. *Ibid.,* 36, 47.
23. Philo: *De Vita Mosis,* 2:59.
24. Ginzberg, *op. cit.,* V, 132.
25. *Book of Adam and Eve,* II, 22:3.
26. Bin Gorion, I, 188, 196.
27. *Midrash Rabba:Bereshith* 34:11; Pseudo-Clement, *Homilies,* 8:15; Bin Gorion, I, 196.
28. *Jasher* 4:5-6; Bin Gorion I, 155.
29. Ginzberg, I, 147.
30. Bin Gorion, I, 152.

children, yet unborn, would live on this planet without a fair chance to decide their course of action by their own free will. To be born into such a wicked and perverted society would leave them very little room to experience the difference between good and bad. It was better that a whole generation would die than that many more would be corrupted and denied their free agency. The Lord therefore decided to make a clean sweep and remove man and animals off the face of the land and start anew. Either choice was a difficult one: to annihilate or to let the transgressions continue and perhaps become even worse. Both alternatives were sorrowful but one way was better, for *us*, not for him.

Noah's Mission to Warn the People of Judgments

But the Lord could not just merely destroy his creation without a proper and formal warning. His sense of justice demanded that he gave the human race a fair chance to repent and thereby avert the oncoming catastrophy.[31] And so the call went out to Noah to take charge of the enterprise of preaching repentance and preparing for the calamity in case the people rejected the Lord. The creation received a reprieve of 120 years and it appears that Noah was called on a mission for that period of time.[32]

And so the new prophet and emissary of the Lord went about his assigned task and declared the warning to the people:

> Ye good for nothings, ye forsake Him whose voice breaks cedars and worship a dry log![33]

> Woe ye foolish ones, tomorrow a flood will come, so repent.[34]

> Repent, for if not, the Holy One, blessed be He, will bring a deluge upon you and cause your bodies to float upon the waters.[35]

Noah was aided in this labor with his grandfather Mehusala as his companion.[36] Noah must have been at least 480 years old at this time and Mehusala 849 yet the two, and possibly others, traversed the earth to offer their contemporaries a choice to the catastrophe.[37]

> Speak to the sons of men and say: Thus saith the Lord, return from your evil life and repent of your works and the Lord will repent of the bad thing which he has

---

31. *Jasher* 5:22; Clemens Alexandrinus, *Stromata,* I, 21; *Apocalypse of Paul,* 50.

32. Origin, *Contra Celsum,* III, 41; Tertullian, *Genesis* 3:30; *Midrash Rabba:Noah* 30:7. The *Apocalypse of Paul* mentions 100 years since he was also using the time to build the ark (50) and in the *Cave of Treasures* 14:5 the time is 130 years.

33. *Midrash Rabba:Bereshith* 31:3.

34. *Midrash Rabba:Ecclesiastis* 9:15, paragraph 1.

35. *Talmud:Sanhedrin* 108a.

36. Bin Gorion, I, 179.

37. Noah was 600 at the time of the flood and Methusala 969 when the first warning was given 120 years prior to the event. See Genesis 7:6.

declared to you and it shall not come to pass. For thus saith the Lord, I will give you a period of one hundred and twenty years. . . . And Noah and Methusala said all the words of the Lord to the sons of men, day after day, speaking unceasingly to them.[38]

Apparently, however, the prophecies and warnings remained largely unheeded. The bulk of the people ignored the preaching and thought that the missionaries were some madmen.[39] The words in the apocryphal texts sound rather discouraging:

But the sons of men would not listen to them nor even lend their ears to their message and they were stiffnecked. . . . But the sons of men did not hearken, neither would they give any attention to the declarations.[40]

Men seem to have been blinded by their longevity. They almost thought that they were immortal.[41] People who lived nearly a millenium and saw their own posterity to the fifth and sixth generation never really considered repenting until old age.[42] Upon seeing their stubborness, the Lord decided to shorten man's life-span to 120 years to remind them of the grace period before the flood and to suggest to their minds early repentance.[43] The Lord could also not hold the antediluvians responsible before their one hundreth birthday as they were deemed innocent up to that age.[44] This period of innocence was also changed with the abbreviation of man's life span.

Very few, if any, converts were made during the 120 year reprieve since none but the few members of Noah's immediate family were saved from the calamity. Apparently all the righteous died prior to the flood so that they did not have to witness the tremendous destruction:

And all men who walked in the ways of the Lord died in those days before the Lord brought the bad thing upon man as he had declared. It was done so that they should not see the bad event of which the Lord spoke to the sons of men.[45]

---

38. *Jasher* 5:7-9, also 5:22-23.
39. *Sibylline Oracles,* I, 177-233.
40. *Jasher* 5:10, 24.
41. *Midrash Rabba:Bereshith* 26:6.
42. Bin Gorion, I, 188. The antediluvians used their longevity to observe the stars and do astonomical work, *Midrash Rabba:Bereshith* 26:5.
43. Philo, *Quaestiones in Genesis,* 1, 91; Lanctantius, *Institutiones,* 2, 14-15; Josephus, *Antiquities,* I, iii, 9. "The good die early in order that they may not degenerate, and the wicked live longer in order that they may have a chance to repent." (*Zohar:Bereshith* 56b).
44. *Midrash Rabba:Bereshith* 26:2. This seems to be the same ratio as some current teachings that accountability begins at age eight. With a life expectancy of about 72 years it amounts to the first one ninth of one's life. With the antediluvian life expectancy of about 900 years, the 100 years of innocence also amounts to about one ninth of a person's life. This could account for the assertion that Noah was not very righteous until age 48 (see note 19). He either repented or he was still within the limits of the age of innocence.
45. *Jasher* 4:20, also 5:6, 21.

The Family of Noah

Even Noah, who was not married when the prophetic call came to him, did not feel inclined to seek a wife and have children. He was worried that they would perhaps join the wicked as so many other worthy sons and daughters had done and be destroyed with the rest in the flood if they did not cease their activities.[46] It was only after the Lord commanded the prophet to find a mate that he finally did so when he was about 490 or 500 years old.

> And Noah, the son of Lamech, refrained from taking a wife in those days to have children, because he said: Surely God will destroy the earth and wherefore shall I have children? And the Lord said to Noah: Take yourself a wife and have children with you in the midst of the earth.[47]

The name of his wife is variously given as Naamah, Emzara, or Noria.[48] Of his three sons Shem, Japheth and Ham, it is Shem who is named first in the Bible (Genesis 6:10). But in the Jewish commentary it is said that Japheth was actually the first-born. Yet he did not receive pre-eminence because Shem was supposedly more righteous than Japhet.[49] When it was time for the children to marry, they found it difficult to find any young ladies worthy to wed. Noah therefore hand picked the wives for his sons from among the daughters of Elyakom, one of the sons of Methusala.[50]

Construction of the Ark

Besides missionary work, Noah also used the 120 year period as a time of preparation for the flood, which seemed inevitable according to the reception he received from his contemporaries. He commenced to plant trees for the eventual construction of the ark and he also laid out plantations for the large amount of food needed in the enterprise.[51] Although there is hardly any material available on the actual work on the ark, it can be assumed that Noah used the best technology and skills of his time, at whatever level of advancement they might have been. He did not seem to have worked alone but employed a number of workers whom he called together every day by means of a loud bell.[52] The time of construction is variously given as having taken either five, fifty-two or one hundred years.[53] It is said

46. Bin Gorion, I, 184.

47. *Jasher* 5:12-15. Here he is 490 years old. In the *Midrash Rabba:Numbers* 14:12 he is about 500.

48. Naamah: *Jasher* 5:15 (a daughter of Enoch), *Midrash Rabba:Bereshith* 23:2. Emzara: *Jubilees* 4:33 (a second cousin). Noria: Epiphanius, *Heresies*, 26, 1.

49. *Midrash Rabba:Bereshith* 26:3.

50. *Jasher* 5:35; Bin Gorion, I, 183.

51. *Midrash Rabba:Bereshith* 30:7.

52. *Cave of Treasures* 14:12.

53. Five: *Jasher* 3:34; Bin Gorion, I, 181. Fifty-two: *Pirke de Rabbi Eliezer*, 23. One Hundred: Origin, *Conta Celsum*, 4, 41; Augustine, *Civitas Dei*, 15, 27; Tertullian, *Adversus Marcionem*, 3, 3.

that Noah worked very slowly on the vessel because he wanted to give the people more time to turn from their wickedness and thereby avert the whole castastropy altogether.[54] A different twist is added by stories which relate that the ark had to be built twice since the first, yet unfinished construction, was burned down by Noah's wife who did not want to see it fabricated at all.[55]

It took a great amount of wisdom and knowledge to build an entity such as the ark.[56] Most texts allude to three levels within the construction but they differ as to the number of rooms or compartments on each. They range from 330 to 360 and 606 all the way to 900.[57]

> And the Lord drew with his own finger for Noah and said: Behold, this is how the vessel should look like; there shall be a hundred-fifty rooms in the right wing and a hundred rooms in the left wing, and it shall be thirty-three rooms in the front and thirty-three rooms in the back. In the middle there shall be ten rooms for food storage.[58]
>
> The first story shall be for lions and beasts and the animals and ostriches all together. The second story shall be for birds and creeping things. And the third story shall be for you and your wife, for your sons and their wives.[59]

Other sources designate the bottom floor for the garbage and refuse, while the middle floor harbored the family and the clean animals and the top floor the unclean ones.[60] Included were also wells "lined with lead" for drinking water and pipes which carried it to different parts of the ark.[61] Even a room for "all the instruments" was provided for but there is no elaboration as to what is being referred to.[62] For a light Noah used precious stones which were shining by a miraculous intervention. During the day they would dim, at night they would give off a soft glow.[63] Other sources mention a pearl instead of a diamond:

> A pearl was suspended in the ark and shed light upon all the creatures in the ark like a lamp[64]

---

54. *Pirke de Rabbi Eliezer*, 23.
55. *Hypostasis of the Archons*, p. 31, line 16; Epiphaneus, *Heresies*, 16, 1. According to the Koran, Sura 66:10, she was assigned to hell.
56. *Midrash Rabba: Bereshith* 31:11; *Talmud: Sanhedrin* 108b; *Pirke de Rabbi Eliezer*, 23; Josephus, *Antiquities*, I, iii, 2.
57. 360 or 900: Bin Gorion, I, 203-204. 330: *Midrash Rabba:Noah* 31:11. 606: Bin Gorion, I, 201. Philo mentions four floors (*De Vita Mosis*, 2, 60).
58. Bin Gorion, I, 201.
59. *Cave of Treasures* 14:9.
60. *Midrash Rabba:Noah* 32:4.
61. Bin Gorion, I, 201; Hippolytus, *Arabic Fragment of the Pentateuch*, 6:18. *Pirke de Rabbi Eliezer*, 23.
62. *Cave of Treasures* 14:10.
63. *Pirke de Rabbi Eliezer*, 23; *Talmud:Sanhedrin* 108b; Bin Gorion, I 209. The word "Zohar" in the Hebrew was evidently mistakenly translated as "window" while it actually means light or stone. (Genesis 6:16) See p. 27, note 80.
64. *Midrash Rabba:Bereshith* 31:11.

When the 120 years drew to a close, the Lord had no other recourse than to proceede in accordance with his intention to eliminate life on the earth and start anew. It was the year 1656 since the mortal period began.[65] Most of all the righteous as well as the patriarchs had been taken from the earth and only Methusala was still alive. But in that year the aging patriarch had an emotional farewell, blessed his posterity for the last time, instructed them once more as to their duties and also gave up the ghost.

> And then came the day of his departure and Noah, Shem, Japhet, Ham, and their wives came, for of all the posterity of Seth only these eight were left who had not been corrupted. . . . They met with Methusala and were blessed by him. He embraced them and kissed them with sadness and wept because of the wickedness of the children of Seth. . . . And when he had spoken all these words of instruction he died with sadness of heart and tears in his eyes.[66]

The destruction of mankind could now begin but out of respect for the great Methusala the Lord decreed a mourning period of seven days and another grace period for the wicked as a last chance to avert their annihilation.[67] But repentance was not forthcoming and after seven days the word came to Noah to gather the animals and prepare for the calamity.

According to the ancient writings Noah received some instructions as to which animals were to be admitted into the ark and which not:

> And you shall go and sit by the doors of the ark, and all the beasts, animals, and the fowls shall assemble and come before you. And the ones which come and crouch before you shall be handed to your sons who shall lead them into the ark, and those which stand before you shall be left behind.[68]

Another advice to Noah was to observe the animals: If a male ran after a female, they were to be admitted, but if a female ran after a male, they were barred from the ark.[69] In all, some thirty-two species of birds and 365 species of reptiles found a refuge on the vessel.[70] Males and females were led to their quarters separately and kept apart throughout the whole journey so that they could not mate during that time.[71] Interesting is also the remark in the writings that the preserved body of Adam was taken aboard the ark as he himself had requested before his death:

---

65. According to the Masoretic Text. It is 2642 in the Septuagint, 2262 in Josephus, *Antiquities,* I, iii, 3; 2000 in the *Cave of Treasures* 17:22.

66. *Cave of Treasures,* Ch. 16.

67. *Midrash Rabba:Bereshith* 32:7; Ginzberg, I, 142, 154. It is a period of forty years in the *Cave of Treasures* 17:4.

68. *Jasher* 6:2.

69. *Midrash Rabba:Noah* 31:3, 32:8.

70. *Pirke de Rabbi Eliezer,* 23; *Targum Yerushalmi,* Genesis 5:20; Philo, *De Vita Mosis,* 2, 12; *Midrash Rabba:Noah* 32:8.

71. *Midrash Rabba:Noah* 31:12. That is the reason for keeping men and women in separate areas of the church or on different sides of the aisle in the early Christian period.

> Hereafter shall a flood come and destroy all creatures and leave only eight souls alive. But, O my son, let those who will be preserved at that time take my body out of this cave with them. Let the oldest among them ask his children and lay my body in the ship until the flood has ended and they leave the ship.[72]

Methusala reminded Noah of this request before his own departure:

> Take with you the body of Adam, our father and place the body in the middle of the ark. . . . Ask your first-born, Shem to take the body of Adam after your death with him and bury him in the middle of the earth[73]

It was a day of sadness when Noah and his family entered the ark, knowing that all life would come to an end. They bid an emotional farewell to their familiar surroundings:

> When they went down from the holy mountain they began to weep that they would be deprived of this homeland and the dwelling place of their fathers. . . . While descending they kissed the rocks and embraced the beautiful trees. So they went down with inner suffering and tears in their eyes.[74]

The Flood Begins

It was on Noah's six hundredth birthday and also the vernal equinox when the doors to the ark were shut and the flood began.[75] The waters fell "like fire from heaven."[76] It raged on the land with tremendous fury so that it appeared to be a "dissolving of the earth."[77] The rain from the skies and the water out of the earth was hot and burned the people.

> Scalding water spurted up from the abyss and when it reached them it burned the skin from the flesh, and then the flesh from the bones, and the bones came apart and no two remained together, and thus they were completed blotted out.[78]

> The waters of the deluge were burning hot and caused their skins to peel off. This was a just punishment for the sins they had committed.[79]

The skies were dark because the sun, the moon and the stars refused to give light during this time and rested.[80] Together with this the flood was accompanied by physical upheavals on the earth:

> The flood caused the whole earth to shake and the sun darkened, and the foundations of the world raged, and the whole earth was moving violently, and the lightning

---

72. *Book of Adam and Eve* 8:11.
73. *Cave of Treasures* 16:14, 22.
74. *Cave of Treasures,* 17:7, 18-19.
75. Philo, *Quaestiones et Solutiones in Genesis,* 2:33, 47.
76. Bin Gorion, I, 195-196.
77. *Midrash Rabba:Bereshith* 28:2.
78. *Zohar:Noah* 66a.
79. *Ibid.,* 62a. Punishment for sexual transgressions, according to this text, was destruction by heat.
80. *Midrash Rabba:Bereshith* 25:2, Noah 33:3; Ginzberg, I, 162.

flashed and the thunder roared, and all the fountains in the earth were broken up, such as was not known to the inhabitants before.[81]

Many of the people ran to the higher elevations but the water caught up with them and everyone drowned. Some 700,000 are said to have gathered around the ark and demanded entry in this desperate situation. However, there was nothing Noah could do for them at this late hour.

Are ye not those who rebelled against God, saying 'There is no God'? Therefore He has brought ruin upon you, to annihilate you and destroy you from the face of the earth. Have I not been prophesying this unto you these hundred and twenty years, and you would not give heed unto the voice of God? Yet now you desire to keep alive! Then the sinners cried out: So be it! We are all ready now to turn back to God if only thou wilt open the door of thy ark to receive us, that we may live and not die![82]

When they commenced to storm the ark and topple it over, the Lord sent wild beasts which attacked them and diverted their attention. Some 409,000 giants were also drowned in the deluge.[83] Millions, or perhaps, even billions of people perished in the waters[84] And the animal life was not spared wither since most of them had also transgressed the laws of their species.[85] According to the legends, though, one other person besides the group in the ark was saved. This was Og, king of Basham, who "sat down on a piece of wood under the gutter of the ark." Noah passed food to him through a hole which gave Og enough strength to survive the ordeal. Later he vowed to become Noah's servant on account of the latter's generosity.[86]

While the elements raged outside, it was not much more tranquil within the vessel as it was lifted up from its resting place and tossed to and fro in the turbulent waters. It swayed from side to side and the animals began to roar and howl with deafening sounds. Even Noah and his family were terribly afraid. They embraced and clung to each other as tears ran down their faces and they prayed fervently for comfort.

And all the living creatures in the ark were terrified. The lions roared, the oxen lowed, the wolves howled, and every living being in the ark cried and lamented in its own language so that their voices were heard at a great distance. And Noah and his sons cried and wept in their fright and they were afraid that they had reached the doors of death. And Noah prayed to the Lord and cried out because of this and said: O Lord, help us, for we have no strength to overcome this what has come upon us. . . . O Lord, answer us, light up your face toward us, be gracious to us and redeem us and help us.[87]

---

81. *Jasher* 6:11; also Bin Gorion, I, 184.
82. Ginzberg, I, 158.
83. 3. Baruch 4:10.
84. Barring diseases and large scale wars, the population could have easily reached several billion by the time of the deluge; see the tables in Cleon Skousen's *The First 2000 Years*, pp. 139-145.
85. See above. Animals were also no longer necessary on the earth without man since they were created especially for his sake; Ginzberg, V, 180.
86. *Pirke de Rabbi Eliezer*, 23.
87. *Jasher* 6:30-31.

The Lord heard their pleadings and soon the violent movements subsided and the ark floated quietly.[88] The inhabitants of the ark slowly gained their composure and adjusted to their new living conditions. Noah was in charge of the wild animals, Shem cared for the domestic ones, Ham for the birds and Japhet for the reptiles.[89] However, all the animals were quiet while in the vessel, so that Noah was able to walk among the snakes and scorpions with the greatest of ease and without any worries.[90]

The real problem during this time concerned the feeding of all these different types of beasts, birds and reptiles since there were so many of them and each required a different type of food and at different times of the day. Noah walked about exhausted and with bloodshot eyes because of the time-consuming work of feeding his charges.

> Throughout the twelve months which Noah spent in the vessel his eyes found no sleep by day or by night, neither did his sons which were with him, for they had to feed the animals, the beasts and the birds.[91]

According to some texts Noah had to have various kinds of food ready for the great number of animals and their different tastes and usages.[92] While other writings assert that the staple food for animals and humans alike were dried figs.[93] Even though the animals were very patient with the slow feeding process due to the small number of people, Noah was struck by an upset lion one day who had been angered by the extremely long waiting period for his meal. Another version claims that a huge elephant accidentally sat down on Noah's leg one night and injured him so that he developed a limp.[94]

A further problem which the inhabitants of the ark faced were the chilly temperatures about the ship. For some reason it was extremely cold so that Noah suffered greatly and coughed blood on account of the frost.[95] Sexual relations were apparently forbidden during the time the ark was afloat. This prohibition covered the animals as well as Noah and his family. In the face of all the living creatures being destroyed by the flood, it was determined improper to propagate offspring at this time of great mourning.[96] The only one who violated the rule was Ham, who was afterwards cursed with a black skin for his disobedience. The dog and the raven

88. Bin Gorion, I, 186; Ginzberg, I, 162.
89. Ginzberg, V, 181-182.
90. *Ibid.,* 182.
91. Bin Gorion, I, 210. *Talmud:Sanhedrin* 108b.
92. E. g. Bin Gorion, I, 204.
93. *Midrash Rabba:Noah* 31:14; *Jasher* 5:31; Augustine, *Civitas Dei* 15, 27.
94. *Midrah Rabba:Noah* 30:6.
95. *Ibid.,* 32:11.
96. *Midrash Rabba:Noah* 31:12, 34:7, 36:7; *Pirke de Rabbi Eliezer,* 23; *Talmud:Sanhedrin* 108b; Philo, *Quaestiones,* 2, 49.

happened to observe Ham and his wife and, following the example of man, also decided to mate whereupon they were also cursed.[97]

The End of the Flood

Finally, after one year and eleven days, the flood ended.[98] Strong winds appeared and scattered the waters and they slowly receded.[99] To find out whether the dry land had appeared yet, Noah sent out a raven with the commission of a scout. But the bird did not really want to fulfill his instruction and objected to the patriarch's desires. He thought that he received the assignment because he mated on the ark, contrary to the instructions, and also because there was only one pair of raven aboard the vessel, since they belonged to the unclean birds.

> The Lord, thy Master, hates me, and thou dost hate me, too. Thy Master hates me, for he bade thee take seven pairs of the clean animals into the ark, and but two pairs of the unclean animals, to which I belong. Thou hatest me, for thou dost not choose, as a messenger, a bird of one of the kind of which there are seven pairs in the ark, but thou sendest me, and of my kind there is but one pair. Suppose now, I should perish by reason of heat or cold, would not the world be poorer by a whole species of animals?[100]

Yet, Noah sent the raven out on his mission. While flying around the bird saw the carcass of a man floating on the water and he settled upon the body to feed himself of something different than he had received for a year aboard the ark. He forgot his assignment and did not return to Noah to report his observations.[101] Therefore the dove was sent out next and she was more faithful in executing her orders. Upon returning Noah found an olive leaf in her bill.[102]

Since the flood had been universal, the ark had drifted to a different part of the earth and it landed in a strange place which Noah and his family did not recognize, on Mt. Ararat.

> And I will bring them to a distant land, and the land in which you live now shall remain desolate and without one inhabitant in it.[103]

---

97. *Ibid.*

98. *Pirke de Rabbi Eliezer,* 23 (p. 168, note 12) One lunar year plus eleven days equal one solar year.

99. Bin Gorion, I, 219.

100. Ginzberg, I, 164.

101. *Ibid. Pirke de Rabbi Eliezer,* 23.

102. *Ibid.* The olive leaf probably represented Christ in an analogy which showed that his first coming was rejected (the raven's mission) but his second coming accepted (the dove's mission).

103. *Book of Adam and Eve,* I, 53:7. II, 21:7. Plato asserted that the flood had only been local (*Laws* 677a). However had the flood not been universal, there would have been no need for the ark. Noah could have simply left the flood area or moved to higher elevation.

The remnants of the ark on Mt. Ararat were supposedly seen at that place by the Assyrian king Sennacherib and also Josephus mentioned that the remains were at that location.[104]

Upon landing Noah did not leave the ark immediately but, according to the apocryphal texts, waited until he was asked by the Lord to do so:

> As I entered the ark at the bidding of God, so will I leave it only at his bidding.[105]

Even then he is hesitant for the destruction which greets him on the earth is total. The family is horrified by what they see and they weep bitterly when they remembered the beautiful land which they left a year before.[106] Of course the Lord could have saved Noah and annihilated the wicked by some other method, but he used the tremendous devastation of the world-wide flood as a sign of his power and as a warning and constant reminder of the wickedness and stubborn refusal to repent.[107] Noah then built an altar and offered sacrifices on it to signify a new beginning and a rededication of the land to the Lord and his creatures.[108] A Jewish commentary, however, asserts that the old patriarch was not able to officiate at the altar himself because of the injury he had received on the ark. Therefore his son Shem acted as a substitute for the prophet.[109] Noah asked the Lord to never have such a destruction by water on the earth again and God made a covenant to that effect with the prophet.

> He put forth his right hand and swore to Noah that he would not bring the waters of the flood over the earth.[110]

The rainbow then became the sign of this covenant.[111] It is said the rainbow would only be visible in times of wickedness as a reminder of the destruction by the flood. It would not be seen when the inhabitants of the earth were righteous.[112] The Lord promised also other things:

> All the days of the earth seed-time and harvest would never cease, and cold and heat, summer and winter, and day and night would not change their order or cease forever.[113]

---

104. *Talmud:Sanhedrin* 96a; Bin Gorion, I, 242; Josephus, *Antiquities* I, ii
105. *Midrash Rabba:Noah* 39:3.
106. *Zohar:Noah* 29a.
107. Ginzberg, V, 174. note 19.
108. *Jubilees* 6:1-3
109. *Midrash Rabba:Noah* 30:6, 36:4. According to the Hebrew law only priests in perfect mental and physical condition may participate at the sacrificial altar.
110. *Pirke de Rabbi Eliezer*, 23; *Midrash Rabba:Noah* 39:3. This promise was later on misused by the Egyptian when they enslaved the Hebrews: no matter how badly they behaved, a new flood would not occur! (*Midrash Rabba: Exodus* 1:18).
111. Genesis 9:13; Isaiah 54:9.
112. *Midrash Rabba:Noah* 35:2.
113. *Jubilees* 6:4.

Though God promised that no future flood would destroy the whole globe again, he reserved the right to send local calamities if it became necessary to warn the people of their neglects.

> If I shall at any time send tempests of rain in an extraordinary manner, be not afraid at the largeness of the showers, for the waters shall no more overspread the earth.[114]

Mankind was now allowed to eat meat while before, it appears, they were counselled to live mainly on fruit and grain.[115] Yet, they were still forbidden to consume blood as this contained the spirit of life. The practice of eating blood had been a source of trouble to the Lord among the wicked before the flood and it had been one reason for their total destruction.[116] Then the Lord blessed Noah and his children to "be fruitful and multiply." But, as the Midrash points out, he did not tell them to have dominion over the animals as he did to Adam.[117] They and man would from now on live separately and one would not obey the other:

> The fear of you and the dread of you I shall inspire in everything that is on the land and in the sea![118]

Life After the Flood

After all the instruction the eight souls went their way to find a new home in a new land. They began to have children and spread out over the "four quarters of the earth."[119] Thus the recolonization commenced and later Noah was hailed as the "preserver for the continuance of the race,"[120] "the founder of the new universe,"[121] "the second root of the human race,"[122] and even as "the last and the first."[123]

The colonists probably took with them as many of the conveniences, the technology and the knowledge which they had managed to preserve through the destruction by the water. Among them was an understanding of the herbs and their purposes. Most of all the trees and herbs have a purpose for their existence, the angel Raphael told Noah, and they could be used to cure various illnesses.[124] Noah thereby became the great possessor of

---

114. Josephus, *Antiquities,* I, iii, 8.
115. Compare Genesis 1:29 and 9:3-6. The *Book of Jubilees* gives long admonitions and instructions in regards to the eating of meat and blood (ch. 6).
116. Clement, *Recognitions, I, 30.*
117. *Midrash Rabba:Noah* 34:12.
118. *Jubilees* 6:5
119. *Zohar:Noah* 61a.
120. Clement, *Recognitions,* 4, 12; 1, 29.
121. Origin, *Homilies in Ezekiel,* 4, 8.
122. Jerome, *Against Jovin,* 1, 17.
123. Philo, *Quaestiones in Genesis,* 1:96.
124. Bin Gorion, I, 114; Ginzberg, I, 173.

knowledge in medicine and the use of natural remedies against diseases and sickness.

> God caused drugs to spring forth from the earth, by which the physician heals the wounds and the apothecary compounds his preparations.[125]

Noah also brought with him the ordinances of the priesthood which he handed down to his posterity:

> And in the twenty-eight jubilee Noah began to give the ordinances and commandments and judgments which he knew to his grandsons.[126]

One of the first things to grow after the flood was the fruit of the vine, the grape, and so Noah decided to plant a whole vineyard of it. While the vines were growing, Satan appeared on the scene to make sure that wine would be made, distributed and used in order that he could again commence to bring about a decadant society.

> Satan: What are you planting here? Noah: A vineyard. Satan: What is the quality of that that it produces? Noah: The fruit is sweet, in a dry or wet condition. It makes wine which makes people happy. Satan: Let us get into partnership in planting this vineyard! Noah: agreed.[127]

After the fruit was ripe Noah took it and seems to have had a jolly good time one day when he consumed a great amount and was, for all practical purposes, drunk. Apparently in this state he went into the room of his wife in order to have relations with her and gain another son. It was at this time that either Ham or his son Canaan saw Noah uncovered on the bed and tried to do violence to the patriarch.

> He entered and saw the nakedness of Noah and he made a thread where the mark of the covenant was and emasculated him.[128]

It appears that the motivation was to prevent Noah from having any more children. Even if Ham was not involved directly, but his son Canaan, he was still to be blamed for he mocked and made fun of what had happened to his father. When Noah woke up from his drowsiness, he recognized what had occurred and he proceeded to tell Ham what would happen and he cursed Canaan for this crime:

> You prevented me from begetting a fourth son, therefore I curse your fourth son.[129]

> The descendants of Ham through Canaan therefore have red eyes, because Ham looked upon the nakedness of his father, they have misshaped lips, because Ham spoke

---

125. *Midrash Rabba:Bereshith* 10:6.
126. *Jubilees* 7:20.
127. *Bereshith Rabba:Noah* 36:3-4; *Pirke de Rabbi Eliezer,* 23. Ginzberg, V, 190.
128. *Ibid.*
129. *Midrash Rabba:Noah* 36:7.

with his lips to his brothers about the unseemly condition of his father. They have twisted curly hair, because Ham turned and twisted his head around to see the nakedness of his father, and they go about naked because Ham did not cover the nakedness of his father.[130]

The offspring became therefore as "black as a raven." [131] It is written in some ancient texts that Noah was, from that time forward, a eunuch.[132] Another writing asserts that Ham was cursed for yet another offense which had something to do with the priestly garment of Adam which had been handed down to him over time.

And while leaving the ark, Ham stole those garments from Noah and he took them and hid them from his brothers, and when Ham had his first-born son Cush, he gave him the garments in secret.[133]

After having been cursed by the patriarch, Ham took his family and moved away into a new and distant area. Also Japhet supposedly migrated to a different land because he was jealous of Shem who appeared more righteous than the others.[134]

And Ham knew that his father had cursed his son, and he was angered that he had cursed his son, and he parted from his father, he and his sons with him, Cush and Mizraim and Put and Canaan. And he built a city for himself and called it after his wife Neelatamauk. And Japhet saw it and he became envious of his brother and he built a city for himself and he called it after his wife Adataneses.[135]

As the people spread out and multiplied they also began to become wicked again. It did not take many generations until the earth was filled again with evil and violence, much to the dismay of Noah who had to see how his posterity fell away from the truth. Twice he witnessed therefore how his contemporaries degenerated and saddened the Lord.[136] To warn the people and leave a record of his life and conditons on the earth during his mortal probation, the aging patriarch decided to write a book. It contained his life's experiences, his counsel and medical remedies.[137] Noah worried deeply about his descendants and their departure from the commandments:

And behold, I see your works before me and that you do not walk in righteousness but you have begun to walk in the path of destruction, and you separate each other and are envious of each other and you are not in harmony each of you with his brother. For behold, I see the demons and how they begin to seduce you and your children, and

130. Ginzberg, I, 169.
131. Bin Gorion, I, 241; *Pirke de Rabbi Eliezer,* 23.
132. *Zohar:Bereshith* 73b; Theophilus, *To Antolycus,* 3, 9.
133. *Jasher* 7:27-28. The garments were later passed on to Nimrod.
134. Ginzberg, I, 170-171.
135. *Jubilees* 7:13-15.
136. *Midrash Rabba:Bereshith* 26:1
137. *Jubilees* 1:13-15; Eusebius, *Chronicon,* I, 19ff; Jellinek, *Bet-ha-Midrash,* III, 31-32.

I fear for you that you might begin to shed blood of men after my death, and that you, too, might be destroyed from the face of the earth.[138]

When it came to problems among his children as to what area of the earth belonged to whom, Noah settled the conflicts by dividing the land among his sons.

And it came to pass in the beginning of the thirty-third jubilee that they divided the earth into three parts, for Shem, Ham, and Japhet, according to the inheritance of each. . . . And he called his sons, and they came to him, they and their children, and he divided the earth into lots. . . . And they reached forth and took the writings with the lots from Noah as he had them assigned.[139]

Finally, after some 350 years since the flood, the great Noah felt his end approaching. He called a meeting with Shem, his last righteous son, gave him some last instructions, and then his spirit left this mortal existence.[140] Millions of people were living on the earth at this time, yet most of them already in apostasy.[141] The old patriarch, though, remains one of the most famous persons ever to walk the earth. The knowledge of his accomplishments spread and his memory remained alive, not only among the Jews and the Christians but also in the legends of the ancient East. His deeds were immortalized in Mesopotamia as Utnapishtim, in Palestine as Leviathan, and finally in Greece as Deucalion.[142]

---

138. *Ibid.*, 7:26-27.
139. *Ibid.*, 8:10-12. Here the division (Genesis 10:25) is not a separation of the continents as most often interpreted.
140. *Cave of Treasures*, ch. 22.
141. Ginzberg, I, 175.
142. See the *Gilgamesh Epic: 1. Enoch* 60:7; Homer, *Illiad* 13:45ff; 14:321ff; Pausanias *Description of Greece*, I, xviii, 7.

Abraham

Abraham, the tenth from Noah in the line of the patriarchs, was the next opener of a dispensation which was named after him. The familiar story of apostasy and a subsequent restoration is being repeated during the life-time of this great individual.

The wickedness which had existed before the deluge was again being revived within a few generations after the re-establishment of civilization with Noah and his family. The true God became all too rapidly forgotten and the generations immediately preceding the birth of Abraham were serving other gods as is apparent from this passage in *Jubilees:*

> And they made for themselves molten images, and everyone worshipped the idols which they had made for themselves, and they began to make graven images and un-clean representations, and evil spirits helped and seduced them to commit transgressions and uncleanliness.[1]

Another text records the same occurrences:

> And all the sons of the earth transgressed against the Lord and they rebelled against him and they served other gods, and they forgot the Lord who had created them. And the inhabitants of the earth made for themselves at that time everyone his own god; gods of wood and of stone which could neither speak nor hear nor help, and the sons of men served them and they became their gods.[2]

Prominent among the apostates from the true faith is the famous Nimrod, who is mentioned in Genesis 10:8-9. While in the Biblical account he is referred to as a "mighty hunter before the Lord" the apocryphal narratives are not very complimentary concerning his activities. In fact, Nimrod is portrayed as the monstrous and wicked initiator of idol worship throughout his domain. He is the first ruler and king after the flood and he himself instituted the adoration of his own person and he bacame the living god to his people.[3]

Even the patriarchs appear to be taken in by his schemes, particularly Terah, the father of Abraham, who is, in most accounts, a high dignitary

---

1. *Jubilees* 10:4.
2. *Jasher* 9:6.
3. *Ibid.,* 7:39-45.

at the court of Nimrod. As such he strongly believes in Nimrod's and the idols' divinity and transmits this acceptance to his household. He marries Edna, the daughter of a certain Abram.[4] Another text lists Amathla, the daughter of Barnabo, as his wife.[5] One of these ladies, then, was the mother of Abraham or Abram as he was first called.[6] His brother Nahor was one year younger and his other brother Haran two years.[7]

Early Life of Abram

That Abram would be somebody special had already been prophecied by his ancestor Reu who made the following statement about Abram:

> He shall be called perfect and spotless and shall be the father of nations and his covenant shall not be dissolved and his seed shall be multiplied forever.[8]

However, before the prophecy could be fulfilled the boy had to go through severe problems and tests. Many of these are mentioned in the Bible. Yet, the scriptures do not relate in any way the early years of the future prophet and patriarch. The account in Genesis omits a great part of Abram's life and starts rather late with his marriage and the move of his residense from Ur in Chaldea to Haran in the Northwest. To discover what precipitated this event we have to let the stories from the apocryphal works speak.

According to those sources the troubles of Abram began immediately with his birth. In the night in which the boy was born Terah had a party in his house to which all the great and important men of the town had been invited. While the birth was being celebrated a large star was moving across the heaven which seemed to swallow some of the other celestial bodies in the sky. The astrologers in the group hurriedly analyzed the event and came to the conclusion that the new born boy would grow up to become a high and mighty leader, who would possess the whole earth and that he would defeat the kings and inherit their lands. Such a thing had to be made known to Nimrod and the next day they assembled before his throne and related to the king the events of the night and their interpretation of it. Naturally Nimrod was worried and fearful of his power and status. He summoned Terah to the palace and demanded the child so he could kill him before the prophecy would be fulfilled. In exchange Terah was to receive his house full of silver and gold. The desperate Terah tried to dissuade the king from his plan by means of a story:

4. *Jubilees* 11:15.
5. Bin Gorion, II, 26.
6. *Ab* = father, *Ram* = high. Terah called him thus because he had just been named to a high official position at the court and he was jubilant about his appointment; bin Gorion, II, 26.
7. *Midrash Rabba:Noach,* 38:14.
8. Pseudo-Philo, 4d.

Ayon, the son of Mored, came to me yesterday saying: Give me the great and beautiful horse which the king gave you and I will give silver and gold for it. I answered him: Wait until I see the king concerning this affair and receive his advice as to what I should do. And now, my Lord and king, I have it known to you and I will follow the advice you will give me in this matter. And the king heard the words of Terah and his anger was kindled and he answered him saying: Are you silly or ignorant or lack understanding to give that beautiful horse in return for silver and gold. Are you so short of silver and gold to do such a thing. . . . What is silver and gold that you should give away the beautiful horse which I gave you, of which there is none other on the earth like it?

Then Terah countered Nimrod and said:

I ask you, my Lord, why did you tell me: give me your son so that I can kill him and I will give you silver and gold in his place? What shall I do with silver and gold after the death of my son? Who shall inherit it after my death? Surely, after my death the silver and gold will return to my king who gave it.

Nimrod saw himself trapped but still he would not give in. Therefore Terah asked the king for three days to think about whether to hand his son over to be killed or not. This Nimrod granted but after three days he sent a message to Terah demanding the infant or else he would take him by force and even anihilate the whole household. Terah, thereupon, took the baby of a servant, born at about the same time, and handed him over to the king who killed the baby immediately. The real Abram, instead, was taken to a cave in the desert where he was kept hidden from the world.[9]

A variation of this story depicts Nimrod himself as the astrologer who learned from the heavenly constellations of the imminent birth of Abram. He and his counselors determined that the infant had to be killed. All expecting mothers in the realm were commanded to appear in a special building where they were kept until they delivered their children. All the male babies were then slaughtered by the guards while the female ones were given presents. Amathla, however, was fearful for her unborn's safety and retreated into the desert into a cave when her time to give birth drew nigh. Abram was born in the cave and left there by his mother who intended to return periodically to care for her son. While she was gone angels provided the little boy with food. Thus Abram was saved from the destruction, while some 70,000 other newborn babies were killed by the wicked Nimrod.[10]

The chronology of Abram's youth is not quite clearly established in the different texts but it appears that somehow Abram came upon Noah

---

9. *Jasher* 8:1-35. Note the resemblance to the infant story of Christ in the Bible. Here also a star marked the birth, the king became worried and tried to kill Jesus who was saved.

10. Bin Gorion, II, 37ff. Again the story is reminiscent of the slaughter of the infants by Herod at the time of Christ as well as of the birth of Moses and his abandonment on the river.

and his son Shem who were dwelling in a cave somewhere near Ur.[11] It is recorded:

> When Abram came out from the cave, he went to Noah and his son Shem, and he remained with them to learn the instruction of the Lord and his ways, and no man knew where Abram was, and Abram served Noah and Shem, his son, for a long time. And Abram was in Noah's house thirty-nine years.[12]

He was taught about the true God of heaven by the only beings who had lived before and after the flood, who held the priesthood and had received revelations. But we also hear that Abram was taught and administered to by angels themselves.[13] Other writings claim that Abram came upon the idea that the idols which were erected everywhere, could not be real gods and if there was one at all it had to be somebody else. Here Abram came upon the truth by logic since his own family and associates were not able to teach him the truth. Only after he had discovered God in his own mind did he receive revelations and spent time with Noah in the cave.

In other writings we find young Abram at home with the rest of his family enjoying life as if nothing has happened. However, that he is no ordinary young man becomes apparent again at the age of fourteen, when Abram is found among the inventors. It appears that the whole region was plagued by ravens in those days, which devoured the seed when it was planted and thereby caused tremendous problems with the harvests.

> And the seed time came for the sowing of seed on the land, and they went forth together to protect their seed against the ravens. . . . And a cloud of ravens came to eat up the seed, and Abram ran toward them before they had reached the ground, and he shouted at them before they had reached the ground and eaten the seed: Do not settle here but return to the place from where you came, and they did turn back. And he made the clouds of ravens turn back seventy times that day and of all the ravens in the land where Abram lived, not even one touched the ground. And all who were out with him in the land and saw him talk to the ravens and watched them return, praised his name and he became famous throughout all the land of the Chaldeans.

Having become a celebrity, Abram's service in keeping the ravens from settling on the ground was in great demand in the area. He was fully occupied for the remainder of the sowing season and was therefore acclaimed throughout the country as the savior of the harvest. Then he actually went ahead and invented a special ploughing instrument which prevented the birds from picking up the seed:

---

11. Abram and Noah were contemporaries for some 58 years, as Noah lived for 350 years after the flood (Gen. 9:28) while Abram was born about 292 years after the flood (adding the ages of the patriarchs at the birth of their oldest son in Gen. 5:32, 11:10-26).

12. *Jasher* 9:5-6.

13. Beer, *Leben Abrahams,* p. 3.

14. *Jubilees* 11:18-21.

Abram taught those who made equipment for oxen, the carpenters, and they built a special instrument above the ground, with the front toward the plough, so that the seed could be placed upon it, and the seed then fell on the ground and was covered with soil, and the ravens could no longer get to it.[15]

The Tower of Babel Built

The period of Abram's youth seems to have been the time when the tower of Babel was constructed. It was Nimrod again who was in charge of this ambitious project which was to show the greatness of the Chaldeans and it would also make the name of Nimrod famous over all the world. The tower was either designed because the people were afraid of another flood and hoped to escape the devastation and drowning,[16] or else, it was meant to be a device to mock God: on top of the structure a temple with the statue of an idol was to be erected which would symbolize god in the heavens.[17]

To show their disrespect and insolence they talked like this:

We will ascend into heaven and fight against him (God). . . . We will ascend to heaven and place our own gods there and serve them. . . . We will ascend to heaven and smite him with bows and spears. . . . And when they were building they built themselves a great city and a very high and strong tower; and because of its height the mortar and the bricks did not reach the masons until those who went up had climbed for a whole year. . . .

One day, while Nimrod and others were on top of the tower they commenced to fulfill their intentions and they shot an arrow into the sky to mock the Lord. But God wanted to scare them and he sent the arrows back smeared in red color—blood! The Chaldeans, however, were not afraid but jubilant and claimed from that time forth that they had killed God.[18] Nimrod consequently asserted that he was the new god, the successor of the old one who was killed!

The wickedness of the people at the time is also indicated by the following statement from the book of *Jasher*:

And if a brick should fall from their hands and became broken, they would all weep over it, but if a man fell off and died, no one of them would even look at him.[19]

An ancient legend tells us that when all the people were called to help with the construction of the tower, Abram and eleven other men refused to do so. Nimrod had them apprehended and put in jail to be burned if they

---

15. *Ibid.*, 23.
16. Bin Gorion, II, 64.
17. *Ibid.*, 47-48.
18. *Jasher* 9:26-27, 29.
19. *Ibid.*, 28.

did not decide to change their minds. One sympathetic leader decided to free them one night and claim that they had escaped. All the other eleven took the opportunity to hide in the mountains, except for Abram. "If there is a sin on my head, then I will die here," he said. When it was time for the execution he was thrown into the fire, but an earthquake occurred at just that time, which freed Abram from the burning but 584 spectators were killed when the fire spread.[20]

The confusion and mixing of the language happened some time later, but apparently still during the younger years of Abram's life. The event was recorded thusly in the legends:

> And from that day forth each man forgot his neighbor's tongue and they could not understand and speak one language, and when a mason asked someone: give me a brick, he gave the other some clay, but if he said: give me some clay, the other would hand him a brick. Thus, when the mason received the stone or the clay, just what he had not asked for, he would throw it back at the other who had handed it to him and killed him. And this happened for many days and many were killed.[21]

After the scattering, Nimrod and a part of the people stayed in Babel. However, he did not learn anything from the experience and did not return to the true God but remained an idol worshipper. His son Mardon was considered to be even worse in his practice of idolatry and cruelty.[22]

Abram Questions the Worship of Idols

In some of the texts Abram had not taken abode with Noah up to this time but was left to himself to discover the true God of heaven. Many very interesting stories were being handed down as to how he was able to discern that idols were not real gods. In most of the writings Abram lives at home with the rest of his family. His father Terah is not only an official at the court of Nimrod but also an idol maker who manufactures and sells statues of all kinds and all types of material. One text mentions that Abram stayed at the house of his father until he was fourteen but then left in disgust over the worshipping of idols in the home.[23] Terah appears to have had a special room for these statues:

> And Terah had twelve big idols made of wood and stone. According to the number of months he worshipped each for a month. And every month he offered sacrifices and bowed down before them. And he did this all his days and all his house did evil before the Lord and there was none found in the whole country who knew the Lord save Noah and his house. . . .[24]

---

20. Bin Gorion, II, 78-82. Note that the number of people who refused to build the tower was twelve!
21. *Ibid.*, 58. See also *Jasher* 9: 33-34.
22. *Ibid.*, 74.
23. *Pirke de Rabbi Eliezer*, ch. 26.
24. Bin Gorion, II, 32-33; also *Jasher* 9:7-8.

One day Abram was in a room with the idols and he noticed that the god Merumath had fallen over and was lying on the floor near the feet of the god Nahon. It was much too heavy for the lad to move and place it again in its original position. So he mentioned the mishap to his father and both of them moved the statue. While they were doing this, however, the head of the god came loose and fell on the floor. Abram was still quite perplexed about this but Terah did not seem worried and merely asked for his tools and made another Merumath without a head and then positioned the old one on top of the new statue.[25] This incident must have remained with Abram for he paid better attention now to the power of these idols who appeared to be quite helpless by themselves.

Another time he was sent to the market to sell five gods. While engaged in talking to some merchants his donkey got upset and jerked so that the idols fell off the animal onto the ground where three of them shattered. That was bad news for the lad because he was supposed to return to his father with the money. Luckily the merchants who had caused the mishap paid him for all five statues. The three broken ones Abram threw into the river where they immediately sank to the ground. Again, the young boy was troubled by this experience:

> And I said in my heart: "What evil deed is this that my father is doing? Is not he rather, the god of his gods, since they came into existence through his chisels and laths and his wisdom; and is it not rather fitting that they should worship my father, since they are his works? Behold, Merumath fell and could not rise in his own temple, nor could I, by myself, move him until my father came and the two of us moved him. . . . And the other five gods were broken in pieces down from the ass, which were able neither to help themselves . . . nor did their broken fragments come up out of the river." And I said in my heart: "If this be so, how can Merumath, my father's god, having the head of another stone, and himself being made of another stone, rescue a man, or hear a man's prayer and reward him?"

When Abram returned home he was eager to tell Terah about his discovery about the powerlessness of the idols. However, it did not turn out the way he had expected.

> Hear, O my father, Terah! Blessed are the gods of thee, for thou art their god, since thou hast made them, for their blessing is ruination, and their power is vain. They who did not help themselves, how shall they, then, help thee or bless me? I have been kind to thee in this affair, because by using my intelligence, I have brought thee the money for the broken gods." And when he heard my word, he became furiously angry with me because I had spoken hard words against his gods.[26]

Another time Abram was asked by Terah to collect some firewood to warm up the meal for lunch. Among the chips he found the discarded statue

---

25. *Apocalypse of Abraham*, edited and translated by G. H. Box, ch. I.
26. *Ibid.*, ch. II-IV.

of the god Barisat and he decided to place the idol near the fire while he went to ask his father a question. Before he left, he admonished the god: "Pay careful attention, Barisat, that the fire does not die down until I come; if, however, it dieth down, blow on it that it may burn up again." Upon returning Abram found that the idol had meanwhile toppled over and fallen into the fire where it was burning along with the chips! Again, it gave Abram occasion to reflect on what had happened and the seeming powerlessness of these statues which were made by Terah:

> How then can that which is made by him—manufactured statues—be a helper of my father? Or shall the body then be subject to the soul, and the soul to the spirit, and the spirit to folly and ignorance![27]

He went to Terah and argued the case against the idols before him in brilliant rhetorical logic:

> Behold, the fire is more worthy of honor than all things formed because even that which is not subject unto it and things easily perishable are mocked by its flames. But even more worthy of honor is the water because it conquereth the fire and satisfieth the earth. But even it I do not call God because it is subjected to the earth under which the water inclineth. But I call the earth much more worthy of honor because it overpowereth the nature of the water. Even it, however, I do not call God because it, too, is dried up by the sun and is apportioned by man to be tilled. I call the sun more worthy of honor than the earth because it with its rays illumineth the whole world and the different atmospheres. But even it I do not call God, because at night and by the clouds its course is obscured. Nor, again, do I call the moon or the stars God because they also in their season obscure their light at night. . . .[28]

While Abram's father is not very impressed by his son's logic, the lad himself continues to ponder the existence of God and what he must be like even though he himself is quite confused as to the real nature of divinity. At times he would sit at night and observe the celestial bodies and wonder about them. The sun, the moon, and the many stars would rise and set and come and go. Surely, if there were a real God some place he would not be on this earth but he has to run the whole universe! "There must be a God over all of these," he exclaimed.[29] And again he surmised about the worthless idols:

> These gods are wood, through which my father Terah is deceived; and these gods have no souls in themselves, and possess eyes that do not see, and have ears that do not hear, and possess hands that handle not, and have feet that walk not, and possess noses that smell not, and there is no voice in their mouth. Therefore I am of the opinion that in truth my father Terah is deceived.[30]

---

27. *Ibid.*, ch. V-VI.
28. *Ibid.*, ch. VII. See also Bin Borion, II, 92-93.
29. *Midrash Hagadol,* edited by Schlechter, p. 189. Also in *Jubilees* 12:16-17.
30. From the *Paleas,* as cited by G. H. Box, *Apocryphon of Abraham,* p. 94.

One day Abram sets out to test the idols. He asked his mother to make a beautiful and tasty dish of meat which he then placed in front of one of the idols. He waited all day long but the statue did not move to partake of the food. However, he was patient and thought that perhaps the gods did not like that particular dish or that it was not big enough of a helping for them. Consequently he repeated the exercise the following day with the same negative result.[31] And again he spoke his mind to his father:

> What help and benefit do we have from these idols which you worship and before which you bow yourself? There is no life in them. They are dumb forms and mislead the heart. Do not worship them. . . ." And his father answered him: "I know it my son, but what shall I do? The people made me serve them. And if I tell them the truth they will kill me because their soul clings to them to worship and adore them. Keep silent, my son, unless they kill you." [32]

This seems to have hurt Abram for his own father knows that something is wrong but he does it regardless because he is afraid of the people and what they would think and do. Here we have another story of a son being more courageous than his father. Perhaps that is the reason that some ancient writings assert that from this time forward Abram had very little trust and faith in the words of his father and mother.[33]

Abram is less afraid of the consequences of his newly acquired insight. He knows that he is right and he sets out to make it known. This will ultimately present problems for him, for as long as he makes his views known in the family circle it remains a private affair but once he carries his anti-idol campaign to the public he is bound to run into troubles. However, the lad is not afraid but embarks on a private crusade for the truth. His first actions are designed to let people know how little value there is in possessing and worshipping the statues. One day a man came to the store to purchase an idol. "How old are you," asked Abram. "About fifty years old," answered the man. "Woe unto such a man," exclaimed Abram, "you are fifty years old and you would worship an object only a day old!" Ashamedly the man left the store after he realized what Abram was trying to say.[34]

A similar incident is recorded in another text. A man came to buy an idol and he specified: "It has to be stronger than I am." "Take this one," answered Abram, "it is the tallest. How old are you?" "I am seventy years old." Then Abram asked: "About this god that you bought. Shall he pray to you or you to him?" "I shall pray to him." "That is foolish," remarked Abraham, "You are seventy years old and the god is only a day old and you

---

31. *Jasher* 11:24-30.
32. *Jubilees* 12: 2, 3, 6, 7.
33. Bin Gorion, II, 95.
34. *Midrash Rabba:* Noach 38:13.

want to pray to him?'' Again the man saw the logic and left without a purchase.[35]

When Abram was twenty years old Terah was very sick one day and the children were asked to go out and sell some extra idols to meet the expenses. Haran did sell some but Abram did not because he would always ask the question: "How old are you," and then the people felt ashamed to buy a god of wood or clay or stone. While out with the idols, Abram took two of the gods, put a rope around their necks and dragged them, heads down, through the dust and mud of the road crying: "Who will buy an idol in which there is no benefit, to itself or to the person who buys in order to worship it? It has a mouth but it speaks not, eyes but they see not, feet but they walk not, ears but they hear not.''[36]

There is a recorded instance where he actually made a convert for the cause. An old woman came one day to buy a god from him. Abram recognized her as someone who had previously bought one from his brother. "What happened to the big idol you bought from Haran," he asked. "Thieves came in the night and stole it while I was taking a bath," the woman replied. "If this is so," said Abram, "how can you worship an idol that cannot save itself from thieves, let alone save others like yourself? How is it possible for you to say that the image you worship is a god?" "If what you say is true whom shall I serve?" asked the woman. "Serve the God of all gods, the Lord of lords, who hath created heaven and earth," was the answer. When she mentioned that she had always thought that this god was Nimrod, he replied: "Who is Nimrod, the dog, who calls himself a god to be worshipped?"

Attacking Nimrod in public was dangerous and sooner or later would lead to trouble. Yet Abram was not concerned with personal safety but only to make the truth known. This woman believed in his words and became a disciple and missionary of the cause and began also to preach.[37]

In some of the legends it is Nimrod himself who hears about Abram and the troubles he is causing concerning the idols. He therefore summons him to the palace to be interrogated and punished. In other stories it is Abram's father Terah who discredits his own son at court. It occurred after this one particular incident in his house: Abram is tired of the idols at home and he is ready now to show by some drastic action how worthless these statues really are. One day, while Terah was gone, he walked into the room with a huge hammer and began to smash and break all the statues with the exception of the largest one. Then he placed the hammer into the hands of this god and left. When Terah came home and saw what had happened he was terribly upset and accused Abram of breaking them.

35. Bin Gorion, II, 103-104.
36. *Zohar*, I, 77.
37. Ginzberg, *Legends of the Jews*, pp. 196-197.

And Abram answered Terah his father and said: not so, my Lord, for I brought some tasty meat to them, and when I came close with the meat so that they could eat, they all stretched forth their hands at once to eat before the great one had stretched forth his hands to partake. And the large god saw their greed and his anger was kindled and he went and took the hammer that was in the house and returned and broke them all. And, behold, the hammer is still in his hands as you can see. And Terah's anger was kindled against Abram and he said: . . . Is there in these gods life, soul or power to do all you told me? Are they not made of wood and stone and have I myself not made them. . . ? And Abram answered his father and said: And how then can you serve these idols in which there is no power to do anything? Can those idols in which you believe, save you? Can they hear your prayer when you call upon them them? Can they save you from the hands of your enemies that you should serve wood and stone which cannot speak nor hear?

This broke the camels back and, apparently, Terah had had enough. He went to the palace and denounced his son before Nimrod: "Send for him that he may come before you and judge him according to the law so that he may end his evil doings." [38] This was done and Abram was brought before the king.

Abram is Brought Before Nimrod to be Judged

Evidently by this time Abram had received some knowledge or actual revelation from the Lord. As before mentioned, he either knew about the true God from Noah or it was made known to him at about this time. One story tells that Abram was engaged in talking and pondering the truth one day when he received a revelation:

Then a voice came to me speaking twice: "Abraham, Abraham!" And I said: "Here am I." And He said: "Behold, it is I. Fear not, for I am before the worlds, and a mighty God who hath created the light of the world. I am a shield to thee and a helper. . . ." [39]

Another version describes it this way:

And it came to pass while I spake thus to my father Terah in the court of my house, there came down the voice of the Mighty One from heaven in fiery cloud-burst, saying and crying: "Abraham, Abraham!" And I said: "Here am I." And He said: "Thou art seeking in the understanding of thine heart the God of Gods and the Creator. I am He." [40]

Thusly fortified in his belief Abram is not a bit afraid to stand before Nimrod and repeat what he had been preaching all the time.

And the king said to Abram: What is this that you have done to your father and his gods? And Abram answered and said: The large god which was with them in the house did to them exactly what you have heard. And the king said to Abram: Do they have power to speak and eat and do as you have said? And Abram answered the king and

---

38. *Jasher* 11: 39-51; also *Midrash Rabba:* Noach 38:13, 19.
39. *Apocryphon of Abraham,* ch. IX.
40. *Ibid.,* ch. VIII.

said: If there is no power in them why do you serve them and cause all people to err because of your foolishness? Do you think that they can help you or do anything small or great that you have to worship them? . . . O foolish, simple and ignorant king, woe to you forever! I thought you would teach your servants the true way but you have not done this: instead you have filled the whole earth with your sins. . . .[41]

Abram reminded Nimrod of the flood and that it occurred exactly because the people then had done the same wicked deeds. He preached to him and asked him to turn from his evil ways. Naturally that was not what Nimrod liked to hear in the presence of his court. Evidently no one had in all these years spoken up against idols and wickedness.[42]

Another text depicts Nimrod as the accuser when Abram was brought before him: "Don't you know that I am god and Lord of all things, that the sun, the moon, and the stars all obey me, and you dared to destroy my images?" the king asked. Abram answered him:

My lord and king, I did not know how great your power is, but I want to say something so that your greatness may be revealed. . . . Since the earth was created the sun rises in the morning and sets in the evening. Command now, therefore, my lord, that he should rise in the evening and set in the morning. Then I will bear testimony that you are the Lord over all works. . .

Nimrod was, of course, baffled and helpless to oblige. No one had challenged him before to prove his powers. When he could not do what Abram had asked the latter ridiculed him:

You are not the lord of the world, you are the son of Cush, a mortal man. If you were the lord of the world you would have saved your father from death. But, just as you were not able to save him, you will not escape death yourself![43]

With that stinging criticism Nimrod had Abram thrown into the dungeon while his fate was being deliberated by the court.

A very interesting account of Abram before Nimrod is this one: When the young man arrived before the throne he bore strong testimony that the king was not a god but there was a real God in the heavens. So powerful was the speech that all the idols in the throne room fell over and broke into pieces. When Nimrod and the court saw these things they became very much afraid and all fell on the ground as if they were dead. Nimrod's heart stopped and his spirit left his body for two hours while he was lying on the floor. Then he came to himself again and said to Abram: "Was that your voice which I heard or was that the voice of your God?" And Abram

41. *Jasher* 11:53-57.
42. Josephus, *Antiquities,* I, vii, 1:"He was the first that ventured to publish the notion, that there was but one God, the creator of the universe; and that, as to the other gods, if they contributed anything to the happiness of men, that each of them afforded it only according to his appointment, and not by their own power."
43. Bin Gorion, II, 105-106.

answered him: "That was the voice of one of the least servants among his creatures." Whereupon Nimrod said: "Truly, your God is a great and powerful God and He is the King of all Kings."[44]

However, in most stories the king becomes annoyed and angry at Abram's refusal to acknowledge the legitimacy of idols. The inevitable happens: the young rebel has to be taken off the streets and away from the people who might become converted to his belief. In some texts Abram is first being thrown into jail for a time while it is hoped that he might recant and while his eventual fate is being deliberated. Supposedly he was in prison without food and water. However the angel Gabriel was sent by the Lord to supply him with those items for a longer period of time. When Abram was finally taken from jail everyone was truly amazed that he was still alive. This so impressed the warden of the prison that he became converted to the truth.[45] It is recorded that Abram was in the dungeon for some ten years before his fate was finally decided upon.[46] An alternate story says that he was in prison for ten days rather than years.[47]

Nimrod's counselors decided that Abram should be burned to death as this was the penalty for offending the gods.[48] Thus it appears that he was assigned to be killed by this method for the second time in his life, the first having been when he refused to help build the tower.

> And the king did so and he commanded his servants that they should prepare a fire for three days and three nights in the king's furnace, that is the Casdim; and the king ordered them to take Abram from prison and bring him out to be burned.[49]

The situation became a bit comical, however, when the guards dragged Abram out to the fire and attempted to throw him in. It was found that the fire was much too hot to even approach. In the midst of the despair as to what action to take now, we are told that Satan appeared on the scene as a pious advisor to the king. He suggested that a catapult be built by which a person could be thrown into the fire without anyone having to walk too close and be harmed. This was done and Abram was about to be catapulted when Satan took one last chance at converting the truth-seeker. In his all-too familiar style and rhetoric he enticed the condemned: "Worship me and I will save you!" But Abram is not impressed and dismisses the temper: "May the Eternal One rebuke thee, thou vile, contemptible, accursed blasphemer!"[50]

44. *Ibid.*, 44-45.
45. Ginzberg, pp. 198-199.
46. *Pirke de Rabbi Eliezer,* ch. 26.
47. Bin Gorion, II, 114.
48. To burn a person in front of an idol seems to have been a common Near Eastern tradition of appeasing the angry gods (e.g. the Moloch worship). The slaughter was regarded therefore as a sacrifice, a ritual killing.
49. *Jasher* 12:6.
50. Ginzberg, p. 200.

When Abram appeared before the court to be burned the astologers of Nimrod recognized in him the man at whose birth the special star crossed the sky. It was Terah's son, who was believed to have been killed! The king is quite outraged and threatens Terah with death. Being quite afraid, the patriarch blames Haran as the one who gave him the idea to this plot.[51] Nimrod therefore decided to spare the life of Terah since he had brought the whole affair to the king's attention, and he took Haran instead to be thrown into the furnace with Abram.

> And they bound their hands and feet with cords, and the servants of the king lifted them up and cast them both into the furnace. And the Lord loved Abram and he had compassion with him, and the Lord came down and delivered Abram from the fire and he was not burned. . . . And Haran died after they had cast him into the furnace, and he was burned to ashes because his heart was not perfect with the Lord.[52]

Why was Haran not righteous enough to be saved from death together with Abram? The apocryphal writings explain that he had not believed in his brother and his crusade against idolatry but was waiting for someone to win the fight before he would take sides.

> And Haran at that time felt inclined to follow the ways of Abram but he kept it to himself. And Haran said in his heart: Behold, the king has taken Abram because of the things which Abram did, and if it so happens that Abram wins against the king, I will follow him, but if the king wins this conflict I will follow after the king.[53]

A different passage contends that Haran was killed one night when Abram was still living with his father and decided to burn the house with all the idols to show that they were not able to help themselves from being reduced to ashes. Haran, however, ran to extinguish the flames and was burned to death. In both accounts, therefore, he does not willingly follow Abram but his heart is still set toward idolatry.[54] It is also written that Haran was the first person to die while his father was still alive.[55]

Meanwhile, Abram is not harmed by the fire at all. The furnace was transformed into a virtual paradise when God commanded the fire to stop and the wood and the logs brought forth buds, leaves, and fruit.[56] Other texts are not that exuberant but they do agree that Abram walked about in the fire quite unmolested:

---

51. This would be quite impossible according to the *Midrash Rabba:* Noach 38:14 where Haran was born after Abram. Bin Gorion, II, 32 states, however, that Haran was thirty years older than Abram.

52. *Jasher,* 12:23,24,26.

53. *Ibid.,* 12:18-19.

54. *Jubilees* 12:12.

55. Bin Gorion, II, 97 (other than Abel, naturally!). In Genesis 11:28 it states that Haran died *before* his father. The Hebrew word פני (face) is used, which would then read "in the face of" or "in the presence of his father." The apocryphal stories do indicate that Haran died with his father Terah present.

56. Ginzberg, p. 201.

And Abram walked in the fire for three days and nights, and all the servants of the king saw him walking in the fire and they came and told the king and said: Behold, we have seen Abram walking about in the fire and even the lower garments which he wears are not burned but only the rope with which he was bound has burned.[57]

Nimrod was quite baffled and surprised about this new twist to the affair which he had hoped to have solved quickly and permanently. Abram the spoiler and trouble maker was expected to be eliminated easily while it now appeared that the challenge which the king faced could not be so smoothly met as he had thought. He ordered Abram to be taken out of the furnace:

And the servants of the king approached Abram again to bring him out, but the flames caught hold of them and burned them so that eight of them died. And when the king saw that his servants could not approach the fire without getting burned he called out to Abram: Servant of God, come out of the fire and come before me![58]

The result of the whole affair was a complete turnabout of the previous condition. Abram emerged victorious while the mighty Nimrod and his idols turned out to be the losers. The scene which emerged when Abram left the furnace depicted Nimrod and his court bowing down to Abram, thinking him to be a god and it took his persuasive powers to keep them from worshipping him. They finally became convinced that Abram was merely the servant of a powerful God and they released him with great honors:

And the king gave Abram many presents and he gave him two servants from his own house, whose names were Oni and Eliezer. And all the kings, princes, and noblemen gave Abram many gifts of silver and gold and pearls, and the king and his princes sent him away and he went in peace.[59]

Abram Leaves Ur of Chaldea

After this incident Abram decided to move away from Chaldea and settle somewhere else. He either does so because of his experience with Nimrod or because of a famine which must have occurred at about this time. It is said to have been the worst up to this period and also a world-wide famine.[60] That the wickedness of the people had something to do with it is also an old teaching. For, when apostasy and the violation of the commandments becomes wide spread, the earth itself will either become also corrupt or will deliberately withhold her bounty from the wicked.[61] Abram

---

57. *Jasher,* 12:27.
58. *Ibid.,* 12:31-32.
59. *Ibid.,* 12:39,40. What happened to Oni is not known but Eliezer is repeatedly referred to in most all texts. He seems to have remained with Abram throughout his life.
60. Ginzberg, I, 22.
61. See *Jasher,* 2:7, 9.

then moves to Haran, and this is the place where the narrative commences in Genesis. The entire youth of Abram with his experiences and his conversion from idolatry have apparently been omitted in the scriptures.

Before leaving Ur, Abram must have married Sarai who is very often referred to as his sister or half-sister. The *Book of Jubilees* refers to her as "the daughter of his father."[62] Since Terah is mentioned to have had two wives it is possible that both were children of different mothers by the same father. In the *Book of Jasher* Sarai was the third child of Abram's brother Haran, and she was born when Abram was ten years old.[63] Accordingly, she would then be Abram's niece. The explanation is that Terah adopted Haran's children after the latter's death, and that thereby Sarai became the legal sister to Abram. At the same time Nahor married Haran's other daughter, Milcah.[64] Sarai was a very beautiful lady. Compared to her other women looked like apes, we are told, and even Eve was inferior.[65]

Before leaving for Haran, Abram also received the priesthood. His own father Terah was not in any position to confer it upon him. It could have been Shem who ordained the new patriarch and prophet. Some of the ancient writings mention that Shem, the son of Noah, was the same person as Melchizedek, the king of Salem, to whom Abram later paid tithes.[66] Therefore it is possible that Abram was ordained by Shem, who himself had received a different name, as Abram was to experience later.[67] It is also claimed that Abram still spoke the holy language,[68] which was supposedly Hebrew.[69]

An interesting little story concerns the use of astrology in those days:

> The Chaldeans, more than other nations, were possessed by the study of astronomy, and attributed all the events to the movements of the stars by which they imagined all the occurrences in the world to be governed. . . . But while they engaged themselves in investigating the arrangement which existed in them in relation to the periodical revolutions of the sun and the moon and the other planets and stars, and the changes of the seasons of the year, and the benevolence of the celestial bodies toward the things on the earth, they were led to believe that the world itself was god, and in their philosophies they mistook the creation for the creator.[70]

---

62. *Jubilees*, 12:9.
63. *Jasher*, 9:4. The marriage is referred to in 12:44. Josephus mentions the same relationship in *Antiquities*, I, vi, 5.
64. *Jasher*, 12:44.
65. *Zohar*, I, 117b.
66. Genesis, 14:18-20; also Hebrews 7:1-6.
67. *Jubilees*, 13:25; *Pirke de Rabbi Eliezer*, ch. 8, ch. 27; *Zohar:* Hadash Noah, 29b; *Targum Yerushalmi*, Genesis 14:18; *Jasher* 16:11-12 refers to him as Adonizedek (Lord of righteousness? *Adonoi* = Lord, *Tsedek* = righteous) instead of Melchizedek (King of righteousness? *Melech* = King).
68. *Midrash Rabba: Lech Lecha*, 42:8.
69. *Jubilees*, 12:26.
70. Philo, *De Abrahamo*, 15.

Even Abram seems to have been caught up in astrology, for we read that he had to be told by the Lord one day not to concern himself with it unduly:

> Abram sat throughout the night of the new moon of the seventh month to observe the stars from the evening to the morning, in order to see what the character of the new year in respect to rain would be. And he was alone when he sat and observed. And a word came into his heart which said: All the signs of the stars, and the signs of the moon and of the sun are all in the hands of the Lord. Why do you try to interpret them? If he desires it to rain it will from morning to the evening. And if desired he withholds it. All things are in his hands.[71]

While in Haran, Abram appears to have been quite well respected and liked by the local population:

> And the people of the land of Haran saw that Abram was good and upright with God and men, and that the Lord, his God, was with him. And some of the people of the land of Haran came and joined Abram and he taught them the instruction of the Lord and his ways, and these people remained with Abram in his house and they loved him.[72]

He was the first person after the terrible flood to be a missionary who made the true God known to the world.[73] Sarai was also engaged in missionary work. It is written that Abram preached and worked mainly with the men, while Sarai did the same among the women.[74] She was also regarded as a prophetess since she made numerous predictions which came to pass. Unfortunately none of these have been transmitted to us. The people often referred to her as "Iscah," the seer.[75]

However, Abram and his household, including Lot, Haran's son, soon left the area and moved to Canaan which was promised him as his homeland. It had been settled, though, by others and was not available to Abram at that time. The rabbis tell us that, when the earth was divided by Noah, Canaan, the son of Ham, did not go to his assigned place to live but settled in the area of Syria and Lebanon, which had been reserved for the generations of Shem. Therefore, Abram was temporarily kept from his inheritance and remained a guest and sojourner in Canaan until the Lord would forcefully remove the population in years hence.[76] As a great test of Abram is counted his willing and unquestioned obedience to the commands of the Lord when he was asked to move. He did not ask why and where to but he packed his possessions and went wherever he was directed.[77]

---

71. *Jubilees,* 12:16-18.
72. *Jasher,* 13:2.
73. *Midrash Rabba: Lech Lucha,* 43:7.
74. *Ibid.,* 40:14; *Pirke de Rabbi Eliezer,* 43:181a.
75. Ginzberg, I, 203.
76. *Midrash Rabba: Lech Lecha,* 41:5.
77. *Ibid.,* 39:10.

In Canaan, Abram saw that the land of his inheritance was a good land and he was very thankful for the promise, that it would be his and belong to his seed forever.

> And he saw and noticed that the land was very large and very good and everything grew on it: vines, figs, pomogranates, oaks, hollies, turpentines, and oil trees, and cedars, cypresses, date trees, and all the trees of the fields, and there was water in the mountains. And he blessed the Lord who had lead him from Ur in Chaldea and had brought him to this land . . . and he built an altar on the mountain and he called the name of the Lord: You, the eternal God, is my Lord. And on the altar he made a burnt offering to the Lord so that He would be with him and not leave him all the remainder of his life.[78]

Wherever he went along the roads and made his abode for a time, he erected altars where he offered up sacrifices to the Most High.[79] In a vision he was shown the place on Mt. Moriah where the temple would later on be built by Solomon and he dedicated the spot for it.[80] In addition, Abram was shown and received the entire temple ceremony and worship.[81]

Abram Moves to Egypt

Apparently a famine broke out in Canaan, and the prophet was commanded to go to Egypt, which was seemingly not effected by the conditions elsewhere. Abram did not complain but took this move as a further opportunity to learn from other people and cultures and also preach to them.[82]

For five years the household settled at the fringes of Egypt, in a place called Zoam.[83] Then Abram decided or was forced to emigrate into the country proper. Before crossing the border he announced his plan that Sarai should not be known as his wife but as his sister for he was fearful that someone would kill him in order to snatch Sarai away.

> And Abram commanded the same to all those who had come with him to Egypt because of the famine. Also his nephew Lot he commanded it and said: If the Egyptians ask you concerning Sarai, tell them that she is the sister of Abram.[84]

Nevertheless, he still did not trust the situation and took other extraordinary precautions, namely he hid his wife in a large chest while they were passing the border guards. He was supposed to pay a tax on all the items he brought with him. When he was asked what was in the large chest he

---

78. *Jubilees,* 13:6-9.
79. *Ibid.,* 39:15.
80. Beer, p. 20.
81. Baring-Gould, *Legends of the Patriarchs,* p. 164.
82. *Midrash Rabba: Lech Lecha,* 40:2; *Pirke de Rabbi Eliezer,* ch. 26.
83. *Jubilees,* 13:10.
84. *Jasher,* 15:6.

answered that it contained barley and he was ready to pay a tax on it. Then the customs official insisted that it might be wheat. In order that the chest should not be opened, Abram consented to it and was ready to pay a tax on wheat, whereupon the official said that perhaps there was pepper hidden in it and he wanted to check it out. Abram refused for the chest to be opened but wanted to pay the high tax on pepper. Now the official became very suspicious and guessed that the emigrant was trying to smuggle gold into the country. Abram was even ready to pay the great amount of tax put on gold. By now, however, the official would not accept any other alternative than for the chest to be opened for inspection. Abram refused and it was forced open by the guards who found Sarai inside.[85]

> And when the officers of the king beheld Sarai they were taken in by her beauty and all the princes of Pharaoh came to see Sarai because she was very beautiful. And the king's officials went and told Pharaoh what they had seen and they praised Sarai before him and Pharaoh ordered her to be brought. . . . And Pharaoh saw Sarai and she pleased him very much and he was gripped by her beauty and the king was happy because of her and he gave presents to those who had brought him the news concerning her. The whiteness of her skin appealled most to the Egyptians since they were dark, being from the lineage of Ham.[86]

Here is a description of Sarai which was given to Pharaoh by a certain Hyrcanus when he told the king about this woman:

> How radiant and beautiful her face is, and how soft the hair of her head, how lovely are her eyes and how graceful her nose and all of her shining face. How full is her breast and how beautiful the whiteness of her skin, how beautiful her arms and how delicate her hands. How lovely are her palms and the long fingers of her hand. How perfect the legs are and how nice her thighs. No virgin or bride at marriage is more beautiful than she. Her beauty is above that of all the women, she surpasses all of them. And still, with all of her beauty she is intelligent and very graceful.[87]

Naturally Abram was heartbroken when Sarai was taken from him by Pharaoh. *The Dead Sea Scrolls* record:

> But I wept bitterly, I, Abram and also my nephew Lot, that night when Sarai had been taken away from me by force. During that night I prayed and pleaded and asked for compassion as my tears ran down my cheeks.

He also asked the Lord to be with Sarai while she was at the royal court:

> Blessed are you, Most High God, my Lord forever. You are the Master over all things and you have power to be judge over all the kings of the earth. And now I file a complaint with you, my Lord, against the Pharoah and king of Egypt for he has taken

---

85. *Midrash Rabba: Lech Lecha,* 40:5; *Zohar,* I, 82b.
86. *Jasher,* 15:14-15.
87. From the *Dead Sea Scrolls,* the *Genesis Apocryphon,* XX, lines 2-8. Sarai is already about 70 years old at this time. She was born ten years after Abram and he was 75 when he left Haran (*Jasher,* 13:26). However, Pharaoh might have also been about that age. She was still considered irresistibly beautiful when past 90 (Graves and Patai, *op. cit.,* p. 18).

my wife away from me by force. Carry out your justice over him and stretch forth your hand against him and the court. May he not be able to defile my wife tonight, so that it might be made known about you, my Lord, that you are the Master over all the kings of the earth.[88]

Sarai, in the palace, said an equally entreating prayer and asked the Lord for protection:

O Lord God, you told my husband Abram to leave his homeland and his father's house to go to Canaan, and you promised him you would bless him if he kept your commandments. Now, we have done as you have commanded and have left our families and land and went to a foreign land and a foreign people unknown to us. We came here to survive the famine and now this bad thing has happened to us. Therefore, O Lord God, help us and save us from the hands of this ruler and protect me because of your mercy.[89]

And so it happened. According to the *Book of Jasher*, an angel was with Sarai all the time to smite with a plague the person who would touch her:

And the king approached to speak with Sarai and he stretched out his hands to touch her, when the angel plagued him severely and Pharaoh was terrified and did not reach out again for her. And when he came near to her again the angel hit him so that he fell on the ground and it happened thus the whole night and the king was again terrified. And the angel during that night plagued all the servants of the palace because of Sarai and there was much lamentation in the house that night.[90]

The Dead Sea Scrolls record the event as follows: "He was not able to approach her or have relations with her even though they were with each other for two years."[91] Finally, Pharaoh caught on that something was the matter with Sarai:

And the king stayed away from Sarai and the plagues of the angel of the Lord discontinued from him and the court. Then Pharaoh knew that he had been plagued because of her and he was greatly surprised about it.[92]

In one account, it was Sarai herself who finally confessed to the inquisitive king that Abram was actually her husband and that the terrible plague had come because of her and Abram.[93] In another version, Pharaoh

---

88. *Ibid*, XX, 10-16.
89. *Jasher*, 15:17-18.
90. *Ibid.*, 15:23-25. This passage in *Jasher* clarifies the obscure and rather laconic sentence in Genesis 12:17. Some sources mention that the plague was leprosy (*Midrash Rabba: Lech Lecha*, 41:2; *Zohar*, I, 82a).
91. *Genesis Apocryphon*, XX, 17.
92. *Jasher*, 15:28.
93. *Ibid.*, 15:27.

called his astrologers and diviners together to find out the relationship between the two.[94]

The king thereupon sent for Abram and gave him Sarai back while at the same time he asked to be cured permanently from the illness which had befallen him. He realized the power of Abram and his God and the prophet graciously forgave Pharaoh for taking Sarai by force and at the same time restored the king's health by the laying on of hands: "And I layed my hands upon his head and the plague was removed from him . . . and he was cured." [95] At the same time, he bestowed on Abram many riches and privileges:

> Because of his love for her, Pharaoh wrote in the marriage contract, giving her much wealth in silver, in gold, in man-servants, in land, and he gave her the land of Goshen as a possession. Therefore did the children of Israel live in the land of Goshen, in the land of their mother Sarai.[96]

In addition, Sarai was given as a handmaiden one of Pharaoh's own daughters by a concubine, namely Hagar.[97] Abram must have remained in Egypt a little while longer because Josephus wrote that he taught the Egyptians many things which he had learned in his life. Abram would not be Abram without trying to teach the people wherever he went the truth about God and his ways.

> (Pharaoh) gave him leave to enter into conversation with the most learned among the Egyptians; and, as a result of these conversations, his virtue and reputation became even greater than they had been before. . . . Abram conferred with all of them, and refuted their logic which they had used to justify their own practices, and he showed that such logic was wrong and without any basis. Therefore he was admired by those people as a wise man and one of the greatest intellects when he was able to talk on any subject, and not only showing that he understood it but was able to bring others to the same belief. He taught them about mathematics and the science of astronomy, because they had been ignorant of those things before Abram came into the country . . .[98]

It is said that he spent anywhere from five years and three months to twenty years in Egypt.[99]

---

94. Josephus, *Antiquities*, I, viii, 2. However, Josephus also mentions in the same verse that Pharaoh wanted to be related to Abram, implying that he chose Sarai deliberately and knew very well that she was Abram's wife. If this were the case, he only gave up the idea because of the plague. The book of *Jasher*, ch. 14, opens the possibility that the Pharaoh at the time of Abram might have been a Semite like Abram himself, rather than a Hamite.

95. *Genesis Apocryphon*, XX, 29.

96. *Pirke de Rabbi Eliezer*, ch. 26. When the Israelites were in bondage in Egypt later on, they lived on *their own* land. Also *Jasher*, 12:30.

97. *Jasher*, 12:31-32. That Hagar was of royal blood is also asserted by the *Midrash Rabba: Lech Lecha*, 45:1; *Targum Yerushalmi*, 26:1.

98. Josephus, *Antiquities*, I, viii, 1,2.

99. *Jubilees*, 13:11; Ginzberg, p. 224.

Abram Returns to Canaan

Upon leaving the country and returning to the promised land, he retraced his former journey and made stops at all the places where he had camped before:

> I reached Bethel, the same place where I had built an altar, and I rebuilt it and offered a burnt offering to the Most High God, and I called there on the name of the Lord of ages, and I praised the name of God, and I blessed God, and I offered thanks before God for all the flocks and the other good things he had bestowed upon me. He had been good to me and he had brought me back to this land safely.[100]

Here emerges the picture of a very greatful Abram who had been saved from some very perilous situations in Ur and Egypt, but who had, nevertheless, with the help of the Lord, triumphed over both rulers, shown his faith, defended the truth, and tried his best to make converts wherever he could and with whom ever he met. He had met his test twice already: trusting his own life in the hands of the Lord at Ur and then trusting his wife's life to the Lord in Egypt. But his tests were continuing.

Differences of Abram and Lot

While settling down, Abram was confronted by natives of the land who complained that his nephew Lot was allowing his herds to run and graze on their land without regards as to their property.

> And Abram said to Lot: What is this that you are doing to me, to make me disliked by the people of this land, that you tell your herdsmen to feed your cattle in the fields of these people? Don't you know that I am a stranger in this land of Canaan? Why do you do this to me? And Abram quarrelled with Lot every day because of this. However, Lot would not listen to Abram but did continue his practice and the people came again to Abram to complain. And Abram said to Lot: How long will you be a stumbling block between me and the people of this land I ask you, let there be no more problems between us because we are relatives. But I ask you to leave from me and select a place where you and your cattle will live . . .[101]

Thus, Lot moved to Sodom and Abram into the area of Mamre, near Hebron. But soon Abram was again called upon to help. This time he came to the rescue of his nephew Lot who had been taken captive by some of the kings of the area, who made war upon each other. Despite tremendous odds in numbers, Abram won a battle against the monarchs, freed Lot and also all the other spoils which had been taken. When these items were returned to their owners they were, of course, very greatful to Abram, and proposed to make him their king. They built a throne for him and hailed him:

---

100. *Genesis Apocryphon*, XXI, 1-4.
101. *Jasher*, 15:39-42.

"Thou art our king! Thou art our prince! Thou art our God!" Naturally, Abram declined and reportedly said: "The universe has its king and it is its God!" [102]

Because of the drought and the famine, the land in the Near East seemed to have changed. Many areas were converted into deserts and it was very hot.[103] Abram had to work hard to make a living and to cultivate the land. He was constantly found digging wells, planting trees, and irrigating the region he chose as a home.[104] It does not appear to have been as serious near the towns of Sodom and Gomorrah, however. The land was still lush and watery and full of orchards (Genesis 13:10). Yet, in spite of being greatly blessed in this respect, the people of the cities were unusually cruel and unfriendly and not at all inclined to share their prosperity. There are many stories which illustrate their character. Even though they were also very immoral and sinful, it is said that their greed and unkindness were responsible for their subsequent destruction.[105] This was notwithstanding that the cities were extremely rich. There was gold found everywhere. When they went out into the fields to harvest they would invariably find silver, pearls, or diamonds in the ground.[106]

> When a stranger came into the city to sell some merchandise the people would gather, men, women, and children, young, and old, and walk up to the man and take small and trifled items from him until there were no more goods left which he had brought. And when the owner would complain against one of the people, saying: What have you done to me, they would individually show him the small item they had taken and make fun of him and say: I only took this mere bagatelle from you about which it is no use to quarrel.[107]

The story is told of a certain traveler who came to Sodom one night but could not find anyone to take him in for the night, until a citizen by the name of Hedad saw a beautiful blanket which the man had on his horse. He coveted it and therefore asked the stranger in kindest terms to accept his hospitality. While the man took up his abode, Hedad took away the blanket and a rope and entertained the stranger for three days. Then, when he was finally ready to leave, he asked for his blanket but Hedad told him that he must have had a dream because there were no blanket and rope. He even interpreted the dream for the traveler, who was, of course, not satisfied with the outcome. Then Hedad even demanded money from him for the interpretation of that dream. About then, the man's patience ran out and

---

102. Ginzberg, p. 231.
103. Bin Gorion, II, 198.
104. *Jubilees,* 24:18.
105. Bin Gorion, II, 233.
106. *Pirke de Rabbi Eliezer,* chapter 25.
107. *Jasher,* 18:16-17.

he went to the Sodom city judge to accuse Hedad of stealing. However, the judge was naturally on the side of Hedad and condemned the stranger not only to paying the money for the interpretation of the dream but also to pay for board and room for three days.[108]

Sometimes, when merchants entered the city, they would buy all the merchandise from them but afterwards refused to sell them any food and water so that they died. Then they would take back their money from the dead man.[109] It was also against the law to help the poor and unfortunate. Paltit, a daughter of Lot, was killed according to the law when she gave some food to a beggar who was starving.[110] Another girl also showed some compassion toward a needy stranger. Thereupon she was stripped, smeared all over with honey and wild bees were let loose over her until she was stung so many times that she died.[111]

Once Abram sent his faithful servant Eliezer to Sodom to visit Lot. While in the city, Lot was a witness to a crime and he went to help the victim who was lying on the ground. He accused the person who had committed the attack and they got into an argument. The criminal picked up a stone and hit Eliezer on the head so that blood was running down his face. Thereupon Eliezer went to court and complained against the man who had injured him. To his amazement he found, however, that he was the guilty party and that the other man had rendered a valuable service to him by hitting him with a stone and letting the blood flow. Eliezer was convicted to pay for the "medical service." [112]

The law always favored the rich and the poor people had to pay higher taxes than the well-to-do. If a person had two oxen, he had to give one day of service a year as a shepherd. But had he only one ox, he had to render two days of service. The poor, as well as the orphans, worked therefore the longest in the public service.[113] The inhabitants of the cities also did not take care of the animals properly. With the desert everywhere, the animals would come and graze in the abundant fields surrounding the cities, but the Sodomites would drive them away. They begrudged them the little which they ate. Yes, they even put wire-nets around the trees so that the birds could not get to them to eat the fruit and rest for a while.[114] Besides all this, their low morals and excesses in sin added to their infamous reputation:

---

108. *Ibid.*, 18:18-43.
109. *Ibid.*, 19:8-9.
110. *Ibid.*, 19:25-35.
111. *Ibid.*, 19:36-42.
112. *Ibid.*, 19:11-21.
113. *Talmud: Sanhedrin*, 109a,b.
114. *Pirke de Rabbi Eliezer*, chapter 25.

And the Lord was provoked at this and all the works of the cities of Sodom, for they had an abundance of food and peace among them, and still would not share with the poor and the needy, and their evil deeds became an offense to the Lord.[115]

Destruction of Sodom and Gomorrah

To warn the people that He was not going to tolerate their sinful behavior much longer, the Lord repeatedly sent earthquakes into the area for some twenty-five years but the Sodomites did not hearken and repent.[116] When the destruction of the cities was finally imminent, God still did not want to do it without the permission of Abram, who was not very pleased about the idea. He knew how wicked the people were, but he was willing to give them the benefit of any doubt and even advised the Lord not to make any hasty judgments:

You did take an oath that no other flood should come upon the earth to end all flesh in its waters. Should you therefore evade your oath and destroy the cities with fire? Shall the Judge of the whole earth not act more justly himself? Surely, if you want the world to continue you must give up the strict line of justice a little. If you only demand the right, there can be no world!

And the Lord answered him:

You have great contendment in defending my creatures and you do not call them guilty. Therefore, I did not speak with anyone but you for the duration of the ten generation since Noah . . . If you think that I have not acted justly, so tell me what I should do and I will undertake to act in accordance with your words.[117]

Then we hear the very familiar story of Abram trying to bargain with the Lord about the inhabitants in the cities. If there were just fifty righteous people among them the Lord would not destroy them because of Abram's pleadings, not even for forty, for thirty, for twenty or for ten.[118] Finally, the angels were sent to Sodom to find at least ten righteous persons. They encountered a disgusting scene in the city when they visited Lot:

When the Sodomites saw the young men [the angels] and how extremely beautiful they were, and that they stayed with Lot, they decided to take these young men by force to enjoy them.[119]

According to a different version, the Sodomites did not see the angels when they entered Lot's house but his wife gave the news away. With two

---

115. *Jasher*, 19:44.
116. *Midrash Rabba: Vayera,* 49:6.
117. *Midrash Rabba: Lech Lecha,* 39:6; 49:9.
118. According to *Bereshit Rabba: Lech Lecha,* 49:13, Abram would not venture below ten because he knew that the Lord did not spare the people at the time of the flood for the sake of the eight righteous in Noah's family.
119. Josephus: *Antiquities,* I, xi, 3.

extra persons in the home she was short of salt for cooking and went to borrow some from her neighbors. They asked her: "Why did you not come during the day to borrow some?" Lot's wife then mentioned that she had had enough salt until the two guests came. And so the word spread that Lot had company, which was against the law. Then the people came to see who it was and to punish Lot. Later, when the cities were destroyed and Lot's wife looked back, she was turned into a pillar of salt because she gave away the news over a cup of salt, the rabbis say.[120] The destruction came by fire because the punishment for certain kinds of immoral acts was decreed to be fire.[121] Lot and his daughters, who were saved, were supposed to go and live with Abram, the angels had told him. But Lot refused: among bad people he looked fairly good and pious, but among the righteous, such as Abram, he would look bad![122]

The Hospitality and Mission of Abram

Indeed, Abram appears to have been perhaps the only kind and compassionate person in the land. The travelers and strangers who went by his estate were always welcome to stay with the patriarch:

> He received everyone, both the rich as well as the poor, kings and rulers, the crippled and the helpless, friends and strangers, neighbors and travelers, all of them were harbored and sheltered by the devout, holy, righteous and hospitable Abram.[123]

> And he planted a large grove at Beersheba, and he made four gates toward the four sides of the earth, and he planted a vineyard in it, so that a stranger who came could enter any gate which was on his way, and he ate and drank there and comforted himself before he left. The house of Abram was always open to the sons of men who passed by and who came again . . . and any man who was hungry . . . would receive bread from Abram . . . and any man who came naked would be clothed with a garment by Abram.[124]

Even when he moved, as he so often had to, he would dig a well and leave some trees for those who would pass the same way and were in need of refreshment.[125] While the people were staying on his estate, Abram taught the gospel to them: "Abram's house was a rest stop for the hungry and thirsty and also a place of instruction where God and His laws were made known."[126] "Abram . . . made known to them the Lord who had created the earth."[127] For all his hospitality, he would never ask anything in return:

---

120. Ginzberg, I, 254.
121. See Leviticus 20:14, 21:9.
122. *Midrash Rabba: Vayera,* 50:11.
123. *Testament of Abraham,* I.
124. *Jasher,* 22:11-13.
125. *Jubilees,* 24:18.
126. Ginzberg, I, 271.
127. *Jasher,* 22:13.

"Do not thank me but instead give thanks to your host, the Lord. It is He alone who provides food and drink for all his creatures." [128] He does not take the credit for the resources, realizing that he is merely a steward, and that it is the Lord who lets everything grow. The only thing he asked of his guests is to say a prayer of thanksgiving when they have received what they needed: "Invoke the name of the God before beginning and praise him when you have finished." [129]

> He would never eat his morning or evening meal unless he could find a guest to eat with, and often he would walk two miles or more until he found a guest to invite. [130]

It is little wonder, then, that he was called "the friend of God," because he was the friend of man and loved all of God's children. [131]

One day Abram must have been in a bad mood when a traveler came who was a fireworshipper. When the usual question as to the payment for the hospitality arose, Abram told him that all he needed to do was to thank the Lord, which his guest declined to do since he did not know anything about the true God. Thereupon Abram denied him any further hospitality and the guest had to leave. Shortly after this incident the voice of the Lord came to the patriarch, telling him that the traveler was a rascal who did not honor the Lord and did not keep the commandments but that this was no reason to treat any man dishonorably: "He has done you no harm. I have put up with him for a hundred years; can't you do it for just one night?" Abram was shocked and he remorsefully raced after the traveler and pleaded with him to return to the grove and he treated him there like a king. [132]

Abram seems to have undertaken rescue missions in the area. It was not enough for him to merely greet the travelers on his estate but he searched for them in the deseret where some might be stranded and in need of food, water and shade. One day, while he is terribly ill he cannot go out with the party and sends his faithful servant Eliezer out into the hot inferno to search the caravan routes for some lost soul. They return later in the day without having found anyone. Abram could not believe that none should be in need of service. And so, the old patriarch, now 99 years of age, delirious with a heavy fever, makes himself go to find a needy stranger. But also he returned empty-handed later in the evening. However, the Lord knows that Abram would not have even spared his own life this day for the

128. Ginzberg, I, 269.
129. G. A. Kohut, *Jewish Quarterly Review,* Vol. XV, p. 104. See also *Midrash Rabba: Vayera,* 54:6.
130. *The Lata 'if Al-Ma 'arif of Tha 'alabi,* C. E. Bosworth, trans. p. 39, note 8.
131. Ginzberg, I, 261. This phrase is also used in *Jubilees,* 21:15,20; 2. Chronicles 20:7; Isaiah 41:8; James 2:23; and in the Koran 4:124.
132. Kohut, *op. cit.,* p. 106.

sake of a lonely stranger. So the Lord himself with two messengers appeared to Abram that evening. And here, again, Abram was the perfect host: "Let a little water be fetched, and wash your feet, and rest yourself under the tree, and I will fetch a morsel of bread, and comfort your hearts. . . ." [133] For this kindness the Lord promised him the son for whom he had been waiting some 99 years.

Because of his great faith and love Abram became the recipient of special favors and consideration of the Lord. An early Christian text records that the Messiah visited the prophet often and showed him the mysteries of heaven, the origin and the end of the world, immortality, the resurrection and the final judgment. [134] He was a special being from the very beginning when the proposals for the earth were made in the pre-existence. The participants were torn between Satan's plan and the plan of God and it was Abram who supposedly made the deciding speech for the Father's plan and swung the vote to his side. [135] "Were it not for men such as Abram I would not have troubled myself to create the heaven, the earth, the moon, and the stars," the Lord is quoted as having said. [136] And as a great tribute and covenant, Abram was commanded by the Lord to officially change his name to Abraham; likewise Sarai was changed to Sarah. [137] Abraham was even asked to choose the future for Israel, his descendants. The Lord asked him what punishment they should receive if they ever neglected Him, the Lord: hell and torture, or bondage by a stranger. The prophet had to ponder for quite some time but then he selected bondage, which was later fulfilled when the tribes spent some four hundred years in Egypt. [138]

Not only is he important on earth but also in the afterlife. In Jewish tradition it is Abraham who pleads in behalf of the sinners at the judgment. [139] On earth he is the great proselyter and missionary and God is reported as having told him once; "My name was not known among my creation but you have made it known to them, therefore I will treat you as if you had been with me during the creation of the world." [140]

Abraham is Concerned About His Lack of Children

Amidst all these great blessings and privileges from on high, the patriarch was worried: he had been promised that his seed would fill the

---

133. Genesis 18:3-4.
134. *Clementine Recognitions,* I, 33.
135. *Zohar: Lech Lecha,* 86b.
136. Bin Gorion, II, 201, 202.
137. Ab = Father, raham = multitude; Sarah = princess.
138. *Midrash Rabba: Lech Lecha,* 44:21.
139. Ginzberg, I, 304-306.
140. *Midrash Rabba: Lech Lecha,* 43:7.

earth forever, but he did not have a son yet. Even his servants and ac-
quaintances evidently did not believe anymore that he would ever have
children after all these years. Lot's servants, we are told, many times took
sheep and other animals from the estate of Abraham and said as a justifica-
tion: He has been promised all this land but he is without an heir. When he
dies Lot will inherit everything anyway. He is therefore only taking what
will be his shortly![141]

One day Abraham talked to the Lord about it and brought up his concern that the stars once revealed to him when he was still in Ur, that he should
never have any children. The Lord rebuked him saying: "You are a prophet
and not an astrologer!"[142] And then the Lord renewed the promise:

> And he brought him forward and said to him: Look at the heaven and count the
> number of stars if you are able to count them. And he looked to the heavens and saw the
> stars. And the Lord said to him: So will your seed be. And he had faith in the Lord and
> it was counted as righteous for him. . . . And on that day He made a covenant with
> Abraham and Abraham renewed the festival and ordinance for himself forever. And
> Abraham was happy and told his wife all of these things and he believed that she would
> bear children but she did not. . . .[143]

For a while Abraham's faith was still being tested but one day Sarah
offered her maid-servant Hagar to her husband for a wife to bear a son
and heir to the patriarch. Thus, when Abraham was about eighty-six years
old his son Ishmael was born.[144] Thirteen years later he was again a little
worried about Sarah, his first wife, who seemed to be quite downcast and
unhappy since she could not bear a son for her husband while Hagar had
done so. It also appeared that Hagar had become highminded because of
Ishmael and tried to be the first lady in the household. We are told by the
rabbis that Hagar deliberately told untrue stories about Sarah to the towns-
people:

> My mistress Sarah is inwardly not what she is outwardly. She seems to be a righteous
> woman, but she is not. If she had been a righteous woman, why did she wait so many
> years without bearing a child. Yet, I conceived a son in one night![145]

Sarah went therefore to Abraham and complained about the lies of
Hagar:

> For your sake I left my homeland and my father's house and followed you to a
> strange land with trust in God. In Egypt I pretended to be your sister so that no harm

---

141. *Ibid.,* 41:5-16.
142. *Ibid.,* 44:8-12. The stars said that *Abram* would not have any children but *Abraham*
would. This was part of the reason for the name change.
143. *Jubilees,* 14:4-6, 19-21.
144. Genesis, 16:16.
145. *Midrash Rabba: Lech Lecha,* 45:4.

would come over you. When I notice that I would not bear any children, I took the Egyptian woman, my servant Hagar, and gave her to you for a wife, being satisfied with the thought that I would rear the children which she would bear. But now she treats me with contempt even in your presence.[146]

Again Abraham went before the Lord to find out His will concerning Hagar and Sarah, for he realized the problems in his household. He was comforted and assured that Sarah was still the princess of his seed.

Abraham! Do you know not that Sarah was appointed for you as a wife from the time she was in the womb? She is your companion and the wife of your covenant.[147]

Birth of Isaac

Finally both his and Sarah's wish was fulfilled and she conceived and had a son when she was about ninety years old and he one hundred.[148] When the birth was near, Abraham invited many important people from far and near to be at his estate for the event so that no rumors could be spread that the child was not their own but some orphan whom they had found, pretending him to be their son. Among many others, Shem was there and his father Terah came from Haran.[149] Supposedly Abrahm and Sarah both rejuvenated at the time of Isaac's birth. His hair turned black again and the wrinkles in Sarah's face were disappearing.[150]

However, the peace and happiness did not last long:

And God was with Ishmael the son of Abraham, and he grew up and he learned to use a bow and became an archer. And when Isaac was five years old he was sitting with Ishmael at the door of the tent and Ishmael seated himself across from him and he took the bow, drew it, put an arrow in it and intended to kill Isaac.[151]

Sarah saw this and she became worried that one day Ishmael would indeed kill Isaac. The kids were also often quarreling about the inheritance and who would receive how large a share.[152] Sarah therefore requested one day of Abraham that he send Ishmael and her mother away from the estate. Abraham complied for the sake of peace.

And he and his mother went to the land of Egypt where they lived and Hagar selected a wife for her son from Egypt whose name was Meribah. And the wife of

---

146. *Targum Yerushalmi,* 16:5. She wanted to make Hagar a servant again but Abraham refused.
147. *Pirke de Rabbi Eliezer,* ch. 26.
148. Genesis, 21:5.
149. *Jasher,* 21:5-8.
150. Ginzberg, I, 206.
151. *Jasher,* 21:12-14.
152. Philo: *Quaestiones in Genesis,* 100.

Ishmael conceived and had four sons and two daughters and Ishmael and his mother and wife and children went after a while and returned to the desert.[153]

It was taught that Abraham did visit with Ishmael periodically and did not leave him alone for the rest of his life.

And some time after Abraham said to his wife Sarah: I will go and see my son Ishmael because I have the wish to see him since I have not seen him for a long time. And Abraham rode one of his camels into the desert to look for his son Ishmael because he had heard that he was living in a tent in the desert with all his house.

Abraham found the place at noon and inquired after his son. He was told that Ishmael was out and so he went to the tent where he met his wife who did not know her father-in-law. Since he had been riding several hours, he asked for some water to drink. But she answered that she had neither water nor bread and she never rose to meet the stranger or ask who he was. She was also beating the children and cursing them as well as her husband. All this was observed by Abraham who became quite disillusioned and decided to leave a message for Ishmael: "When he comes home tell him to put away the old nail of the tent and replace it by a new one!" Then he rode home. When Ishmael returned that night she told him what had happened and also gave him the message. Ishmael understood. He knew that it had been his father and that he was not pleased with his wife. Therefore he divorced her and took a new wife. After some three years, Abraham again rode out to see his son who was again out on business. Yet this time the woman in the tent immediately rose and came out to him and offered him food and water. Abraham was pleased and this time his message was: "The nail of the tent which you have is very good; do not replace it!" [154]

The Sacrifice of Isaac

Perhaps the greatest test of Abraham was to come shortly and it involved Satan who was always looking for some weak spot in a person. It appears that he wanted to attend the birth of Isaac and came disguised as the poor stranger, ready to take part in the festivities and the celebration. However, according to his accusation, everyone was rather busy with the friends, relatives and important people, to worry about the poor man, and he felt chided and neglected. So he came before God a little while later and lodged a complaint against Abraham, that was very much blessed as to the material things of the world but that refused to harbor and treat kindly a

---

153. See Genesis 21:14-21. This was the last time that Isaac and Ishmael met until they were together for the burial of Abraham at Machpela (Genesis 25:9). Hagar supposedly turned apostate in the wilderness and followed "after the idolatry of her father." (Pirke de Rabbi Eliezer, ch. 27).

154. Jasher, 21:24-48.

poor man while he preferred the rich people. The Lord knew that it was merely one of Satan's ploys but, to be fair, he had to check out the accusation.[155]

Another version says that Satan accused Abraham of having been unfaithful to the Lord since the birth of Isaac.

> And now since his son Isaac was born to him he has left you. He made a great celebration for all the people in the land but he has forgotten the Lord. For all the things he has done he has brought no sacrifices before you, no burnt offerings and no peace offerings, no ox, no lamb, no goat even though he killed much on the day his son was born. Even until now, thirty-seven years since his son's birth, he has not built an altar for you and made no sacrifices for you because he knew that you would bless him with whatever he asked for, and he has forsaken you.[156]

Satan's plan is clear: he accused Abrahm of inhospitality because he was quite rich and therefore needed to have something precious taken away to remind him that everything was merely given as a blessing. The most precious thing Abraham possessed was his son, Isaac. The second accusation was that no sacrifices had been offered. Satan wanted that God would command Abraham to sacrifice again by offering up his most priceless possession, his son.

The Lord consented and so, one night, the voice came to the patriarch to take his son and offer him up as a sacrifice. Abraham was very surprised and it seems that he pretended not to understand: "I ask of you, I beg you, take your son." "Which son?" "Your only son." "But each is the only son of his mother." "The one whom you love." "Is there a difference. I love both." "Take Isaac!" He still did not want to do it and tried to find a way out: "Shem shall do it. He is a high priest!" "I will make you one when you arrive at the assigned place," the Lord replied.[157]

> And Abraham said to himself: How shall I take Isaac from his mother in order to bring him before the Lord as a sacrifice? And he went into the tent and sat there with Sarah and he said to her: My son Isaac is now a grown young man and he has not yet studied the ways of the Lord. Tomorrow I will go and take him to Shem and his son Eber and there he will learn the ways of God . . .[158]

Sarah consented to this idea although she was worried about her son. The next day she saw them off as they left for Mt. Moriah.

> And Sarah went out with them and she accompanied them on the road to say goodbye. And they said to her to return to the tent. And when Sarah heard those words of

---

155. *Zohar*, I, 10a-11b.
156. *Jasher*, 22:51-53.
157. Ginzberg, I, 274; *Midrash Rabba: Vayera*, 55:7.
158. *Jasher*, 23:3-5.

Isaac she wept and Abraham her husband also wept, and also Isaac wept and all those who were with them. And Sarah took her son Isaac and embraced him in her arms and continued to weep with him and Sarah said: Who knows if I shall ever see him again after this day?[159]

After this emotional farewell the two and their servants proceed on their way to the mountain. Meanwhile, Satan saw that Abraham was going ahead with the sacrifice as the Lord had commanded and he became worried that his carefully planned scheme was not working according to his satisfaction. He therefore appeared to the traveling party as an old and humble gentleman and struck up a conversation with Abraham. When he heard the astonishing news of why Abraham was going to Mt. Moriah, he all of a sudden converted into the pious and concerned friend who wants to keep the patriarch from making a grave mistake:

Are you mad or like an animal that you are going to do this deed to your only son? God gave you a son in your old age, and now you want to go and kill him today though he committed no crime and you will make the spirit of your son leave the earth? Do you not understand that this cannot be from the Lord? The Lord cannot do such an evil thing on the earth as to say to a man: Go and kill your child![160]

Abraham was, of course, not impressed. He knew that it was the Lord who asked him to offer his son. He also realized that the stranger was Satan and he rebuked him so that he had to leave. However, Satan was determined not to give up so easily. A little while later he returned and struck up a conversation with Isaac and proceeded to warn him against the evil plans of his father:

Do you know that your old and senile father takes you to be killed today for no reason? Therefore, my son, do not listen to him because he is mad and do not let your precious spirit and your fine body leave the earth.[161]

This desperate attempt did not work either. When Isaac went to his father concerning what the stranger had said, Abraham told him not to listen to the story because that man had been Satan.

However, Abraham could not hide his intention from his son forever. According to some old texts, Isaac was not a young child any more but probably about thirty-seven years old.[162] He finally told him what the Lord had commanded him to do. Isaac's answer was typical of anyone who was associated with Abraham and acquainted with his character:

---

159. *Ibid.*, 23:16-18.
160. *Ibid.*, 23:25-27.
161. *Ibid.*, 23:30-31.
162. *Ibid.*, 21:53. He was twenty-five according to Josephus, *Antiquities,* i, xiii, 2.

> And Isaac said to his father: I will do everything the Lord said to you with happiness and a joyful heart . . . Blessed is the Lord who has today chosen me to be a sacrifice before Him![163]

Isaac is actually cheerful because, of all the people, the Lord chose particularly him for this offering. He considered it a special recognition. It probably also implied that he was pure and worthy because the sacrificial item had to be blameless of any offense before God and the law. Even after Abraham probed his son's real feeling and his conscience, Isaac remained dedicated and obedient to the Lord's will:

> Is there in your heart any thought of word which does not agree with this act? Tell me, my son, I beg you, do not withhold it from me! And Isaac answered his father and said to him: My father, as surely as the Lord lives and as you live, there is nothing in my heart which would cause me to change to the left or the right from what you have said to me. No limb or muscle has moved in me about this and there is no thought of evil in my heart concerning this action. I am happy and my heart rejoices.[164]

Isaac even helped his father to build the altar upon which he would soon be laid.[165] However, he did ask one question: "What will you two do in your old age," referring to his father and his mother. And Abraham answered: "We know that we can survive you only by a few days. He who was our comforter before you were born will be our comforter now and henceforth."[166]

When Isaac was on the altar he asked his father to bind him tightly so that he would not move:

> Father, I am a young man and I am afraid that my body might tremble because of fear of the knife and I might cause you grief, and the sacrifice might be invalid and it will not count as a real sacrifice. Bind me therefore very firmly.[167]

> And Isaac said to his father: My father, when you have killed me and burnt me for an offering, take the ashes which remain of me and bring them to my mother Sarah and tell her: this is the sweet smell of Isaac . . . And Abraham heard the words of Isaac, and he cried when Isaac said these words. And Abraham's tears fell down upon Isaac, his son, and he also wept bitterly, and he said to his father: My father, hurry and do with me as the Lord our God has commanded you.[168]

Even though both father and son were terrified and sad, they were ready and willing to do the impossible with gladness to please the Lord.

---

163. *Ibid.,* 23:52, 56.
164. *Ibid.,* 23:53-56.
165. *Ibid.,* 23:58.
166. Ginzberg, I, 280.
167. *Midrash Rabba: Vayera,* 56:8. How does a man 137 years old bind a man of 37 without his consent?
168. *Jasher,* 23:62-63.

> Abraham stretched forth his hands to take the knife, while the tears came out of his eyes, tears of a father's compassion, and they dropped into Isaac's eyes. But even so, his heart was glad to obey the will of his creator.[169]

Abraham was so determined to follow the commandment that even when the instruction of the angel came to stop the sacrifice, he was not quite sure whether this was not another of Satan's schemes to abbort the offering:

> Abraham, Abraham, do not lay your hands upon the young man. And Abraham answered: God did command me to sacrifice Isaac and you command me not to kill him. The words of the teacher and the words of the disciple, to whose words should I listen?[170]

When the attempted offering ended so abruptly, Abraham asked the Lord: "Shall I go hence without having offered up a sacrifice?" And then God replied: "Lift up thine eyes and behold the sacrifice behind thee." There in the bushes was the ram and Abraham went to sacrifice it in the place of Isaac: "This one instead of my son and may this be considered as the blood of my son before the Lord."[171]

Even at this point Satan still attempted to intervene as recorded by an old text. While the ram was running toward Abraham as the designated substitute, Satan tried to stop it, caught hold of it and entangled its horn in the bushes so that it might not act as a substitute. Now, that the Lord changed the plan, Satan was determined to undermine it and snatched the ram so that Abraham might still have to kill Isaac! However, Abraham realized the plot and took the ram away and sacrificed it.[172] When all the traumatic excitement was over, the patriarch asked the Lord about the whole affair to get a clearer idea of what it was about:

> Thou surely didst know that I was ready to sacrifice my son? And the Lord answered: It was manifest to me and I foreknew it that thou wouldest withhold not even thy son from Me. And why, then, didst Thou afflict me thus? It was my wish that the world should become acquainted with thee, and should know that it is not without good reason that I have chosen thee from all nations. Now it hath been witnessed unto men that thou fearest God.[173]

While still on the mountain, Abraham was told a temple would later on be erected at this spot but also that it would be destroyed at some future time.[174] In addition, the Lord made it known that Isaac's future wife, Milkah, was born this day.[175]

---

169. *Midrash Rabba: Vayera,* 56:9.
170. *Pirke de Rabbi Eliezer,* ch. 31.
171. Ginzberg, I, 282-283. The eternal principle of substitution is brought forth quite clearly: Isaac's sacrifice was to be in the similitude of the Messiah but the ram finally substituted for the substitute. See *Jasher,* 23:75.
172. *Jasher,* 23:75.
173. Ginzberg, I, 283-284.
174. *Pirke de Rabbi Eliezer,* ch. 31. *Midrash Rabba: Vayera,* 56:10.
175. *Midrash Rabba: Vayera,* 57:2.

Satan, meanwhile, was mad and thought about how he could salvage something from the whole affair and hurt Abraham at the same time. He appeared to Sarah in disguise and brought her a false version of what had happened on Mt. Moriah that day:

> And he said to her: Do you know what Abraham has done with your son this day? He took Isaac and built an altar and killed and offered him up as a sacrifice. Isaac cried and wept before his father but he did not look and had no compassion on him . . . And Sarah cried out and wept bitterly because of her son and she threw herself on the ground and put dust on her head and said: O my son, Isaac, my son, had I died instead of you . . .[176]

Yet, she knew that her husband was a prophet and would not do such an act unless it had been commanded to him by the Lord. She had complete faith in him and, although she was shocked and sad, she did not complain too much but trusted in the Lord:

> You are just, O Lord our God, for all your works are good and righteous. I am also rejoicing in accordance with your word which you have commanded and while my eyes weep bitterly my heart is happy.[177]

The Death of Sarah

To find out what really happened and to receive the remnants of her son, Sarah traveled to Kireath Arba. While looking and waiting for Abraham, Satan appeared again to her. Since she took the news quite well the first time, he devised a different plan and this one worked. He told Sarah that he had made an error the first time he came and that Isaac had not been killed but was still alive.

> And she heard the message and her joy and happiness was so great that her son was still alive that her spirit left her and she died and was taken home to her people.[178]

Abraham and Isaac, meanwhile, descended from the mountain and made their way toward Beersheba, probably happy and glad that everything had turned out so well after all. But the disappointment was great when they heard the news about Sarah and realized that it did take one life after all.

> And Abraham looked for Sarah and could not find her and he asked for her and he was told that she went as far as Hebron to look for you both to see where you had gone. And Abraham and Isaac went to Hebron and when they found that she was dead they

---

176. *Jasher,* 23:77, 79.
177. *Ibid.,* 23:82.
178. *Jasher,* 23:86. She was 127 years old at this time (Genesis 23:1). She was 90 when Isaac was born, so he was 37 when this incident occurred.

cried and wept bitterly over her . . . And Abraham and Isaac wept greatly and all their servants wept with them on account of Sarah and they mourned for her a great and heavy mourning.[179]

Abraham bought the cave of Machpelah as a burial place for Sarah and for himself.[180] The actual interment was quite festive: "And Abraham buried Sarah with pomp as only done at the burial of kings. And she was buried in very fine and beautiful garments."[181]

Thus Abraham outlived Sarah by some thirty-eight years. It is written that his brother Nahor and Lot both died about this time also.[182] His father, Terah, evidently already passed away two years before Sarah's death.[183]

Isaac's Marriage and the Last Days of Abraham

As time went by, Abraham was concerned to have Isaac married. His son was away at the house of Shem for three years to learn and study, and during this time, he undertook a search for a suitable companion for Isaac.[184] To accomplish this, Abraham instructed his faithful servant Eliezer to go and find a wife. Eliezer was eager to offer his own daughter as a bride for Isaac but the patriarch declined: "No, you are of the forbidden race and my son is of the blessed race. Curses and blessings cannot unite."[185] Eliezer had to promise Abraham that he would not look for a wife among the Canaanites but that he would return to Haran for that purpose. "And Abraham made him take the oath by the sign of the covenant."[186] So Eliezer went to Haran and found Rebeccah for Isaac.

After Isaac was married and had moved away, Abraham was very lonely. He had become old after his wife died. Up to that time he looked so much like Isaac that people who did not know him could not tell those two apart. It was so confusing that Abraham prayed to the Lord to give him some marks of distinction. The Lord granted his request and changed his hair to white.[187] Now the old patriarch looked his age.

---

179. *Ibid.*, 23:88-90. Philo said that Abraham mourned only for a short period of time, for it was unworthy of a great and wise man to mourn long because he knew that he was only a steward on the earth and the Lord was taking back what had always been his (*De Abrahamo 44*).

180. Genesis 23:3-20. Here we find the patriarch buying land, which was promised him by the Lord as his inheritance, from people who possessed it illegally. It shows the humility and generosity of the patriarch.

181. *Jasher,* 24:13.

182. *Ibid.,* 24:22, 27.

183. *Midrash Rabba: Chayye Sarah,* 58:5.

184. *Jasher,* 24:17.

185. *Midrash Rabba:Chayye Sarah,* 59:9. Here we have one of the finest apocryphal passages showing that a person can be very much blessed in many areas but cursed as to the priesthood because of his lineage.

186. Ginzberg, I, 294. See Genesis 24:3-9.

187. *Talmud: Sanhedrin,* 107b. *Pirke de Rabbi Eliezer,* ch. 52. It was the first time that white hair was used to denote someone of venerable age.

Since his son was happily married it occurred to Abraham that he would also like to get married again. His third wife's name was Keturah and she was evidently from the line of Japhet.[188]

After many years the old patriarch slowly felt his end approaching and he called his relatives to him once more for some last instruction:

> Abraham called Ishmael and his twelve sons, and Isaac and his two sons, and the six sons of Ketuhra, and their sons. And he commanded them to follow the path of the Lord, to live righteously, for each to love their neighbor and to act in love toward all men . . .[189]

He also reiterated the commandments and laws of God and then sent them on their way. But he asked Isaac to remain with him and then, in private, he counseled him on various matters and gave him insight and advice, for Isaac was to be the leader and patriarch following his father.

> I have become old but I do not know the day of my death but my days are full; behold, I am one hundred and seventy-five years old and all throughout my life I have been mindful of the Lord and have tried to do his will all my days and to walk righteously before him. I have hated idols and I have followed the will of him who has created me. He is the living God and he is holy and faithful, and he is righteous beyond anyone, and he is no respector of person and does not accept bribes . . .[190]

He admonished Isaac to be faithful and he enumerated the different laws and traditions which he should follow and concluded by asking a blessing from God:

> May Thy grace and Thy mercy be upon my sons, whom I love with all my heart and my affection, and upon his posterity forever. Do not forsake him or forget him from now until the days of eternity and may Thine eyes be upon him and his seed so that he might be protected, and bless him and make him into a great nation for the inheritance. Bless him with all Thy blessings from now until the days of eternity, and renew Thy covenant and Thy grace with him and with his posterity as Thou wouldst to all the generations of the earth.[191]

Another text describes the last instructions to Isaac thusly:

> Now, my son, listen to my words, and keep the commandments of the Lord your God which I commanded you. Do not turn from the correct way to either the left or the right, in order that everything may be well with you and your children forever. Remember the wonderful works of the Lord and the kindness He has shown to us by helping us out of the hands of our enemies as he let them fall into our hands. Keep therefore all that I have commanded you and do not turn from the commandments of

---

188. Genesis 25:1. It is written that Keturah was actually Hagar whom Abraham now took back *(Midrash Rabba: Chayye Sarah* 61:4; *Pike de Rabbi Eliezer,* ch. 30; *Targum Yerulshalmi).* According to Ginzberg, V, 265 note 309, Abraham married women from all of Noah's descendants: Shem (Sarah), Japhet (Keturah) and Ham (Hagar).

189. *Jubilees,* 20:1, 2.

190. *Ibid.,* 21:1-4.

191. *Jubilees,* 22:28-30.

your God and serve none besides him so that all may be well with you and your seed which comes after you. Teach your children and your seed the laws of God and his commandments and teach the righteous way by which they should walk so that all may be well with them forever.[192]

The Death of Abraham

Finally the life of the great patriarch and prophet came to an end. When the spirit of Abraham was to leave this mortal world, the Lord did not merely summon it but he sent a messenger to accompany him to the other side. According to Jewish traditions, it was Michael who received the commission. Abraham was sitting next to some oxen in a field near Mamre when he saw the stranger come. As was his usual custom, he rose, greeted the traveler and invited him home for refreshments. Slowly he became aware of who the stranger was, but he remained the perfect host which he had always been:

When they came to the house they rested on the court. And when Isaac saw the angel's face he said to his mother Sarah: My mother, the man who sits with my father is not of the same race as those who live on the earth. And he ran and bowed before him and fell to the feet of the angel and the angel blessed him and said: The Lord God will fulfill his promise to you which he has made to your father Abraham and his seed and he will answer the prayer of your father and your mother. And Abraham said to his son Isaac: Isaac, my son, fetch some water from the well and bring it to me in a bowl that we may wash the feet of the stranger, for he is tired since he came from a far away journey. Isaac ran to the well and fetched some water in a bowl and brought it back to them. And Abraham came forward and washed the feet of the angel Michael and he was deeply touched and he wept over the stranger . . .[193]

And Abraham said to his son Isaac: My son, go into the inner chamber of the house and arrange everything nicely. Lay out two couches, one for me and for this man who is our guest today. Prepare a seat and a candlestick and a table full of every good thing. Make the room beautiful and lay out the linen and the purple cloth. Burn the good and expensive incense and bring in the sweet plants from the garden and fill the house with them. Light seven lamps with oil that we may be happy because this man who is our guest today is more exalted than kings and rulers.[194]

So it was done, but after a while Michael wanted to leave and take Abraham with him. However, the aged patriarch was not yet ready. He asked for an extension and answers to certain questions. The Lord granted them and he was shown many things in the heavens and under the heavens. Everyone knew that the great Abraham was stalling. Finally, however, he had to leave this world which he loved so much and where he worked so hard

---

192. *Jasher*, 26:25-27.
193. *Testament of Abraham*, III.
194. *Ibid.*, IV.

and long. "Abraham, come and take my right hand," said the messenger and then he and the great patriarch left this world.

Another text has him depart while he and his grandson Jacob are together:

> And he placed two fingers of Jacob on his eyes and he blessed the God of Gods and he covered his face and stretched out his feet and slept the sleep of the eternity and he was gathered home to his fathers.[195]

Naturally, there was a great mourning in the land when the death of the prophet became known and many great tributes were paid to his righteous life and his love for his fellow man:

> And all the little children and all the people in the land wept because of Abraham, for Abraham had been good to them all; he had been upright with God and with men . . . And he had brought the children of the earth to the service of God and he had taught them the ways of the Lord and he had made the Lord known to them . . . And the Lord delivered the whole earth on account of Abraham.[196]

This was the mortal end of the "friend of God." His fame and his name spread to many distant places where he was also remembered as a saintly being.[197]

---

195. *Jubilees,* 23:1.
196. *Jasher* 26:33, 38.
197. It is said that the Brahmins of India took their name from Abraham.

Moses

The Egyptians Oppressed Israel

The children of Jacob fared quite well while in Egypt. They grew in number and became a mighty force in the country. Joseph was the chancellor under pharaoh for some eighty years before he died at the advanced age of 110.[1] Conditions for the Israelites did not immediately change upon his passing, even though no one in the family occupied any important position at court any more. However, their prosperity and progress caused a great deal of envy among the native Egyptians, who seemed to have long forgotten the great service which Joseph rendered to the country during the times of famine and need. Yet, as long as one of his brothers was still alive, none dared to molest the Israelites. But the situation took an abrupt turn after the death of Levi, the last of the sons of Jacob, at the venerable age of 137. Josephus indicates that the Egyptians were envious of the wealth which the Hebrews had accumulated during their time in the country.

> Now it happened that the Egyptians grew delicate and lazy and gave themselves up to pleasures and particularly the love for riches and gain. They also became jealous toward the Hebrews and envious because of their prosperity for they saw that the whole nation flourished and had become distinguished because of their wealth which they had acquired with their virtues and labor.[2]

The book of Jasher tells of the suppression which began to change the status of the Israelites:

> And it came to pass after the death of Levi, when all of Egypt saw that the brethren of Joseph, the sons of Jacob, were all dead, they began to suppress the children of Israel and to make their lives bitter from day to day. And they took from them all their vineyards and fields which Joseph had given them, and also all the beautiful houses in which they lived.[3]

Not only had the patriarchs died, but also the whole generation of Israelites and Egyptians and the ruling pharaoh who had been kind toward

---

1. *Jubilees,* 46:3
2. Josephus, *Antiquities,* II, ix, 1.
3. *Jasher,* 63:2; Bin Gorion, III, 8.

his Semite guests. When king Magron died, his son, Malol, succeeded to the throne. He, together with his counselors, was not favorably inclined toward the Israelites and the animosities continued with official sanction of the ruler. Of course, the Jewish commentators are not too happy with the situation which shows the favored nation of God at the mercy of the Egyptians, the great enemy of Israel. It was therefore interpreted that the Lord placed his people deliberately into this subserviant position, or let it passively happen, in order to teach and test them:

> There is no nation so despised of the Holy One, as is Egypt; and yet he gave her dominion over Israel while the handmaid is Hagar who bare Ishmael who tormented Israel so cruelly in the past.[4]

According to the book of Jasher,

> . . . This was also from the Lord for the children of Israel, to benefit them in their latter days so that all the children of Israel might know the Lord their God. Also in order to know the signs and mighty wonders which the Lord would do in Egypt on account of his people Israel, in order that the children of Israel might fear the Lord God of their ancestors and walk in all his ways, they and their seed for ever after them.[5]

Pharaoh Malol was only twenty years old when he assumed the reign, and he is said to have ruled for ninety-four years.[6] Apparently some 600,000 Israelites were living in the country when the oppression began.[7] But soon the government found itself in a difficult foreign policy situation. Several kings from the Canaan region decided to make war on Egypt. When the Egyptians assembled to defend themselves against the invasion, they also demanded that the Israelites contribute their share of soldiers to the fighting. This was quite a thing to ask after the persecution had already begun, but the Israelites did contribute a sizeable number of men for the Egyptian forces:

> And the men of Israel and of Egypt went forth, about 300,150 men strong, and they went to battle against these kings and they formed the lines just outside of Goshen opposite from Pathos.[8]

The Egyptians, however, were afraid to rely on the Israelites too much lest they decided to betray them and turn them over to the enemy. Therefore, the Israelites were kept at the rear and at the side of the Egyptian forces and were only to be engaged in an extreme emergency. That situation came faster than anticipated when the Egyptian forces were overcome by the warriors of the invading kings:

---

4. *Zohar: Shemoth*, 17a.
5. *Jasher*, 63:7-8.
6. *Ibid.*, 63:9.
7. Ginzberg, II, 245.
8. *Jasher*, 64:22.

And all the Egyptians cried unto the children of Israel saying: Hurry and assist us and save us from the hands of Esau, Ishmael and the children of Chittim . . . And the children of Israel cried unto the Lord their God to help them. And the Lord listened to Israel and he delivered all the men of the kings into their hands. . . . And all the soldiers of the kings fled from the children of Israel and the children of Israel persued them and continued to kill them up to the borders of the land of Cush.[9]

This show of strength by the Israelites scared the Egyptians, who had not thought that the much smaller Israelite force could defeat the hostile invader. Most of them fled the battlefields and hid themselves in the mountains.

And all of Israel knew what the Egyptians had done to them when they had fled from the battle and left them to fight alone. And so the children of Israel acted cunningly when they returned from the pursuit. They searched for the Egyptians and killed them.[10]

It was after this incident that the Egyptians commenced to wage a full-scale war of oppression against the Israelites. They took counsel with Pharaoh on how to effectively deal with the descendants of Jacob:

And the counselors and elders of Egypt spoke to the king saying: Behold the children of Israel are greater and mightier than we are and you know all the evil which they have done to us on the road when we returned from battle. You have seen their strong power . . . Now, therefore, give us advice on what to do with them until we shall slowly eliminate them from among us, lest they will become too numerous for us. For if the children of Israel should increase even more they will become a menace to us, for if war should happen, they can, with their great strength, join the enemy against us and fight us and destroy us off the land.[11]

At first, they were inclined to kill them all, but one of the counselors at court thought of a different plan:

Now Job was one of the closest counselors of Pharaoh and when the latter formed the intention of exterminating the children of Israel, Job advised him: Do not kill them but take their possessions from them and subject their bodies to severe labor.[12]

Pharaoh's plan, in theory, was this: He wanted to call Egyptian and Hebrew workers together to fortify and beautify the cities of Pithom and Rameses. Everyone was to receive a fair amount of money for the work performed, but only for a short period of time. After a while the Egyptians would withdraw themselves from the work while the Israelites would continue to labor because of their greed for money. The Egyptians would slowly refuse payment for the work and when the Hebrews would complain, the Egyptians were to force them to continue and become their task-masters. That way, Pharaoh hoped, the Israelites would not only become

---

9. *Jasher*, 64:33-37.
10. *Ibid.*, 64:42-43.
11. *Ibid.*, 65:1-6.
12. *Zohar: Bo*, 33a.

slaves for the country but would also be too tired at night to have relations with their wives and thus discontinue to have as many children as before.[13]

> And at the end of a year and four months all the Egyptians had withdrawn them-selves from the children of Israel, so that the children of Israel were left to do the work alone. And after the Egyptians had withdrawn from the children of Israel they returned and became oppressors and officers over them and stood over the children of Israel as task-masters . . . And the Egyptians refused to give any pay to the children of Israel from that time forth. And when some of the men of Israel refused to work on account of the wages not being paid, the servants of Pharaoh oppressed them and smote them and made them return to work by force.[14]

The only tribe which was not engaged in the forced labor were the descendants of Levi. They had resisted the temptation to earn money by working on the cities in the first place, and had thereby avoided becoming serfs to the Egyptians.[15] To make sure that the Israelites would not leave, Pharaoh closed the whole land of Egypt for travelers so that there was no coming or going at all.[16] Josephus mentions that the Hebrews were also forced to work on all manner of other projects in the country from this time forth:

> They made them cut channels for rivers into the earth and built walls for their cities and ramparts in order to restrain the rivers and keep their water from rising over the banks. They made them build pyramids, and by doing all this they wore them out.[17]

Many Israelites died at this time because of the hard labor. Their corpses were not buried but merely discarded outside the city or country boundaries. Apparently the Hebrews were not allowed to take time off to attend to proper funerals.[18] Yet, somehow the tribes managed to still have children in contrast to what Pharaoh had hoped to accomplish. A new order was therefore given that the workers were not to return home to their houses after their labor but sleep in the fields near their construction areas. Pharaoh hoped that this decree would eventually keep the Israelites from having offspring.[19] In addition, a plan was devised by which it were no longer solely Egyptians who exacted the work from the Hebrews, but for special advantages and incentives some Israelites were "promoted" to supervisory activities among their own people. Soon one Hebrew was put in charge over ten Hebrew workers, and an Egyptian directed ten Hebrew supervisors or

---

13. *Jasher*, 65:7-14.

14. *Ibid.*, 65:28-30. The buildings were not constructed very well and seem to have collapsed soon (Ginzberg, II, 249).

15. Bin Gorion, III, 31; Ginzberg, II, 248.

16. *Jubilees*, 46:7.

17. Josephus, *Antiquities*, II, ix, 1.

18. Philo, *Moses*, 1.7.

19. *Midrash Rabba: Shemoth*, 1:12.

one hundred workers.[20] The Israelite overseers were either very kind or very mean toward their fellow tribesmen. The ones who wanted favors from the Egyptians treated the workers cruelly. The ones who had sympathy often took the brunt of the Egyptian wrath when the daily work was not performed satisfactorily or according to schedule.[21]

Yet Pharaoh's intricate plan of controlling the Israelites was only partially effective. The cities and public projects were constructed but somehow the Hebrew population was not decreased or even stabilized. Therefore, the court felt that they had to initiate a new plan to accomplish their objective. They met in a council to decide how to handle the situation.

> And an official, one of the court's counselors by the name of Job from the land of Uz in Mesopotamia ansered and said: . . . Behold, the counsel of the king which he advised before in regards to the work of the children of Israel is very good, and you must remove them from that work. But this is the counsel by which you may reduce their number, if it seems good to the king to execute . . . If it pleases the king, let a royal decree be announced and let it be written in Egypt never to be revoked, that every male child born to the Israelites shall have his blood spilled and killed.[22]

But the Egyptians did not feel inclined to kill the infants themselves and so they charged the Hebrew midwives with the task of carrying out Pharaoh's order. One of the women was the young Jochebed, the future mother of Moses.[23] These midwives did not comply with the instructions of the royal court, using various excuses for their apparent inability.[24]

About this time Pharaoh was having a dream one night which worried him deeply. In it he saw an old man who held a pair of scales in his hands. On one side all of Egypt's nobility was assembled, on the other side one little milk kid was playing, yet the kid was much heavier and tipped the scales down in his favor. Since Pharaoh could not explain this unusual happening, he called in his deviners and astrologers to give him an interpretation of that dream.

> And Balaam, the son of Beor, answered the king and said to him: This means nothing else but that a great danger will come upon Egypt. A son will be born to the Israelites who will destroy Egypt and its people and he will deliver the Israelites out of Egypt with a strong hand. Now, therefore, O King, take advice so that you might destroy the hope of the Israelites before this evil thing will happen in Egypt.[25]

---

20. *Ibid.*, 1:28.
21. *Ibid.*, 5:20.
22. *Jasher*, 66:15-21. The Egyptians let the female infants live because they wanted them to grow up and use them for illicit and sensual relations (Ginzberg, II, 251).
23. Ginzberg, II, 251.
24. *Jasher*, 66:28-31. Josephus mentions that the midwives were Egyptians rather than Hebrews (*Antiquities,* II, ix, 2).
25. *Jasher*, 67:18-19. In some texts this counselor is called Jethro.

Upon hearing this, Pharaoh was even more worried and he hurriedly sent for his two counselors, Job and Uzite and Reul the Midianite. Since the previous strategy had not been effective, a new method had to be found to deal with the male children of the Hebrews. But he received conflicting advice from his aids.

> And Reul the Medianite answered the king and said: . . .If it seems good to the king, let him leave the Hebrews alone and let him not stretch out his hand against them. For these are the ones whom God chose anciently . . .

Then Reul recounted the history of the Israelite ancestors and how God had protected them throughout history. He ended with this counsel:

> Now therefore, if it seems good in your eyes, desist from destroying the children of Israel, but if it is not your will that they should live in Egypt, send them away from here so that they may go to the land ofCanaan, the land in which their ancestors dwelled.[26]

As expected, Pharaoh was not pleased with this advice and he sent his counselor away. Then he turned to Job, who gave him the following suggestion:

> If it pleases the king, let him order that all the Hebrew children born from this time forth be thrown into the water and thus you can destroy them . . .[27]

Pharaoh was much more pleased with this plan and immediately ordered it to be carried out throughout the country. There was weeping and mourning among the Israelites as the royal henchmen came to seek out the newborn infants in Goshen and other areas as hundreds and thousands of little babies were being taken away by force and thrown into the rivers and ponds. But then some of the Hebrew women began to hide their boys from the searchers and the number of children killed decreased quickly. However, the Egyptians countered the Hebrew ploy by this method:

> The Egyptians went from house to house where they thought a babe had been born, taking with them a small Egyptian child and, making him cry, the Hebrew baby would hear the sound and cry with him.[28]

The Birth of Moses

Under these trying circumstances for the Israelites, Moses was born into this world. His father was Amram, the son of Kehath, the son of Levi,

---

26. *Ibid.,* 67:26-40.
27. *Jasher,* 67:49. Water was chosen since God had sworn that He would never again destroy mankind by water and he would therefore not punish the Egyptians by that method.
28. *Midrash Rabba: Shemoth,* 1:20. Some children were said to also have been offered as a human sacrifice to the Egyptian gods (*Pirke de Rabbi Eliezer,* 48).

one of Joseph's brethren. His mother was Jochebed, whom we have encountered before as one of the midwives who refused to kill the newborn infants according to Pharaoh's command.[29] It is said that Amram was one of the few who were not greedy after money when the opportunity came to make bricks. He only finished one brick per day. Later, when the Hebrews were required to make the same number of bricks but without any pay, Amram still only had to finish one a day since that was the total output he produced earlier.[30] The entire tribe of Levi seems to have been that wise in regards to the commands of Pharaoh. Yet, when the order was announced that all male Israelite children were to be thrown into the water, Amram and Jochebed were afflicted the same as was everyone else. In order to spare their eventual offspring this dreadful fate, Amram decided to separate himself from his wife so that they would not have any children. Since he had the respect of the Levites, being a member of the Sanhedrin, many others emulated his example and did the same with their wives.[31] Jochebed had already given birth to two children before the decree was promulgated in the land, namely Aaron and his sister, Miriam.

It was their daughter, Miriam, who spoke out to Amram one day, complaining about the way he had handled the situation.

> Father, thy decree is worse than Pharaoh's decree. The Egyptians aim to destroy only the male children, but thou includest the girls as well. Pharaoh deprives his victims of life in this world, but thou preventest children from being born, and thus thou deprivest them of the future life, too.[32]

Another version says that Amram took his wife back after Miriam one day spoke a revelation concerning a son that would be born to her mother and father:

> And she went forth and prophecied about the house, saying: Behold, a son will be born unto us from my father and my mother this time, and he will save Israel from the hands of Egypt. And when Amram heard the words of his daughter he went and took his wife back to the house . . . three years after he had left her, and he came to her and she conceived. And at the end of seven months from her conception she brought forth a son.[33]

And thus Moses was born. But it was not a happy time in which to be born, and the joy in the household of Amram was only short-lived. After

---

29. *Jasher*, 67:1-2.
30. Ginzberg, II, 260, 261.
31. *Ibid.*, II, 258, 259. In *Pseudo-Philo*, 10c, the opposite is true. The Israelites in general separate themselves from their wives while the Levites, particularly Amram, speak out against this practice and refuse to follow their fellow Hebrews.
32. Midrash Rabba:Shemoth, 1:24.
33. *Jasher*, 68:1-4.

three months, the Egyptian spies came to check on all the households for newborn boys. Jochebed placed the little infant in a basket sealed with tar, and put this mini-ark into the Nile near the royal palace. Miriam remained near the floating vessel in order to see what would happen, and also to ascertain the validity of her prophecy.[34]

Just at that time, the Lord intervened in an almost natural way to influence the outcome of this otherwise probably disastrous occurrence.

> And God sent out a terrible heat in the land of Egypt at that time, which burned the skins of all men by the sun in its course, and it distressed the Egyptians greatly. And all the Egyptians went down to the river to bathe because of the dissolving heat which burned their skin. And Bithia, the daughter of Pharaoh, also went down to the river because of the heat.[35]

The vessel containing the infant Moses drifted by and the princess noticed it floating on the Nile. She had the basket fetched and was very surprised when it contained a little baby. Since she had been childless, Bithia took this discovery as a good omen and decided to keep the child and raise him as her own. Another version asserts that the princess had been stricken with leprosy but, upon touching the vessel with the baby boy, she was miraculously cured. With such a sudden favor bestowed on her, she could not help but retain the child as a sign from on high, although she recognized the baby to be of Hebrew origin by the manner of the diapers and clothes on him.[36]

She had some Egyptian women brought to nurse the infant but he would not accept her. This was the point where Miriam stepped forward from her hidden observation place and offered to bring a Hebrew nurse to take care of the child. The princess consented, and Miriam ran to bring her mother Jochebed back, who was then appointed to take care of the boy for Bithia.[37]

Moses' Youth

The infant grew up in his own household for the next two years.[38] Here he also received his names. His mother called him Jekuthiel, Miriam called him Jered, his father named him Chabar, Aaron preferred Abich Zanuch,

---

34. Ginzberg, II, 265.

35. *Jasher*, 68:15-17; *Pirke de Rabbi Eliezer*, 48. Josephus named her Thermutis (*Antiquities*, II, ix, 5) as it is also rendered in *Jubilees*, 47:5.

36. *Midrash Rabba:Shemoth*, 1:23; Ginzberg, II, 267.

37. *Jasher*, 68:20-23.

38. *Jubilees*, 47:2 lists seven months; *Pirke de Rabbi Eliezer*, 48 has three and a half years.

and others referred to him variously as Abigdor, Abi Socho, and She-maiah.[39] It was the princess who named the boy Moses upon his return to the palace.[40]

> And Moses was in Pharaoh's house as a son to Bithia, Pharaoh's daughter, and Moses grew up along the children of the king.[41]

> Pharaoh's daughter used to hug and kiss him and love him as if he were her own son and would not allow him out of the royal palace. Because he was so handsome everyone was eager to see him and whosoever saw him was not able to tear himself away from him. Pharaoh also used to kiss and hug him. . . .[42]

So much attention was on the little Moses that any extraordinary behavior by him would naturally be noticed by everyone. One such occasion happened a year later when the royal family was having dinner.

> And in the third year from the birth of Moses, Pharaoh was sitting at a banquet with Alparanith, the queen, who was sitting at his right and Bithia on his left, while the boy Moses was lying in her lap, and Balaam, the son of Beor with his two sons, and all the princes of the land were sitting at the table in the presence of the king. And the boy stretched forth his hand toward the king's head and took the crown from the king's head and placed it upon his own. And when the king and the princes saw what the boy had done, the king and the princes were terrified and everyone expressed his astonishment to his neighbor.[43]

This, of course, was an awkward situation for Moses and Pharaoh alike. Balaam and the other court magicians immediately used the occasion to discredit the boy and possibly eliminate him from the court. They announced the truth about Moses:

> This is a child from the Hebrew children. . . and do not let my Lord be mislead that this lad did not know what he was doing. He is a Hebrew boy and he possesses wisdom and understanding although he is only a child, and with this wisdom he has done this and chosen himself to be king over the kingdom of Egypt. . . . If it please the king let us kill him unless he grows up and takes away the government from your hand.[44]

Other counselors were called in to offer their advice on the matter. In some accounts, the angel Gabriel is among the advisors, while in another text it is the already-mentioned Jethro who attempts to come to the rescue of the child by suggesting a different plan:

---

39. *Jasher*, 68:25-31. *Pseudo-Philo,* 11a and Clement Alexandrinus, in *Stromata*, 1:21 mention that Jochebed named him Melkiel.
40. Evidently from the Egyptian *Moy* or *Mui* for water, in Philo, *Vita Mosis*, 1-4; Josephus, *Antiquities,* II, ix, 5.
41. *Ibid.,* 68:32.
42. *Midrash Rabba:Shemoth* 1:26.
Jasher, 70:1-3.
43. *Jasher,* 70:1-3.
44. *Ibid.,* 70:6,7,19.

> If it pleases the king, let him bring men who shall place an onyx stone and a bowl with coal of fire before the boy, and if he shall stretch forth his hand and take the onyx stone then we know that he has acted with wisdom and we must kill him. But if he shall stretch forth his hand toward the coal we know that it has not been done with knowledge and he shall remain alive. . . . And they placed those things before the boy and he tried to stretch forth his hand to the onyx stone but an angel of the Lord took his hand and placed it upon the coal . . . and he took it and put it into his mouth and burned his lips and his tongue and thereby he became heavy in his mouth and slow of speech.[45]

Thus the incident turned out well for the little Moses and the court seemed satisfied that the boy did not act with wisdom when he took the royal crown from Pharaoh. Moses therefore remained the darling of the family and of the country as a whole.

> And while the boy was in the house of the king he was robed in purple and he grew up among the other children of the king. And as Moses grew up in the King's house, Bithia, the daughter of Pharaoh, considered him her son, and all the household of Pharaoh honored him. . . . And Moses was in the king's house going out and coming in. The Lord gave him favor in the eyes of Pharaoh and in all the eyes of his servants, and in all the eyes of all the people of Egypt, and they loved him very much.[46]

While Moses grew up in the court, he evidently received the best education which could be procured at that time. Teachers came from many areas to teach him in the arts of science, astronomy, physics, philosophy, medicines, weapons, administration, and the wisdom of the ancients in general.[47] Manethos is said to have written that Moses also became a priest of Osiris while at the court of Pharaoh.[48]

It is not quite clear in the ancient traditions how Moses became aware of the fact that he was not an Egyptian but a son of simple Hebrew slaves. But the texts do mention that he often ventured out into the area of Goshen where he saw the Israelite workers engaged in their forced labor. He noticed that their strength was slowly draining away because of their continuous and strenuous work. One day he came before his "grandfather", the king of Egypt, to ask a favor for the Israelites:

> It is an admitted fact, that if a slave is not afforded rest at least one day in the week, he will die of over-exertion. "Thy Hebrew slaves will surely perish, unless thou accordest them a day of cessation from work." [49]

---

45. *Ibid.,* 70:25-29, where it is an angel who proposes the plan while in *Midrash Rabba: Shemoth* 1:26 it is Jethro, who had shown his compassion for the Israelites before.

46. *Jasher,* 70:32, 33, 40.

47. Philo, *Vita Mosis,* 1. 5-7; Clement of Alexandria, *Stomata,* 15, 23. Eusebius, *Praeparatio Evengelica,* 410-411. Josephus mentions that the Egyptians received this knowledge from Abraham when he was in the country sometime before (*Antiquities,* I viii, 2).

48. See Jean Doresse, *The Secret Books of the Egyptian Gnostics,* p. 105.

49. Ginzberg, II, 278; also in the *Midrash Rabba:Shemoth* 1:28.

Being one of Pharaoh's favorite grandchildren, the ruler granted Moses his request and ordered a proclamation to that effect:

> To you, all the children of Israel, thus sayeth the king, for six days shall you do all your work and labor, but on the seventh day you shall rest and not perform any work and you shall do so all the days as the king and Moses the son of Bithia have commanded.[50]

Through this action, Moses gained respect and fame among the Hebrews and the Egyptians alike. The Israelites now had a day of rest and the Egyptians remained satisfied since the work output of the slaves did not appear to have diminished.

> And the Lord was with Moses and his fame went throughout Egypt. And Moses became great in the eyes of all the Egyptians, and in the eyes of all the children of Israel, seeking good for his people Israel and speaking kind words of peace to the king.[51]

Moses' Flight From Egypt

Then one day the incident happened which would change the life of Moses and all of Egyptian and Israelite history. A Hebrew taskmaster by the name of Dathan had a very beautiful wife. She came to the attention of a higher Egyptian official who desired her very much and seduced her one day when Dathan was out at work. Upon returning to his home, the husband became aware of what had happened between his supervisor and his wife. Thereupon he went and accused the Egyptian of this crime. But instead of redress, he was severely beaten and probably would have been killed had not Moses just been in the area on an inspection. Dathan ran up to the royal prince and brought his case before him. Enraged by this matter, Moses went after the Egyptian overseer and killed him for the violation of the Hebrew woman.[52]

This incident was witnessed, reported to the authorities, and finally reached the court of Pharaoh, where it was also detected that Moses was not an Egyptian but a Hebrew slave. The irate king withdrew the princely authority and rank from Moses and degraded him to the status of a simple Israelite. Then he was tried for killing an Egyptian, which, of course, was punishable by death. Yet, before the execution could be carried out, Moses, by divine intervention was able to flee and leave the country.[53] The age of Moses at this occurrence is variously given as either 18, 20, 21, or 40.[54]

---

50. *Jasher*, 70:47. This day was, of course, the Sabbath, a Saturday.
51. *Jasher*, 70:50-51.
52. *Ibid.*, 71:1-3; *Pirke de Rabbi Eliezer*, 48, Philo, *Vita Mosis*, 1:8; *Midrash Rabba: Shemoth*, 1:29.
53. *Ibid.*, 71:9-10; Clement of Alexandria, *Stromata*, 1:22; Targum, *Yerushalmi*, Exodus 2:12; *Talmud: Sanhedrin*, 58b.
54. See Ginzberg, V, 404, n. 69.

The degradation and the flight of the former prince of the court was a terrific shock for Pharaoh and he immediately responded by tightening the rules and the workload for the Hebrews. The life for the slaves became miserable again and the Israelites felt the loss of Moses especially hard since they had perceived him to be a mediator and friend and perhaps even an eventual liberator from the yoke. Aaron tried to keep up the morale of the children of Israel but they would not listen. They drowned their disappointments in rebellion against God and embraced the Egyptians' idols even more than previously.[55]

Upon fleeing Egypt, Moses went South to the court of king Kikianus of Cush, who was engaged in a war. Having heard of Moses and his great achievements in Egypt, he made Moses more than welcome in his country because Egypt was not very much liked by its neighbors. Any enemy of Pharaoh was considered a friend among the kingdoms at the fringes of Egypt.

> And the king and the princess and all the fighting men loved Moses for he was great and worthy and his stature was like that of a noble lion and his face was like the sun and his strength was that of a lion. And he became a counselor to the king.[56]

Moses Becomes King of Ethiopia

He even advanced to become commander-in-chief to Kikianus.[57] However, after some nine years, the king died while the country was still at war. The soldiers were very much afraid that their enemies would mount a strong offensive once they heard of the death of their leader. They sought

---

55. *Jasher,* 71:12-14; Bin Gorion, IV, 52.
56. *Ibid.,* 72:24. Cush denotes the country of Ethiopia.
57. Ginzberg, II, 285.
   Artapanus tells a different story which is worth mentioning. Chenephres, the husband of princess Bathia, was envious of Moses and sought to eliminate him during a war with the Ethiopians. He had Moses appointed commander of a very weak force of Egyptian soldiers, hoping that he would be speedily killed. But Moses prevailed and became a hero on the battlefield. Upon returning to Egypt proper Moses was more popular than before and Chenephres conspired against him and attempted to kill Moses by means of some hired assassins. But the plot was revealed and Moses fled before the plot could unfold. Seeing that he could not gain respect at court, he left for Ethiopia, which gladly received the former enemy general (in Ginzberg, V, 407, 408).
   Josephus gives yet another twist to the story. Here Pharaoh is in war with the Ethiopians and commands Bathia to lure Moses back to Egypt to aid them in that war which had been going unsuccessfully. Moses did return and led the Egyptian forces to victory. But afterwards Pharaoh became jealous of Moses' popularity and sought to kill him; thereupon the hero left and returned to his exile (*Antiquities,* II, x, xi).

to choose a new leader as quickly as possible to forego any eventual problem. Yet, they were not able to find anyone as great and courageous as Moses, the friend and commander of the king's forces.

> And they hastened and each man stripped his garments off and placed them on the ground, and they made a huge pile and placed Moses on top of it and they stood and blew their trumpets and called out and said: May the king live, may the king live! . . . And they placed the royal crown upon his head and they gave him Adoniah, the widow of Kikianus, for a wife.[58]

Thus Moses became a king after all, a position he should have held but which had been denied him in his land of birth. His extraordinary skill and insight brought him success in his affairs and the people liked and revered him as their king.

> And the Lord granted Moses favor and grace in the eyes of all the children of Cush, and the children of Cush loved him very much, and so Moses was favored by the Lord and by men. . . . And Moses strengthened himself in the kingdom of the children of Cush, and he lead the children of Cush with his unusual wisdom and Moses prospered in his kingdom.[59]

Yet, in spite of all his military victories and just government, the time came when Moses had to leave and assume a new role. One day, after forty years of kingship, his wife Adoniah stepped forward and made it known that it was time for the country to espouse a new ruler.

> And Adoniah, the queen, said before the king and the princess: What is this thing which you, the children of Cush, have done for this time period? Surely you know that for forty years this man has reigned over Cush but he has never come to me and neither has he served the gods of Cush. Now, therefore, you children of Cush, let him reign no longer over you since he is not of our kind. Behold, Menacrus, my son, has grown up and let him rule over you, for it is better to serve the son of your king than this stranger, a slave of Egypt.[60]

The people hesitated at first to follow the queen's advice and disclaim Moses as their king, but after many debates and thoughts they concluded to proclaim Menacrus their ruler. Yet they did not merely dismiss Moses from his office, but asked him to vacate it, and when he consented they celebrated his decision with great honors, gave him many precious gifts, and let him depart the country as a hero and friend.[61] Moses then left Cush when he was about sixty-seven years of age and migrated to the area of Midian.[62]

---

58. *Jasher,* 72:35-36; 73:31.
59. *Ibid.,* 73:3,38.
60. *Ibid.,* 76:4-7.
61. *Ibid.,* 76:9-11.
62. *Ibid.,* 76:12-13.

About this time, a legend says, a group of 30,00 Hebrews from the tribe of Ephraim united in their effort to leave Egypt and seek the promised land of their ancestors. They succeeded in reaching the desert and arrived near the border to the Philistines. They are described as a very brave group of fighters, but having been in the desert and on a march without food for some three days, they had become weak and when they were attacked by a force of Philistine soldiers, most of the Ephraimites were slaughtered. The few survivors returned to Egypt and told of their experiences, which discouraged the Israelites from leaving as they now knew that they could not survive if they attempted to depart from Egypt by their own initiative.[63]

Moses' Experiences in Midian

Moses did not know of this incident since he was to the South of the country at this time. While wandering about in search of a new home he came to the area of the Midianites. It was in this place that he came into contact with Jethro and his daughters. Apparently Jethro had been a heathen priest who became dissolusioned with his occupation because he perceived idol worship as a wasteful and fundamentally wrong approach to gain the favors of heaven. Therefore he resigned his position as priest. The people in the region did not appreciate Jethro's action and treated him as an outcast from this time forth.[64]

At about that time Moses, the ex-king of Ethiopia, arrived in Midian and happened to stop for a rest near a well where a scuffle was ensuing over water rights between the daughters of Jethro and some neighborhood ruffians. Moses jumped into the middle and rescued the girls from the conflict:

> In the name of Divine Justice, he cried, which is exercized even in the desert, and in the name of the Almighty,who has sent me to deliver these innocent maidens, I swear unto you that I will not permit you to do them any harm.[65]

The thankful girls took the weary traveller home to their father and related to him how Moses had saved them from the hands of the rowdy gang. Naturally Jethro was elated to have this strong protector in his home and offered him the best hospitality. During the evening conversation, Moses was asked who he was and where he was from. He decided not to tell them about his Egyptian background, lest they had heard about his expulsion and he mentioned therefore only his experiences in Ethiopia. However, he encountered quite an unexpected and negative result:

---

63. Bin Gorion, IV, 63-65. *Pirke de Rabbi Eliezer,* 48.
64. Ginzberg, II, 289-290. Jethro is also called Reuel (*Jasher,* 76) or Raguel (Josephus, *Antiquities,* II, xi). Perhaps he changed his name, as is often the case after one's conversion.
65. From Angelo Rappoport, *Myth and Legend of Ancient Israel,* II, 252.

And Moses related to Reuel that he had come from Egypt and that he had reigned in Cush for forty years, and that they had taken the government from him and had sent him away in peace with many honors and gifts. And when Reuel heard these words of Moses, he said to himself: I will put this man in prison for he seems to have fled from Cush and thereby I will appease the people of Cush.[66]

Another version describes it this way:

Reuel began to consider the matter and wondered why his guest had been forced to leave both Egypt and Ethiopia. He may have been guilty. . . of an act of high treason, and if I give him shelter and protection, I may find myself in trouble and embroil myself with Pharaoh and with the men of Ethiopia who have wrestled the kingdom from him. . . . I will put him in prison.[67]

That was quite a shock for Moses, who had saved Jethro's daughters from harm. He ended up in a dungeon for a total of ten years. Jethro would have forgotten about the stranger in jail, had it not been for his oldest daughter, Zipporah, who had fallen in love with Moses and saw to his welfare while he was incarcerated. One day she came before her father and told him that someone had to care for the household rather than run off every day to the well to provide water for the flocks. His other six daughters could do the work quite adequately, while she would stay at home and care for the family. Jethro agreed to that quite readily and Zipporah was able to take care of Moses in prison by feeding him special meals and comforting his worried spirit.[68]

And at the end of ten years . . . Zipporah said to her father Reuel, no one inquires or seeks after the Hebrew man, whom thou hast bound in prison for ten years now. Now therefore, if it seem good in thy sight, let us send and see whether he is alive or dead. Her father knew not that she had supported him. And Reuel her father answered and said to her, has such a thing ever happened that a man should be shut up in a prison for ten years without food and then live? . . . And the thing seemed good in the sight of Reuel and he did according to the word of his daughter. . . . And he saw and beheld the man Moses in the dungeon, standing upon his feet, praying and praising the God of his ancestors. And Reuel commanded Moses to be brought out of the prison.[69]

Jethro was now satisfied that no one was in pursuit of the stranger and that he would no longer be in danger for harboring a fugitive. Therefore Moses stayed in Jethro's household as a free man.

One day, while in the garden, Moses noticed a sapphire-looking stick in the ground and he took it and plucked it out of the soil. He did not know it then, but it was the stick which God had given Adam when he was made to leave paradise. It had been handed down through Noah, Abraham, and

---

66. *Jasher,* 76:21-22. On the difference in the name, see note 64.
67. Rappoport, II, 253.
68. Ginzberg, II, 293-294, and others.
69. *Jasher,* 77:28-37.

Joseph. The legend associated with the stick in the ground was that whosoever could unpluck it from the ground would become a great prophet and leader in the hands of God. No one had been able to do this feat so far, though many had tried. When the family noticed that the stick was uprooted and that Moses had done it, everyone was astounded and Moses gained prominence in the eyes of the Midianites.[70] It was therefore little wonder that Moses and Zipporah were married a short time later with the express blessing of the aged Jethro or Reuel.

While Moses had been in Ethiopia and among the Midianites for all those years, the situation in Egypt had turned from bad to worse. Because of Pharaoh's cruelty toward the Israelites the Lord had begun to plague the monarch with leprosy. But that did not deter him, and he became even more vicious.

> And when the Lord had inflicted the plague upon Pharaoh, king of Egypt, he asked his wise men and sorcerers to cure him. And his wise men and sorcerers said to him that if the blood of little children were put into the wounds he would be healed. And Pharaoh listened to them and sent his ministers to Goshen to the children of Israel to take their little children . . . and the physicians killed them and applied the blood to the wounds. . . and the number of the children slain was three hundred and seventy-five.[71]

Yet, the blood of the children did not comfort the pains of the king and he became very irritated and easily angered. Soon boils began to appear on the monarch's body and the agony became almost unbearable. About this time, a report reached the court that the Hebrews were slacking off in their work. This news angered king Malol greatly and he sought to see this for himself and punish the slaves for their idleness:

> Now that the children of Israel know that I am ill, they turn and scoff at us; now, therefore, harness my chariot for me and I will go to Goshen and will see the scoff of the children of Israel and how they are deriding me.

So it was done—the royal party made its way to the land of the Hebrews. But here an incident happened which aggravated the situation even more:

> And the king's horse fell into a low ditch while Pharaoh was on it, and when the horse fell, the king's chariot landed on top of him and the horse also lay upon the king, and he cried out for his flesh was already raw. And the flesh of Pharaoh was torn from him and his bones were broken. . . . And his servants carried him upon their shoulders, a little at a time, and they brought him back to the capital. . . . And they put him in his

---

70. *Ibid.,* 77:39-51. *Pirke de Rabbi Eliezer,* 40. Other texts place the story into a time period before Moses was thrown into prison, but Jethro was not told of the miracle or he would not have treated his guest so strangely.

71. *Ibid.,* 76:28-32. *Midrash Rabba:Shemoth,* 1:34.

bed and the king knew that his end had come. . . . And the wounds were very bad and the flesh began to smell as the flesh of a carcass in the fields at summer time during the heat of the sun.[72]

Before he died, however, Malol commanded that his son Adikam be crowned king and successor. The new ruler was only twenty years old at that time and was described as being very short, with a long beard, and extremely ugly.[73] His worst trait, however, was his extraordinary cruelty and hardness of heart which exceeded even that of his father. He increased the workload of the Hebrews and also the punishment for the nonfulfillment of the assignment:

> And whenever any deficiency was found in the measure of the children of Israel's daily number of bricks, the taskmasters of Pharaoh would go to the wives of the children of Israel and take infants of the children of Israel according to the number of bricks deficient. They would take them by force from their mother's laps and then place them in the building instead of the bricks.[74]

It became a heartbreaking and intolerable situation for the Hebrews since they had hoped that the conditions of their lives would change after the death of the old monarch but, instead, it had even changed for the worse:

> And the labor imposed upon the children of Israel in the days of Adikam exceeded in hardship that which they performed in the days of his father. And the children of Israel sighed every day on account of their heavy work, for they had said to themselves: Behold, when Pharaoh will die, his son will lighten our burden. But he increased the work more than the former. . . .[75]

> And Pharaoh, king of Egypt, increased the labor of the children of Israel in those days, and continued to make his yoke heavier upon them. And he ordered a proclamation to be made in Egypt, saying, give no more straw to the people to make bricks with, let them go and gather it themselves as they can find it.[76]

It was at this point that the Lord remembered his children of the covenant and the time appeared ripe for their delivery from the yoke. They were now sufficiently humble to recall the God of their fathers which they had forgotten while in Egypt. It was, therefore, not because of the Hebrews' righteous living that they deserved to be delivered from their lot, but for the sake of the covenant that God had made with their fathers and for the Lord's name's sake.[77] However, it is admitted that Israel in Egypt had

---

72. *Ibid.,* 76:44-57.
73. He was nicknamed "Akuz the short." (Bin Gorion IV, 71).
74. *Jasher,* 77:16.
75. *Ibid.,* 77:21-23.
76. *Ibid.,* 11,12.
77. *Midrash Rabba:Shemoth,* 1:34-35.

certain merits which justified divine intervention and grace in their behalf, for it is said that some of the Hebrews helped each other in their work: when one man had finished his assigned work and had time left over he would go and help his neighbor complete his number of bricks.[78]

Moses, the appointed deliverer, had lived with the Midianites all these years and was apparently not aware of the hardships of his people and his future role in relation to them. Yet, the Lord prepared the new prophet during his forty years of exile for the difficult task ahead. His experiences in Ethiopia as a ruler and strategist evidently gave Moses knowledge in leadership and skill as an organizer, while life in the desert with Jethro prepared him spiritually and provided advancement in wisdom and thought.

One such story told about the prophet is indicative of the training he received from the Lord in preparation for his work. One day, while Moses was out tending the sheep, he was thinking and meditating about life and its meaning, when he noticed a traveller come and stop at the well to refresh himself. Unnoticed, a purse of money dropped out of his garments and fell on the ground before he continued on his journey. After a short while another traveller appeared. He refreshed himself with the cool water and, while standing near the well, found the money-bag on the ground. He picked it up, rejoiced about the stroke of luck and went happily on his way. Yet another stranger came after a while who also drank of the water from the well and then proceeded to take a nap nearby. Meanwhile the first traveller had noticed the loss of his purse and hurriedly returned to the area since he surmised that he could have only lost it while refreshing himself at the well.

When he saw the sleeping man, he awakened him and asked him whether he had found the money, to which the other replied, truthfully, that he had not. However, the first stranger evidently did not believe the other's assurance and after some accusations and shouting, a fight between the two ensued. It was at this point that Moses came running from his place of meditation to quell the disturbance and calm the tempers because he had witnessed what had happened. But it was too late. The man who had lost the purse had already killed the innocent man when Moses arrived at the scene. The prophet related his observations to the man, who was quite shaken at his deed, and departed in great sorrow over the loss of his possessions and the knowledge of having killed for no cause.

Moses was also shaken by this experience and he wondered deeply about the justice and benevolence of a God who had permitted such an act to happen.

---

78. Ginzberg, II, 300. There are four reasons why the Lord had compassion on his people: The covenant with the fathers, the people's own merits, the merits of future generations and the unlimited mercy of God toward all those who suffer (Ginzberg, V, 414, n. 106).

Lord of the Universe, spoke Moses, "can it be Thy will to punish the innocent and let prosper the guilty? The man who hath stolen the money-bag is enjoying wealth which is not his, whilst the innocent man hath been slain. The owner of the money, too, hath not only lost his property, but his loss hath been the cause of his becoming a murderer. I fail to understand the ways of Providence and workings of Divine justice. O Almighty, reveal unto me Thy hidden ways that I may understand."

And so the Lord proceeded to tell Moses why it was just. The man who had lost the money had inherited it from his father who, in turn, had stolen it from the father of the man who had found it. Therefore that situation had now been corrected. The man who had been killed, had in years past killed the brother of the man who had killed him during the quarrel. Said the Lord to Moses:

Know then, O Moses, that I ordained it that the murderer should be put to death by the brother of the victim, whilst the son should find the money of which his father had once been robbed. My ways are inscrutable, and often the human mind wonders why the innocent suffer and the wicked prosper.[79]

Thus the great prophet-leader was taught the ways and wisdom of God, how to deal with men and how to judge and how not to; all valuable lessons which he could draw from while leading the Israelites to the promised land. He exhibited his training and righteous judgment as he was watched by the Lord. Another story goes like this:

When Moses, our teacher, blessed be he, was tending the flocks of Jethro in the wilderness, a little kid escaped from him. He ran after it until it reached a shady place . . . and the kid stooped to drink. When Moses approached it, he said: I did not know that you ran away because of thirst: you must be weary. So he placed the kid upon his shoulders and walked away. Thereupon God said: Because thou hast mercy in leading the flock of sheep, thou wilt assuredly tend my flock of Israel.[80]

Moses also became very experienced in desert living and survival while grazing the flocks and wandering about in the area in search of suitable patches of shrubbery and water holes.[81]

Moses' Call to Deliver Israel

Finally, after many years of preparation, the time had come for Moses to be officially called on his mission of leading the children of Israel out of Egypt and on to the Promised Land. One day the Lord appeared to the new prophet on Mt. Horeb in the burning bush and gave him the commission to

---

79. Rappoport, II, 263-266. There are many versions of this story, often also told in relations to other men than Moses, such as in the tales of *A Thousand and One Nights;* the *Gesta Romarorum,* 80 (72); Jami, *Subhat ul Abraham.*

80. *Midrash Rabba: Shemoth,* 2:3.

81. Ginzberg, II, 302; Philo, *Vita Mosis,* 1:12.

free his people.[82] However, instead of being overjoyed and feeling extremely blessed and fortunate that he, of all people, had been chosen to accomplish this task, Moses appeared fearful and very anxious to relinquish the calling, according to the ancient texts. He objected to the Lord with these words:

> When Thou didst seek to save Lot, Abraham's brother, Thou didst send angels to deliver them, and now Thou dost send me to deliver 600,000 children of Abraham? Send, therefore, Thy angels, whom Thou dost usually send.[83]

But God eliminated the objection of his prophet. Then Moses pleaded his inexperience and lack of knowledge:

> Lord of the Universe! Who am I to go to pharaoh, and how can I accomplish such a mission as to bring the children of Israel out of Egypt? How could I alone minister to the people? Where shall I take food and drink for them? How shall I be able to protect them against the heat of the scorching sun, against storm, hail, and rain? How shall I be able to provide for the pregnant women, the women in child-birth, the new-born babes, and the little children.[84]

Once the Lord had quieted his fears concerning those items Moses asked for the name of God, in order to tell the Hebrews by whose command he was speaking to them, and God told him:

> Know then, that my name is according to my acts. Elohim is my name when I judge my creatures, and I am the Lord of Hosts, Zebaoth, when I lend strength to men in battle, enabling them to rise and conquer their enemies; I am Yahveh or Adonai, when I have mercy upon my creatures; and I am El Shaddai, when I am the Lord of all strength and power.[85]

After that request had been granted, Moses still felt inadequate and suggested that his brother Aaron might be more suitable for the assignment, since he could talk better and would therefore be a much more qualified messenger. The Lord partially agreed to that suggestion and designated Aaron to be his assistant and companion on this mission. Thereupon Moses saw that it was useless to object any further and he accepted the divine calling. It appears that Moses was told by the Lord what would happen in Egypt and how the exodus would take place. He was warned by God that his mission would not always run smoothly, and that many obstacles had to be overcome, even with the people whom Moses was to liberate:

> My children are obstinate, bad tempered, and troublesome. In assuming leadership over them, you must expect that they will curse you and stone you![86]

---

82. Mr. Horeb is also known as Sinai, possibly from S'neh = thorn bush (*Pirke de Rabbi Eliezer*, 41)

83. *Midrash Rabba:Shemoth*, 3:16.

84. Rappoport, II, 272.

85. *Ibid.*, II, 273.

86. *Midrash Rabba:Va'era*, 7:3.

That was not a bright prospect for the prophet, but he submitted to his role and promised to bear it. The greatest opposition, of course, was to come from the royal court, and Moses was told at this time that Pharaoh would harden his heart and not let the children of Israel go, just so that he would not be surprised and doubt the powers of the Lord.[87] Yet Moses was afraid that he would say things about God's great powers before the king, and the Lord would not uphold him when it was time to show the might of the true God of heaven. Therefore, the Lord had to swear that what Moses said to Pharaoh would take place.[88] It is also asserted that God rehearsed with Moses the plagues and miracles he was to perform in Egypt, so that the prophet would be assured of his work and their affects.[89] Finally, Moses was moved up into the celestial sphere and shown the different heavens, hell, paradise, the future, and the mysteries of God.[90]

Having been thus prepared, the prophet returned to his family and told them about his calling, and after having received the blessings of Jethro, his father-in-law, he took his wife Zipporah and his son Gershom and left for Egypt. On the way, we read, Moses encountered Satan, who tried to dissuade the emissary of God from carrying out his mission and even attempted to kill him. However, Moses was successful in overcoming the evil influence with the help of the Lord and continued on his journey.[91] As he was coming close to Goshen, his elder brother Aaron was being made aware of Moses' mission and his imminent arrival:

> And the Lord appeared to him in that place and He said to him: Go now toward Moses in the wilderness, and he went and met him in the mountains of God, and he kissed him. And Aaron lifted up his eyes and he saw Zipporah, the wife of Moses and her children, and he said unto Moses: Who are these unto thee? And Moses said unto him: They are my wife and son, which God gave me in Midian; and the thing grieved Aaron on account of the woman and her children. And Aaron said unto Moses: Send away the woman and her children that they may go to her father's house, and Moses harkened to the words of Aaron, and did so. And Zipporah returned with her children, and they went to the house of Reuel, and remained there until the time arrived when the Lord had visited his people.[92]

Aaron evidently felt it was unwise for Moses to be worrying about his family amidst the difficult times which awaited the two messengers from God.

---

87. *Midrash Rabba:Shemoth*, 3:9.

88. *Pirke de Rabbi Eliezer*, 45. The only thing God did not promise him was that he would take him into Canaan and to prolong his life beyond 120 years.

89. Rappoport, II, 273-274.

90. *Midrashim Gedullat Moshe.*

91. *Jubilees*, 48:3.

92. *Jasher*, 79:14-18.

Moses' Confrontations With the Pharaoh

After his wife and children had departed, Moses and his brother continued on to the dwelling places of the Hebrews. There they met with the elders and representatives of the tribes who in the main were overjoyed with the prospect of being liberated from their yoke. Yet some of them remained sceptical about the whole affair and most of them lacked the courage to accompany Moses into the court of Pharaoh when they were asked to do so by the prophet. Some of them went for part of the way but as they were nearing the palace, they withdrew one by one, and finally it was Moses and Aaron alone who asked for an audience with Pharaoh.[93]

It just so happened that the day of the visit to the court was also the anniversary of the king. Representatives from all over the ancient world had assembled to bring their gifts from their various countries and monarchs and to praise and congratulate Pharaoh. Soon it was their turn to pay homage to the king:

> Moses and Aaron were still standing at the door of Pharaoh's palace, whereupon his servants came and said: Two elders of the Hebrews are at the gate. The reply was: Let them enter. When they entered, he looked at them as if expecting that they wished to crown him or give him their credentials, but they did not even greet him. He said to them: Who are you? They replied: We are the ambassadors of the Lord. What do you want? he asked. They replied: Thus sayeth the Lord: Let my people go. Then Pharaoh became very angry and said: Who is the Lord that I should hearken to his voice to let Israel go? He has not the sense to send me a crown that you come with mere words? Tarry a while that I may search the records. So he went into the palace chamber and scrutenized every nation and its gods. . . . He said to them I have searched for his name throughout my archives but have not found him.[94]

Thereupon he quizzed the brothers about their god: Is he young or old? How many cities has he captured? How many nations has he subdued? What is his occupation? Everytime Moses and Aaron answered, but pharaoh maintained that he did not know that god and would therefore not bow to their requests. It was a difficult situation and finally the prophet was required to show the king the power of the Lord and he performed the miracle with the staff which was transformed into a snake. But the Egyptians were "masters of sorcery" and had learned ways to perform astounding miracles themselves.[95] Therefore, Pharaoh mocked Moses and Aaron about their performance. He called his children, aged four and five, and they displayed their magical talents before the throne by duplicating what Moses had done: their staffs converted into snakes.[96]

93. Ginzberg, II, 330-331.
94. *Midrash Rabba: Shemoth*, 5:14.
95. *Zohar: Waera*, 30b.
96. *Midrash Rabba: Va'era*, 9:6. "Do not think that the magician's performance was a mere make-believe," says the *Zohar*, "their rods actually did become serpents." (*Waera*, 28a).

The court was amused and Moses was for a moment bewildered, but then he commanded his snake to swallow up the serpents of the king. With great astonishment and horror the court watched this new miracle and this time the king became worried: "What will happen if he now says to his rod: 'Swallow up Pharaoh and his throne?' It would at once swallow me up!"[97] But the royal magicians were not disheartened. They counseled the king to dismiss the prophets and asked them to return the following day, under the pretense that the court wanted to discuss their demands. After the brothers had left, Pharaoh met with his head magicians, Balaam, Jannes, and Jambres.[98] They were not very impressed with the performance of Moses and told Pharaoh not to worry: "He is just another magician like we are." They counseled him to not let the children of Israel go but, instead, to harden their lot and increase their assignments.[99] Since the king usually acted on the advice of his sorcerers and magicians, he did as they advised him and ordered it done.[100]

When Moses returned to the palace the next day, he was informed of the king's decision. It was heartbreaking for him for he felt that his worst fears were substantiated and that the king would never let the Hebrews go in spite of all the miracles, since his court was full of witchcraft and could countermand all that he would do. Besides, the workload of his fellow Israelites had been increased and they were wroth at Moses because of their shattered hopes in a delivery from bondage. They accused him:

> You are responsible for the widespread stench now issuing from the Israelite corpses used as bricks for building when our tale was not complete. The Egyptians had but a faint suspicion that we were waiting for our redemption. It is your fault if they are fully conscious of it now.[101]

Disappointed and embarrassed, the story goes, Moses left Egypt and returned to Midian for six months.[102] Other writings assert that he remained in Egypt among the Israelites for a period of two years.[103]

During this time Moses was questioning his own ability and that of the Lord to really bring about a delivery from the captivity. He asked the Lord:

> What has this nation of Israel done that it is oppressed more than any other nation in history? . . . Why are not the descendants of Esau and Ishmael held in bondage, too?

---

97. *Ibid.*, 9:7.
98. *Zohar: Ki Tisa*, 191a; *Jasher*, 79:27.
99. The magicians considered Moses to be just one of theirs. Since he had been brought up in the palace he had been familiar with their witchcraft and merely perfected it while away from Egypt.
100. *Zohar: Beshalah*, 46b.
101. Ginzberg, II, 337.
102. *Midrash Rabba: Shemoth*, 5:19.
103. Such as in *Jasher*, 79:56-57; 80:1.

Are they not likewise the seed of Abraham? . . . Why did you send me there as Thy messenger? Thy great, exalted, and terrible name is feared in all the earth, yet Pharaoh heard me pronounce it, and he refuses obedience.[104]

And also:

O Lord of the world, I know well that Thou wilt bring Thy children forth from Egypt. O that Thou wouldst make use of another instrument, for I am not worthy of being the redeemer of Thy children[105]

God had to strengthen Moses and give him confidence that the mission could be completed and that Moses would be able to do it:

I will send you to Pharaoh, and although I will punish him according to his desert, yet you must not fail in the respect due to him as a ruler. Furthermore, be careful to take the elders of the people into your counsel, and let your first step toward redemption be to make the people give up the worship of idols.[106]

The Lord would only liberate a people which believed in Him and followed his precepts and ordinances. Therefore it was essential that Moses taught them about the true God and his laws because the children of Israel had become neglectful and factually ignorant of many of the teachings and ordinances which their fathers had practiced. They had not kept the law of circumcision,[107] and had become virtually pagans.[108]

While they were in captivity in Egypt, they had worshipped foreign gods and had forgotten the essentials of the faith. . . . So when Moses came, he had to teach them that in the universe there is a supreme God . . . gradually they learned the ways of the Holy One.[109]

But it was not easy for Moses to teach his fellow Israelites, and we read that he once complained to the Lord in exasperation: "See, the children of Israel will not hearken unto me. How, then, should Pharaoh hearken unto me?"[110]

The Plagues

Yet Moses succeeded and the time was at hand again for him to appear before the king and negotiate the release of the Hebrew nation from Egypt. The well-known stories of the plagues imposed upon the country follow. They

---

104. Ginzberg, II, 338.
105. *Ibid.,* II, 339.
106. *Ibid,* II, 340, 341. See also *Midrash Rabba: Bo,* 16:2.
107. *Midrash Rabba: Shemoth,* 1-8.
108. *Zohar: Ahare Moth,* 70a.
109. *Zohar: Terumah,* 161a.
110. Ginzberg, II, 341.

are broadly treated in apocryphal writings and commentaries. A few interesting insights will suffice to shed some extra light on the times of those memorable events.

Moses warned the king and his court for some three weeks before each of the plagues scourged the country, and the plague itself usually lasted about a week.[111] The first one was the turning of the water into blood. We are told that the Israelites gained monetarily from this miracle because the Egyptians would offer them riches and wealth for some water that had not become red, for it appears that the water which the Hebrews used was not subject to the conversion.[112] But this event did not impress Pharaoh and his court very much, because the magicians were able, by the help of the evil powers, to duplicate it. And thus it was with most of the early plagues which menaced the country—the sorcerers were able to do likewise:

> Every plague which the Holy One, blessed be He, brought upon them, they also produced until He brought upon them the boils and they were not able to stand and do likewise.[113]

The later miracles were evidently beyond their skill to perform, partially because the Lord smote them with an illness and they were not available to the court.[114]

> As soon as the magicians realized that they were not able to produce the gnats, they recognized that the deeds were those of God and not witchcraft. They no longer claimed to compare themselves with Moses in producing the plagues.[115]

They were still able to produce the frogs, we are told, but their greatest problem with all the sorcery was not to bring it about but how to stop it again. Yet most of their "miracles" were outright deceptions and optical illusions, though they impressed the king and his court.[116] Some of the plagues caused tremendous annoyance to the population, as can be seen by the example of the frog pest:

> Through the croakings of the frogs no one in Egypt could converse with his neighbor, through them the very soil became polluted, and babes and young children died from their chatter.[117]

They tried to kill them at first, but for each one eliminated six new ones would spring forth. By attempting to kill the frogs, therefore, they only succeeded in multiplying them.

---

111. *Ibid.,* II, 348.
112. *Midrash Rabba Va'era,* 9-10. Josephus, *Antiquities,* II, xix, 1; Philo, *Vita Mosis,* I, 26.
113. *Pirke de Rabbi Eliezer,* 48.
114. *Jubilees,* 48:9-11.
115. *Midrash Rabba: Va'era,* 10:7.
116. Ginzberg, II, 355; V, 429, n. 185.
117. *Zohar:Waera,* 3a

The plagues which God brought upon the Egyptians were the means of establish-
ing peace . . . there was a dispute between the Ethiopians and the Egyptians, the latter
said: Our borders extend til here, while the former claimed: Our borders extend to here.
But when the frogs came the dispute was settled, for the plague only visited the Egyptian
borders and thus the Ethiopians knew which was not theirs.[118]

When the frog-plague ended and the animals died, they decayed very
rapidly in the hot sun and there was a terrible and nauseating stench all
over the country.[119] But the game proceeded, since Pharaoh always promised to free the Israelites but rescinded his orders as soon as the scourge
had subsided by the intervention of Moses and Aaron. It became a mere
game, and Pharaoh soon began to avoid the prophets in his palace. He
would rise very early and go out to the banks of the Nile so that he would
not have to meet the brothers. But Moses realized what the king was
attempting to do, so the two would also appear on the Nile in the early
morning hours, telling Pharaoh to let the people go.[120] Moses knew very
well that the monarch would promise anything they asked, but then not
keep his word until the plagues became so extreme that the state of affairs
in Egypt did not allow any other option. He told the king once:

Do not think that I am unaware of what your actions will be after this: I know full
well that you will not fear God after this just as you have not feared Him hitherto, but I
will do this in order that you may recognize the greatness of God.[121]

At one time, before the terrible and last plague was placed on Egypt,
pharaoh told Moses:

If you desired a thousand or even two thousand men I would have granted them,
but if you seek the whole 600,000 then I cannot permit it.[122]

Because of the stubbornness of the king, Moses had to allow the last
scourge to come upon the country. He had hoped to avoid it and gave
Pharaoh many chances and opportunities to reconsider, but nothing had
worked. Therefore he announced the tenth plague, the death of the firstborn in each household. The king was upset and threatened to kill Moses
and his brother if they should come before his face again. Then Moses
answered: "Thou hast spoken well; I will see thy face again no more."[123] It
was a prophetic statement, for Moses never looked at the face of Pharaoh
again after this last meeting.

---

118. *Midrash Rabba: Va'era*, 10:2.
119. *Ibid.*, 10:6.
120. *Ibid.*, 11:1.
121. *Ibid.*, 12:5.
122. *Midrash Rabba:Shemoth*, 5:17.
123. Ginzberg, II, 261.

This final plague on the land killed the firstborn in each family in that one unforgettable night. Unlike other miracles which had been brought about by Moses and Aaron, this was the one which the Lord himself directed while all the Israelites were in their homes. Not only did all the firstborn males die, but also the females, we are told in the commentaries.[124] The Egyptians had pleaded with Pharaoh to let the Hebrews go as soon as they heard the rumors about the final and most costly plague, but the king dismissed their petitions and even clubbed the people's representatives who had gone to the palace for this request.[125] So afraid were the Egyptians that they even hid up their firstborn children in the temples, but it was of no avail.[126] When the angel of death had struck the land, some one million Egyptians had lost their lives.[127]

It came as a terrible surprise to Pharaoh as even his own son had not been spared. Only Bithia, the old foster-mother of Moses, escaped the troubles of the plague by divine intervention.[128]

> Pharaoh, on seeing the havoc wrought upon his own household, himself arose and with bitterness and fury smote those princes and nobles who had advised him to persecute Israel.[129]

It had become a terrible catastrophe because of Pharaoh's stubbornness and the inappropriate advice of his court and the magicians. But this time the king recognized that he could no longer afford to harden his heart. He assembled his court and the whole entourage made their way to Goshen to petition Moses and Aaron and to announce to them that this time, for sure, the Israelites would be allowed to leave. Indeed, they urged them and pleaded with them to leave. Pharaoh recalled that he had sworn not to let Moses live if his face would behold him again; therefore, he and the prophet could not meet each other in the open. Moses stayed in the house, which he was not allowed to leave until sunrise, and talked to the king through a curtain.[130] It was a complete reversal of the situation now, as we find Pharaoh telling the Hebrews to leave:

> Ye children of Israel, ye are your own masters. Prepare for your journey, and depart from among my people. Hitherto ye were the slaves of Pharaoh, but henceforth ye are under the authority of God. Serve the Lord your God![131]

---

124. *Midrash Rabba:Bo,* 18:3.
125. Ginzberg, II, 367.
126. *Midrash Rabba:Bo,* 15:15.
127. *Jubilees,* 48:14.
128. *Jasher,* 80:48-49.
129. *Zohar: Beshala,* 45a.
130. *Targum Yerushalmi,* Exodus 12:29; *Midrash Rabba: Shir,* 24a.
131. Ginzberg, II, 369-370.

Another version relates Pharaoh's desires in this way:

> Rise up and take your brethren, all the children of Israel who are in the land, with their sheep and oxen, and all belonging to them, they shall leave nothing behind, only pray for me to the Lord your God. . . . And the Egyptians sent the Israelites forth, with great riches, sheep and oxen and precious things . . . and the children of Israel asked of the Egyptians, vessels of silver, and vessels of gold, and garments, and the children of Israel stripped the Egyptians.[132]

The Exodus

While Israel was busy preparing for the exodus and amassing as much property as could be carried with them, including gold and silver and precious stones, Moses was occupied in finding the body of Joseph, who had become chancellor of Egypt many decades earlier and who had been buried in the country. His body had been entombed in a royal mausoleum like one of the great kings.[133] But there were so many other mummies buried there that Moses found it difficult to identify the coffin of the great Israelite ancestor, but by a miracle he was shown to the right tomb.[134]

There were no obstacles placed before the tribes as they were about to leave the country on such a grand scale. Everyone seemed happy to see them go. Pharaoh, it is said, even accompanied them part of the way to be sure that they were really leaving![135] As joyful as the occasion must have been for the Hebrews, they found it difficult at first to really grasp what was happening:

> When the children of Israel went out of Egypt their spirits were broken because of their past sufferings and there was no energy left in them and no will to participate in the joy, singing and exultation of Moses and Miriam. But when all the celestial hosts and chariots . . . began to sing and to praise the Lord for his glorious deeds, the Holy One awakened the spirit of the Israelites, putting new life into them.[136]

Some texts mention that Pharaoh had been given the impression that the tribes merely wanted to go into the desert for three days in order to worship their God; that it was not a general and final departure but a short journey or vacation.[137] Yet that position seems untenable in view of the fact that every single Hebrew went, together with all of his property and the many gifts he had received or appropriated. Had it actually been only for the purpose of a brief pilgrimage, there would have been no requirement to take all household equipment with them, and not all the people would have

---

132. *Jasher,* 80:56-61.
133. *Midrash Rabba: Beshallach,* 20:19; *Zohar: Beshalah,* 46a.
134. Ginzberg, III, 5.
135. *Ibid.,* III, 6.
136. *Zohar: Beshalah,* 45a.
137. See, for example, *Jasher,* 81.

participated. Therefore, it appears that the idea of an exodus, even in the eyes of Pharaoh, must have represented a permanent loss.

However, when the shock of the past plagues and constantly-changing events had subsided and the king was in a more somber mood and deliberating the whole outcome, he became convinced that it was a mistake after all to have sent 600,000 men and their families out of the country. A powerful economic element had left which would be very difficult to replace. In addition, his pride was hurt when he thought of all the other monarchs in the Near East who might be laughing at him for giving leave to a group of slaves because of some magic and trickery, for as far as he was concerned, that was all it was. He was a ruler over many nations, tribes and cities, and any one of these could now rebel and ask to be free of the domination of Egypt and attempt a like turn of events. Pharaoh seemed gullible and Egypt appeared weak! He could not let that happen. Israel had to be shown who was stronger and the world should observe the might of Egypt!

> And Pharaoh's heart and the hearts of all his subjects were turned against Israel, and they repented that they had sent Israel away; and all the Egyptians advised Pharaoh to pursue the children of Israel to make them return to their burdens . . .[138]

Soon the chariots were assembled and the soldiers ready for the march in pursuit of Moses and his people. In one day they caught up with the Hebrews, who had three days to walk toward the Red Sea.[139]

Seeing the Egyptians advancing in the distance created terror among the Israelites and they cried out to Moses:

> What have you done unto us? For they are coming to do unto us all that we have done unto them, for we have slain their firstborn, taken their money and fled. . . . It was then that they stood still and did not know what to do for the sea had closed them in and the enemy pursued them.[140]

The children of Israel were divided in their opinion as to what to do in the situation. One group was for drowning themselves in the water, rather than be recaptured by the Egyptians. Another faction wanted to appeal to the Egyptians to spare them and take them back as slaves. Still another wanted to fight a battle rather than commit suicide or ask for mercy, and yet a fourth wanted to intimidate the Egyptians by much noise and threats of further plagues.[141]

It was a dangerous situation, and even Moses did not know what else to do. So he knelt down and prayed a long, ritualistic prayer to the Lord. God answered him by saying:

---

138. *Jasher*, 81:19.
139. Ginzberg, III, 12.
140. *Midrash Rabba: Beshallach*, 21:5.
141. *Jasher*, 81:26-33; *Targum Yerushalmi, Exodus*, 14:13.

> There is a time to pray briefly and a time to pray at length. My children are in distress, the sea shuts them in and the enemy is pursuing, and you stand here adding prayer upon prayer. . .All that Israel has to do is to go forward. Therefore, let them go forward! Let their feet step forward from the dry land to the sea and thou wilt see the miracles which I will preform in them.[142]

Another prominent writing tells the story like this:

> After this Moses rose up from amidst the people and he prayed to the Lord, saying: O Lord God of the whole earth, save thy people whom thou didst bring forth from Egypt, and let not the Egyptians boast that power and might are theirs. So the Lord said to Moses: Why dost thou cry unto me? Speak to the children of Israel that they shall proceed, and do thou stretch out thy rod upon the sea and divide it, and the children of Israel shall pass through it.[143]

And so it happened. One of the greatest miracles of all time began to unfold before their very eyes, as the sea parted upon the command of the prophet and Israel proceeded to pass to the other side on dry land. It is even mentioned that the waters divided into twelve parts, one for each of the tribes.[144]

Thus Israel went across and the Egyptians thought to do likewise in their pursuit of their former slaves, but their doom was spelled out. Yet, when the Lord was just about to close the waters in over them, the angels in heaven stopped him and inquired as to why he would want to save one group and destroy the other, seeing that both were probably unworthy of divine intervention:

> Why dost thou desire to punish Egypt and divide the Red Sea for Israel. Have not all sinned against thee? Those are idolaters and so are these. Those are murderers and so are these.

It was difficult for the Lord to answer, but Israel was chosen and He responded: "For Abraham's sake." [145] We are also told that the Egyptians deliberately persecuted Israel because they knew that the Lord had sworn after the great flood that he would never again destroy the earth by another deluge, no matter how wicked.[146] Yet, God had spoken about the whole earth and not any particular group of people, and thus He was free to do so when the situation warranted it. Drowning the Egyptians was in memory of the many children of the Hebrews who were drowned by the commands of the pharaohs.[147]

---

142. *Midrash Rabba: Beshallach*, 21:8.
143. *Jasher*, 81:34-36.
144. *Ibid.*, 81:38.
145. *Zohar: Terumah*, 170b.
146. See the chapter on Noah; *Midrash Rabba: Beshallach*, 22; Shemoth 1:9.
147. *Pirke de Rabbi Eliezer*, 42.

The destruction of the Egyptian forces by the water was a horrible sight. The Israelites saw the Egyptians "floating like skin-bottles upon the surface of the water . . . and the Israelites went and saw them and they recognized them." Apparently they were able to identify specific people among the bodies which were washed ashore, such as some court and military officials and the task-masters.[148] Only Pharaoh was spared, but he had to watch the elimination of his army and his friends and court. He is quoted as having said:

> Let neither man nor beast, herd nor flock, taste anything; let them not feed nor drink water; for I know there is no god beside Him in all the world; all His words are true, all his judgments are true and faithful.[149]

It had been a spectacle which was not soon to be forgotten, and the news of what had happened to Pharaoh and his armed forces spread throughout all the lands. The kings of Edom, Moab, Canaan, and Amalak offered their advice to the Egyptian king as to how best attack and re-capture the twelve tribes, but Pharaoh was without military might and his spirit was broken.[150] Of the great leaders at this time, we hear:

> All the kings of the earth heard of the departure from Egypt, and the dividing of the Red Sea, and they trembled and feared and fled from their palaces.[151]

Now Israel was free and would remain so for a long period of time, for it is written that "the enemies of Israel have no power over them until Israel weakens the might of the Shekinah," until they forget the Lord and force Him to deny the people their blessings since He cannot grant them, in the interest of justice, to those who are unworthy of them.[152] The people had lived in Egypt for a period of either 210 or 400 years; exactly which figure is still debated by the scholars.[153] Yet, Egypt appears to have occupied an im-portant place in the lives of many of the great leaders of Israel, and a central position even for Christianity. The descendants of Noah went there after the flood, Abraham dwelled and taught there, Joseph was an important administrator in the country and married an Egyptian woman (of whose children, Ephraim and Manasses, many in the world today are the off-spring), Jacob and his posterity lived in the country for centuries and Israel had its very beginning as a nation in Egypt, Moses grew up and learned

---

148. *Ibid.*
149. Ginzberg, III, 29-30.
150. *Midrash Rabba: Beshallach,* 20:18.
151. *Pirke de Rabbi Eliezer,* 42.
152. *Zohar: Ahare Moth,* 75b. Shekinah refers to the Spirit of the Lord.
153. See Genesis 15:13, Exodus 12:40. Most of the apocryphal writings seem to prefer 210 years such as *Pirke de Rabbi Eliezer,* 48; *Midrash Rabba: Bo,* 18:11; *Jasher,* 81:4.

much for his great mission in that country, and finally Christ himself spent two or more years of his early childhood there during the Herodian persecution in Palestine. "Nobles shall come out of Egypt," the scriptures read.[154]

The Old Testament was there translated into the Greek language, and this Septuagint version spread from Egypt and became a valuable book, even in the non-Hebrew world. Egypt also took rather quickly to Christianity in its early days under the apostles and other missionaries.[155] Surely it was a land of much wisdom and knowledge and the great men of later ages appear to have undergone the almost obligatory pilgrimage to the country of the Nile such as Thales, Solon, Pythagoras, Aristotle, Herodotus and others. Even the Jews admitted that Egypt takes a central position as to wisdom, even though much of it was perverted and used unrighteously:

> We have learned that these ten species of Wisdom came down to this world, and all were concentrated in Egypt, save one which spread through the rest of the world. They are all species of sorcery and through them the Egyptians were more skilled in sorcery than all other men.[156]

When leaving the country forever, after the miraculous occurrence at the Red Sea, Moses lead the children of Israel in a series of songs of jubilation and thankfulness. It was a kind of antiphonal singing by which the prophet would sing or chant half a verse and the people would either repeat or respond to the first part.[157] It is even written that they had a mixed chorus and used musical instruments such as cymbals.[158]

But the good mood and the festive spirit did not last long. Soon voices emerged which were opposed to the prospect of going further into the unknown in a search for a new place of residence. Why march through the inferno of an unchartered desert and endanger oneself to the prospects of death and hardships? Would it not be better to return to Egypt now that the country had been defeated and humiliated and take over the land with which they were familiar?

> He has already given us the spoils of Egypt. He has made us ride on clouds of glory. He has divided the sea for us and has punished the Egyptians, and we have cited a song before Him. Let us, therefore, now go back to Egypt. . . . They are all dead. Let us return to Egypt.[159]

---

154. Psalms 68:32.
155. "Moses was learned in all the wisdom of the Egyptians" (Acts 7:22), and the Lord said: "Out of Egypt have I called my son" (Matthew 2:13-15), and also Isaiah gives importance to the country (Isaiah 19:19-20).
156. *Zohar: Ahare Moth*, 70a.
157. *Targum Yerushalmi, Exodus*, 15; Philo, *Vita Mosis*, 2:34; *Jasher*, 81:43-44.
158. *Pirke de Rabbi Eliezer*, 42.
159. *Midrash Rabba: Beshallach*, 24:2.

They were persuaded not to return, but their rebellious attitude and occasional ungratefulness became evident and continued to be a source of frustration and anger to both Moses and the Lord, as it is written:

> After all the mighty deeds and wonders which the Holy One, blessed be He, did unto Israel in Egypt and at the Red Sea, they repeatedly tempted the Omnipresent ten times . . . moreover, they slandered the Holy One.[160]

Israel in the Wilderness

God did his best to make them feel comfortable in the desert. A pillar of fire showed them the way to go by night so that they did not have to worry that they were lost and doomed but that the Lord was with them and guided them.[161] During the day, a large cloud led the way and also protected them from the glaring sun, and provided shade and coolness.[162]

But after some days they ran out of the food which they had taken with them from Egypt for the journey, not knowing where they would be led and how long their journey would last. The murmurings commenced again:

> We migrated, expecting freedom, and now we are not even free from the cares of subsistence; we are not, as our leader promised, the happiest, but in truth the most unfortunate of men. After our leader's words had keyed us to the highest pitch of expectation, and filled our ears with vain hopes, he tortures us with famine and does not provide even the necessary food.[163]

Thus the food was provided for by the Lord in form of the manna which fell from heaven. It was a miraculous substance which came down to the ground daily. It needed no preparation such as cooking and needed not to be carried with them but appeared new from day to day. Another remarkable property was that it assumed the taste and flavor of anything the person wanted. He only had to think of it as something that tasted like meat or vegetables or cake and the manna would assume that particular flavor.[164] Therefore, the same food had a different taste to different people. It only lasted for the day and therefore did not require storage and transport. At first, some of the Israelites did not believe that it would appear daily and so they hoarded it and even attempted to gather more for themselves than they needed and then attempted to sell the surplus to others who were not as skeptical and enterprising. Yet it did not work and they were punished by

---

160. *Pirke de Rabbi Eliezer,* 44.
161. *Ibid.,* 42; Michael was in charge of the pillar of fire enterprise.
162. Clement, *Recognitions,* I, xxxv.
163. Philo, *Vita Mosis,* 1:35; Josephus, *Antiquities,* III, i, 3-5; *Midrash Rabba: Beshallach,* :25:4.
164. *Zohar: Beshalah,* 62b; Josephus, *Antiquities,* III, i, 6.

the Lord for their greedy attitude in regards to the free gift of God.[165] For forty years the manna provided food for them and their cattle in the wilderness.

The Ten Commandments

After many weeks in the desert and the many miracles Moses had to perform by the power of God, the wandering group were visited by Jethro, who had come to meet Moses and had brought with them Zipporah and the children. It was a great reunion and Jethro was of much help to Moses as a general counselor. But Israel moved forward and came to Sinai where the commandments and laws were to be given to the chosen people. Moses ascended the mountain and God told him about his plan and what it would require. He commanded Moses to make it known to Israel and receive their commitment to obey the ordinances and the laws.

> The beginning of all things is hard, but as soon as you will have grown accustomed to obedience, all else will be easy for you. If you will now observe the Abrahamic covenant, the Sabbath, and the commandment against idolatry, then you will be my possession; for although everything belongs to me, Israel will be My special possession. . . I will reign over you, as My possession, I and none other, so long as you keep yourselves aloof from other peoples. If not, other peoples will rule over you. But if you obey me, you shall be a nation, not only free from care, but also a nation of priests, a holy nation.[166]

And thus Moses did. He brought the message of God to the people. First he announced it to the elders, as a matter of courtesy, and then to all Israel, including the women. When he had received their approval, he again went up onto the mount and reported to God.[167] Another version recounts that Moses was instructed by the Lord to offer the women the choice of acceptance first; afterwards to present the choice to the men:

> Men, as a rule, hearken to the counsel of women and if the women accept my commandments, they will not be able to imitate their mother Eve who, when she sinned, excused herself with the words: The commandment had not been given to me, but to my husband alone. The women, too, will instruct their children in the Law.[168]

The children of Israel then committed by voice vote to an oath to abide by the words and laws of God. It was a ritual acceptance and a covenant. Moses asked them whether they would keep the code of behavior and they responded with a unison "yes." [169] After this procedure, the Lord went

165. *Targum Yerushalmi,* Deut. 21; Ginzberg, III, 46-48.
166. Ginzberg, III, 86-87. He mentions further that Israel was not to have a cast of priests as other cultures, but that every man would be a priest.
167. *Ibid.,* 87.
168. Rappoport, II, 305.
169. *Ibid.,* 307; Bin Gorion, IV, 224; *Pirke de Rabbi Eliezer,* 41.

ahead with the actual announcement to his people. The earth became calm and quiet, nature rested for a moment as the birds ceased to sing and all the other animals stood silently waiting for the creator of all things to speak. And then the voice of the Lord resounded over the breadth of the earth like thunder. It chilled every spine and echoed in every heart: "I am the Lord, your God!" Not only the children of Israel were awed and fell to the ground, but the sound of the Lord's voice penetrated every being on the face of the earth. Not only Israel was shocked by the presence of God and his power but all the inhabitants of the earth were frightened. They thought that the end was near and that the final destruction was at hand, as during the time of the flood. The kings called on their diviners and seers to ascertain the meaning of this unusual occurence. When they found out that it was Israel which was receiving the law at this time, they were very much relieved and returned to their business.[170]

Everyone understood and perceived the word of God according to his grade of readiness and level of glory he could withstand.[171] Interesting, also, is the statement that the Lord, when he introduced himself, spoke in Egyptian because this was the language which the people had adopted while in bondage.[172] Yet, the whole experience of actually witnessing the call from God proved too much for the Israelites:

> Israel asked of God two things: that they should see His glory and hear His voice; and they did see His glory and heard His voice . . . but they had no strength to endure this revelation, for when they came to Sinai and God revealed himself to them, then their souls fled because He spoke with them.[173]

After Israel perceived that they did not possess the strength and fortitude to endure the immediate presence of the Lord, they fled, fell to their faces, wept and entreated Moses to become an intermediary between them and God and receive the law for them and merely communicate it to the people.[174] Therefore, the prophet left them and proceeded up the mountain to receive the law and the necessary instruction alone.

For forty days the prophet remained on Mt. Sinai and saw and heard some of the most unspeakable things for a human being to know. As Enoch before him, Moses was received into the glory of the Lord, walked the different heavens, and obtained instructions and knowledge in each of them under the tutorage of the angels. He also encountered hell with the power of the devil and the fallen angels who tried to mislead and punish

---

170. *Ibid.*; Ginzberg, III, 91; Josephus, *Antiquities,* III, v, 2-3.
171. *Zohar: Jethro,* 94a.
172. See Ginzberg, III, 94-95.
173. *Midrash Rabba:* Yithro, 29:4. Bin Gorion records that the Israelites actually *saw* the voice of God (IV, 225).
174. Rappoport, II, 308; Bin Gorion, IV, 227-228; Ginzberg, III, 106ff.

him.[175] During the forty days, Moses studied the Torah and its teachings in the presence of the Lord himself. He also met Michael and Gabriel, Metatron and other of the great assistants of God. He was allowed to look behind the veil and hear the most unspeakable things.[176] While in the celestial temple, the prophet was shown the colors which were to be used in the earthly tabernacle, namely violet, red, blue and white.[177] Though he was forty days on the mount, he was not hungry or thirsty since the visitors to each other's spheres act always in accordance to the customs of the place they are in or, in modern speech: when in Rome do like a Roman.

> Is it then possible for any man to be forty days without food or drink? . . . If thou goest into a city thou must act according to its customs. When Moses ascended on high, where there is no eating and drinking, he emulated the heavenly example, and when angels descended to earth where there is eating and drinking, they ate and drank.[178]

While the survival of the forty days presented no problem to Moses, it did, however, affect the thinking of the Israelites around Mt. Sinai since they knew nothing of this law of the spheres. That Moses could be without food for so many days seemed incredible to the people and the suspicion grew among them that something must have happened to the prophet and that he had probably died.

The realization that this might be true affected the jubilant and festive crowd like a shock wave. Many would not believe it but many agitators and dissatisfied people, such as the notorious Dathan, who would have rather stayed in Egypt, and the magicians Jannes and Jambres, who were envious of Moses because of his miracles and the status and adoration he enjoyed among the Israelites, did their best to stir up the multitude into a panic. What if the great prophet and leader was dead? Who could take his place? Who could lead them out of this desert? The rebellious had an answer for that: "Let us make ourselves a god!"

The mass of the people had been whipped into a frenzy. When some of the more sensible people warned that Israel ought not go back to worshiping idols, the agitators accused them of seeking the nation's destruction in the wilderness and demanded their death. Some brave and righteous Israelites, among them the kind and noble Hur, were killed by the fanatical mob.[179]

Then the people turned to Aaron, the brother of Moses, who was an accomplished goldsmith and artist, to make them an idol which they could

175. Rappoport, II, 308ff; Bin Gorion, IV, 231ff; Ginzberg, III, 109ff.
176. Bin Gorion, IV, 241-244.
177. Ginzberg, III, 117.
178. *Midrash Rabba: Ki Thissa,* 47:5.
179. *Ibid.,* 41:7; *Pirke de Rabbi Eliezer,* 45.

see and which could be paraded in front of the multitude to lead them out of the wilderness, since this was the method they had seen the Egyptians follow while they were still inhabitants of that country. Aaron was naturally horrified by the thought of offending the true God of heaven by making an idol which the Israelites could worship. Yet, being mindful of the violent death the great and righteous Hur had suffered at the mob's hands, he thought it best not to agitate them further but to gain time.

> Aaron argued with himself saying: If I say to Israel give me your gold and silver, they will bring it immediately, but if I say to them give me the earrings of your wives and of your daughters, the matter will forthwith fail.

And so it was. He announced that he would do according to their wishes but he gained another precious day by asking the gold of the Hebrew women and children. A quarrel ensued in the camp over the gold as the women were not willing to offer up their jewelry for a golden image. But the time Aaron gained by his trick was running out and Moses still had not returned a day later. Meanwhile, the men tried to remedy the stalemate:

> The men saw that the women would not consent to give their earrings to their husbands. What did they do? Until that hour the earrings were also in their own ears after the fashion of the Egyptians and the Arabs. And they broke off their earrings which were in their own ears and give them to Aaron.[180]

Aaron, seeing no choice open to him, now commenced his assignment with all possible slowness. It is said that he was willing to take a grevious sin upon himself rather than allow the whole people to commit such an enormous sin as to worship an idol. He was still hoping that Moses would appear while he was making the golden image.[181] But the image was finished before the prophet returned from the mountain. It was in the form of an Egyptian Apis bull, 125 hundredweight heavy.[182] Some texts even assert that there were thirteen images made—one for each of the tribes and another one for all of Israel.[183]

It is said that the idol was hollow and that either a man or Satan himself was able to crawl into the image and speak from it so as to make believe that it was a true and living god.[184] But it was not enough for the tribes to have the idol which they could adore. They also demanded that an altar would be made upon which sacrifices could be offered up to the calf-god. Again, Aaron worked extremely slowly so that Moses had another chance to return in time and abort the renewed blaspheme. But the prophet did not

---

180. *Pirke de Rabbi Eliezer,* 45.
181. Ginzberg, III, 121.
182. *Zohar: Ki Tisa,* 192b; *Clement, Recognitions,* I, 25.
183. *Targum Yerushalmi: Sanhedrin,* 10, 28b.
184. Bin Gorion, IV, 257.

appear at this time either. The altar was finished and sacrifices were offered, among them the precious manna which the Lord had so graciously supplied throughout the journey.[185] Immoral acts were also committed by the people and innocent blood was shed in their ordinances to the idol.[186] However, most of the elders of the tribes, and all of the Levites, refused to participate in the worship and general mass hysteria surrounding the golden calf.[187]

The Lord, meanwhile, was aware of the sacrilegious doings of his chosen people and it hurt him deeply that they were, in effect, bowing down before a man-made idol at the very time when he was instructing his prophet, and so soon after the whole nation had heard his voice and had made a covenant to receive his laws. When God informed Moses of the conditions at the foot of the mountain, the prophet refused to believe that his people had actually stooped so low: "Unless I see it with my own eyes, I cannot believe it!"[188]

And thus the disappointed leader descended from Sinai and went to witness the great sin before the Lord of the world. As he approached the camp and saw the calf and sacrifices and the lewdness, the tablets of the law which he had taken with him became heavy and he could no longer carry them. He dropped them and they broke and were no more.[189] A deeply disappointed and angry Moses then acted promptly to end the orgies and idolatry. The earth swallowed up the guilty and the righteous rejoiced and heralded the return of the prophet-leader. For forty days Moses stayed among the remnants of his people and taught them to be strong and faithful to their God.[190] Then he proceeded to ascend the mount again to beg the Lord for forgiveness in behalf of Israel and to ascertain God's will and plan for his people.

Of course, the Lord was displeased and angry. He now referred to the tribes as "Moses' people," whereupon the prophet responded:

> As long as they were righteous you called them *My People* but now that they have sinned you say *Thy People*. They are Thy people and Thine inheritance![191]

But the Lord was angry enough to destroy them all and Moses had to calm him so that they could be received back into the favor of their God.

---

185. *Targum Yerulshalmi: Sanhedrin*, 10, 28b.
186. *Midrash Rabba: Ki Thissa*, 42:1.
187. *Pirke de Rabbi Eliezer*, 45; Bin Gorion, IV, 258; see Exodus 32:26.
188. *Midrash Rabba: Ki Thissa*, 46:1. It is said that Moses needed to see the idolatry for himself so that he could act as a witness against the people.
189. *Pirke de Rabbi Eliezer*, 45, 46; *Targum Yerushalmi*, Exodus 31:18; 32:19. Pseudo-Philo 12, 5 reports that the writings on the tablets vanished when Moses reached the camp.
190. Bin Gorion, IV, 266.
191. *Pirke de Rabbi Eliezer*, 45.

Lord of the universe! Did you not bring them out of Egypt which is a place of idol-worshippers? They are still young . . . be patient with them a while longer and be with them and they will do good deeds before you![192]

Such pleading aided in comforting the Lord to the point where he was no longer adament in destroying them completely or even abandoning his covenant with them. Though quite disappointed, God agreed to offer the tribes a second chance, not like unto the first opportunity, but a more stringent and preparatory way leading to the eventual acceptance. Moses, too, was deeply disappointed that his people had rejected their God so blatantly.[193] For another forty days, the prophet remained on Mt. Sinai where he received new laws and instructions for Israel.[194] The day of a renewed acceptance before the Lord is said to be a renewal of the Day of Atonement, as the events occurred on the same day.[195]

The procedure of acceptance by the people was reminiscent of the first introduction before the rejection and the apostasy. Moses initially communicated the divine laws to Aaron and his two sons, Eleazer and Ithamar. Afterwards the elders of the tribes received the same introduction and finally Israel as a body. Then Moses withdrew and delegated the further instructions first to Aaron, second to his two sons, and thirdly to the elders. This way everyone received the law and repeated it four times.[196] Before they agreed to the commandments, a cloud of dew came down from heaven, according to the legends, and cleansed and purified the people.[197] The law was given on Friday, the sixth of the month, at the sixth hour and the following day was declared the first day of rest.[198] Yet, we are told that it took only forty days that Israel kept the law and then it was already broken for the first time.[199]

The Construction of the Tabernacle

After a while it was time for the Tabernacle to be erected—an edifice in which the holy ordinances could be performed. According to one text, the people themselves pleaded with the Lord to allow them the construction of a temple:

---

192. *Midrash Rabba: Ki Thissa,* 43:9. He actually accused God of contributing to the rebellion by having made Israel so rich in gold when they left Egypt (Ginzberg, III, 131).
193. See the *Apocalypse of Paul,* 48.
194. Ginzberg, III, 133; *Pirke de Rabbi Eliezer,* 46.
195. *Pirke de Rabbi Eliezer,* 46.
196. Ginzberg, III, 144.
197. *Zohar Leviticus: Emor,* 97a.
198. *Pirke de Rabbi Eliezer,* 46.
199. *Ibid.,* 41, 45.

> O Lord of the World! The kings of the nations have palaces in which they have set a table, candlesticks, and other royal insignia, that their king may be recognized as such. Shalt not Thou, too, our king, Redeemer, and helper, use royal insignia, so that the dwellers on earth may recognize that Thou art their king?[200]

At first, God did not think that the people needed such a house of representation but, after repeated requests, he consented and permitted it to be erected.

According to another writing, the Lord himself asked for the construction of an earthly house for him to dwell in whenever he left his mansion on high:

> I order them to build me a tabernacle not because I lack a house, for even before the world was created I built my temple in heaven. But as a token of affection for you I will leave my heavenly temple and dwell among you.[201]

And so it was done. The task of constructing the tabernacle and its furnishings was assigned to Bezalel, son of the martyred Hur.[202] Yet, Moses had already seen the model for the earthly temple while he was in the celestial region, and was therefore able to tell the architect how it should be built.[203] The Lord told Moses:

> Make one after the pattern in blue, purple, scarlet, as thou hast seen above, copy the pattern below . . . if thou wilt make a replica of that which is above, I will leave my heavenly assembly and will cause my spirit to dwell among you below.[204]

> The Holy One showed Moses each single part of it in its exact supernal form, after which Moses constructed the earthly tabernacle.[205]

The material for its construction was collected from the people, who parted freely of their precious substances and treasures. In fact, they gave so freely that material was left over after the tabernacle was finished, so that much ended up in the temple treasury.[206] Another version mentions that Moses was able to construct a like tabernacle with the extra contributions and there were then actually two buildings erected.[207] It took six months for the sanctuary to be ready for the dedication.[208] The consecration ceremonies lasted for seven days, and each day the tabernacle had to be

---

200. *Midrash Aggada: Exodus,* 27:1.

201. *Midrash Tanchuma: Naso,* 11, "I have in the heavens a temple, a hall, and a throne."

202. Ginzberg, III, 154ff.

203. *Midrash Rabba: Shemoth,* 40:2. See also Philo, *Moses,* 2, 3 and *Quaestiones in Exodus,* 2, 52. See Exodus 25:40.

204. *Midrash Rabba: Terumah,* 35:6.

205. *Zohar: P'Qude,* 221a.

206. *Midrash Rabba: Pekude,* 51:2. See also Exodus 36:7.

207. *Midrash Rabba: Shemoth,* 51:2.

208. *Midrash Rabba: Pekude,* 52:2. It might be that it took three months to build it and three months to wait for the proper time of dedication.

erected and taken down again.[209] The Holy of Holies in the sanctuary became forever associated with the name of Moses for it was here that he received some of the important revelations:

> Moses would come in and stand in the tent. A voice would then descend from heaven, as though through a tube of fire, to between the two cherubim and Moses would hear the voice speaking to him from within the ark of covenant.[210]

At other times he would actually be transfigured in the holy place:

> No one can see Moses because a veil overspreads his face and seven clouds of glory surround him . . . the more illuminating the exposition given of the Torah, the more those clouds are lit up, and they become more and more transparent until the veil becomes visible, and from the midst of that veil they see a light brighter than that of all other lights, and this is the face of Moses. No one actually sees his face, but only the light which proceeds from the veil behind all the clouds.[211]

It is written that "just as the Lord called unto Moses and spoke with him, so did Moses call God and spoke with him."[212] And he received some of the grandest revelations of all time from the Lord:

> For he showed him many admonitions together with the principles of the laws and the consummation of time . . . and likewise the pattern of Zion and its measures . . . also he showed to him the measures of fire and also the depths of the abyss and the weight of the winds and the number of the drops of rain . . . and the height of the air and the greatness of paradise and the consummation of the ages and the beginning of the day of judgment . . . and the earths which have not yet come . . .[213]

But, at times, even Moses was frightened by the visits of personages from the other realms whom he received. Once an angel came and scared the prophet:

> On seeing him, Moses was struck dumb with awe and would have thrown himself down from the cloud but the Holy One, admonished him, saying: Moses, thou didst speak much with me at the bush and didst that I should reveal to thee my holy name and wast not afraid and art thou now afraid before my servants?[214]

It must not be an easy matter to be confronted with visions and meet the visitors from other spheres, and therefore we hear that "Moses began to quake with mighty dread but the Holy One took hold of him," or "Moses trembled and could not utter a word."[215]

---

209. *Midrash Rabba: Naso,* 18:5. Some teachings even mention that it happened two or three times daily.

210. *Ibid.,* 14:19.

211. *Zohar: Shelah Lecha,* 163a.

212. *Midrash Rabba: Beshallah,* 21:2.

213. *Apocalypse of Baruch,* 59:4-9.

214. *Zohar: Beshalah,* 58a.

215. *Ibid.*

But the great prophet also had his troubles on earth, particularly with some of the Israelites who were not very diligent in keeping their covenants and oaths, and who deliberately attempted to do him harm. It began already after the tabernacle had been constructed and dedicated. Voices were heard, and became louder, which accused Moses of having taken for himself some of the material donated for the building of the sanctuary. He and his son Amram were, in effect, accused of enriching themselves in the enterprise. Moses, therefore, gave a very accurate and detailed account of the expenditures and satisfied the people that none of the donations was used for personal gain.[216]

The Accusations of the Rebellious Israelites

Of course, it was a disappointment for the prophet when the Lord did not choose him but rather his brother Aaron and his two sons to be the high priests. God told him:

> I might have installed thy brother as high priest without having informed thee of it, but I hand over the appointment to thee, so that thou mayest have an opportunity of showing the people thy humility, in that thou dost not seek this high office for thyself.[217]

This act of courtesy to Moses helped him in avoiding the accusations of being powerhungry.

Yet, there were enough men among the Israelites who would have gladly been appointed to a high office themselves, even to that of prophet and leader. The story concerning the troubles with Korah may show the problems Moses had to endure repeatedly during the sojourn in the wilderness. Korah was a cousin of the prophet and one of the wealthiest men in the tribe of Levi. He therefore assumed that he should have been invested with some power and status among the children of Israel:

> Moses is king, Aaron is high priest, and I have always hoped that I would be appointed the leader of my tribe. Yet Moses has given this honor to Eliphaz, the son of Usiel, the younger brother of my father. He seems determined to slide me and thinks contemptuously of me, even though I have many riches. I will therefore stir up a revolt against Moses and thwart all his plans.[218]

And thus he went and commenced to spread vicious stories about the leaders of the Israelites, primarily about Moses. Besides murmuring concerning the wanderings in the desert and the unavailability of the promised land, he invented evil and false stories about the leading authorities of the Israelites. One of them, which he told in the camp, was as follows:

---

216. *Midrash Rabba: Pekude,* 51:2, 6.
217. *Midrash Rabba: Shemoth,* 37:1-4.
218. *Midrash Tanchuma: Korah; Midrash Rabba: Korach,* 18:2.

There was a poor man in my neighborhood who toiled hard all his life but remained poor to his last day. When he died, his wife and her two orphan daughters only had a small field among their few possessions. The widow then decided to cultivate the field to find sustenance for herself and her two children. But when she started ploughing the field Moses came and told her: You cannot plough the field with an ox and an ass together! So the woman hired only an ass and ploughed the field. Then it came time to sow and again Moses came and said to her: You cannot sow the field with two kinds of seed! So she only sowed one kind. When it came time to reap Moses came by and told her not to gather everything but leave the gleanings for the poor. She obeyed him and reaped only part of the harvest and placed it in her barn. When she was about to thresh it Moses appeared and asked her to give him the heave-offering and the second and the third tithe for the priests. She did that but thought to herself: There is very little left of this field and it will not yield much for me and my daughters if I am always to pay such high taxes and give such a large portion to the priests. I will sell the field and buy instead two ewes whose milk we will drink, my two daughters and myself, and of their wool we will clothe ourselves! Thus she did. She sold the field and bought the two sheep. But when her sheep brought forth young ones, Aaron, the high priest, came and said: Give me the firstborn of your sheep for they belong to me according to the law which says that all firstborn males born of thy flock shall be sanctified unto the Lord! The poor woman handed the firstling over to Aaron. When the time for shearing came she hoped to weave some woolen garments for herself and her daughters, but Aaron came again and demanded his share of the shearing. . . . The woman did as she was asked but she was grieved in her heart and thought to herself: The priest is robbing me constantly and leaves me but little for myself and my children. I will slaughter the two sheep and eat their meat and the priest will cease to rob me! But she had barely done so when Aaron appeared once more and demanded the shoulder, the two cheeks and the maw as his share. This is the law, he said . . . When the poor widow heard this she exclaimed: Woe unto me! I had hoped never to see the face of the priest again who has been robbing me all my life, but he has come again! I cannot give you the share that you asked for I dedicated the whole sheep to God! Then Aaron replied: If that is the case, the whole sheep is mine because everything devoted to God in Israel belongs to the priest. Such is the law! Then he took the sheep and walked away leaving the widow and her orphans weeping bitterly.[219]

With stories like these Korah naturally inflamed the minds of those who were spiritually weak and he began to collect a group of followers who would go about the camp speaking out against Moses and the whole treck to the promised land: "You have laid upon us a burden that is greater than that of the Egyptian slavery. We were better off under the Egyptians than under your rule!"[220] Even though these troublemakers seem to have been mostly in the minority in the camp, they caused enough trouble and heartaches to make life miserable for the prophet. Instead of leading the people, he saw himself often in the position of having to defend himself and his actions.

Korah said quite openly that he did not consider Moses to be a true prophet:

219. *Midrash Tehillim*, 1:14.
220. *Midrash Rabba: Korach*, 18:4.

Laws so irrational cannot possibly come from God. The laws which you teach are therefore not God's work but your own. Therefore you are not a prophet and Aaron is no high priest.[221]

Among his constant adversaries were also Dathan and Abiram, who had already opposed him in Egypt before the exodus. They gladly joined the ranks of the dissatisfied and made their opposition to the prophet known:

Why do you set yourself up as master over us? What have you done for us anyway? You have led us out of Egypt, a land like the garden of the Lord, and you have not brought us to Canaan but into the middle of the desert where we are plagued daily. Already in Egypt you have tried to assume leadership over us as you are doing it now. You have beguiled the people when you promised them a land of milk and honey and in their delusion they have followed you.[222]

But not only Korah, Dathan, Abiram and others murmured and rebelled against Moses, but also his own brother and sister. Aaron and Miriam also became infected with a spirit of criticism.

Even though Egypt had treated the Israelites harshly and with contempt, the rebellious among the tribes wished that they were still in the land of the Nile:

Who shall give us flesh to eat? We remember the fish which we ate so freely in Egypt, and the cucumbers, the onions and the garlic. But now our souls are dry for there is nothing at all except this manna![223]

It was not that life in Egypt had been better, because it had not been, but some of the people became tired and dissatisfied with the strict observance of the law. They had imagined their exodus and the road to the promised land differently. Any accusation now served their purpose in showing their opposition to the situation they were in. And even the great Moses grew tired at times of their murmurings and disobedience. He thought that perhaps someone else might be better suitable to lead the people and asked the Lord whether he could be relieved of his duties. Finally God saw it fit not to release Moses but to give him additional assistants to help carry out the responsibilities and the great burden of presidency:

I gave you enough understanding and wisdom to guide my children alone, so that you might be distinguished by this honor, but you wish to share this guidance with others . . . they shall bear the burden of the people with you, that you do not have to bear it alone.[224]

---

221. *Targum Yerushalmi: Sanhedrin*, 10, 27-18a.
222. *Midrash Bamidbar Rabba*, 18:10.
223. Ginzberg, III, 245.
224. *Ibid.*, III, 248., 248.

And so Moses was allowed to select 70 elders to help him lead and guide the affairs of the nation. It helped somewhat to have these counselors and administrators on his side, yet Moses himself continued to bear the heavy responsibility of his office. And he handled it well and with dignity for most of the forty years in the wilderness. Only once did he offend the Almighty, when he performed a miracle for the multitude in need of water and seemingly took the honor of it to himself.[225] But, in spite of that, he remained the "confident of God,"[226] and "exceedingly meek, above all the men on the face of the earth."[227]

The Call of Joshua

After forty years of wanderings, the life of the great prophet leader was coming to an end. Many problems had been overcome, wars won and battles fought. Aaron had already passed on, and the children of Israel were nearing the frontiers of the promised land. But Moses was not yet ready to give up. If he did not enter the final destination together with his people it might indeed look to his critics that he had been wandering about the wilderness without any guidance and direction from God. Therefore, he pleaded with the Lord to allow him to step into the chosen land, even though he recalled the word of God that he would not be allowed to do so. But the Almighty stood firm to his word in spite of the repentance and the pleadings of his prophet:

> With all your creatures you deal with the quality of mercy and you forgive their sins once, twice even three times, but you will not forgive me?
>
> O Lord of the world! How often did Israel sin before you and when I begged and implored mercy for them before you, you forgave them, but not for me! For my sake you forgave the sins of sixty thousand and you will not forgive my sin?[228]

But the Lord held to his original decision. He had long forgiven Moses, but he had other plans for the prophet and needed to call him home. Adam had also transgressed but once, and God forgave him; nevertheless he had to die because it was part of the overall plan of which mortals are not always aware.

Joshua was chosen by the Lord as the new successor to the great Moses and for the next thirty-six days, we are told, the old prophet, now a hundred and twenty years old, worked for Joshua to teach him what he knew. He

---

225. Numbers 20:12. He was called "Moses" because he was saved out of the water, delivered a nation by passing through the water, and was punished because of water (*Midrash Rabba: Chukkath*, 19:14).
226. *Midrash Rabba: Pekude*, 51:1.
227. *Zohar: Balak*, 205b. See Numbers 12:3.
228. Ginzberg, III, 424-425.

cleaned his house, washed his clothes, polished his shoes and performed many of the menial functions of everyday service for Joshua, his former aid and right hand. It was embarrassing for Joshua but Moses could not be swayed: "Love thy neighbor as thyself," he said, "and let thy pupil's honor be as dear to thee as thine own."[229]

On the morning of Moses' last day, he wrote some items and deposited them in the ark of covenant.[230] Then he assembled Israel and in a spectacular ceremony before the people he invested Joshua with the authority as the new leader to take them into the promised land.[231] Then, in the company of Joshua, Moses ascended Mt. Nebo to await his impending fate. But before he was taken, the Lord showed the aging prophet the promised land so that he might see from on high what he would not be permitted to experience. He also saw a vision of the future, the history of the whole land.[232]

Then Moses directed some last words of instruction and comfort to Joshua before the two had to separate after some forty years together as a great team of leaders:

> Behold, my son, the people whom I deliver into thy hands. They are the people of the Lord. They are still in their youth and therefore inexperienced in keeping the commandments. Make sure that thou dost not speak harshly to them, for they are the children of the Holy One . . .[233]

> Moses took Joshua's hand and placed him before himself and said to him: Do not think of ourself as less than you are. Do not be troubled. Listen to my words: God created all the people of the world including us and he saw the end from the beginning, including us, and nothing has been overlooked, even the smallest item. The Lord knew everything in this world beforehand and so it will happen. Do not be afraid![234]

He comforted Joshua, who was worried about the burden of his new assignment. Then Moses proceeded to bless each of the tribes once more, as he had done so many times before.[235] He concluded by saying: "Happy art thou, Israel, for who is like unto thee, a people saved by the Lord. . . ."[236] Finally the last moment came and the great Moses departed from this world at the hour of the Sabbath afternoon prayer.[237]

---

229. *Ibid.*, III, 438.
230. *Midrash Rabba Debarim*, 9:9.
231. Ginzberg, III, 440-441.
232. *Ibid.*, 443.
233. *Ibid.*, 451.
234. *Assumption of Moses*, 12:2-5.
235. Ginzberg, III, 455ff.
236. *Midrash Tannaim*, 222.
237. *Zohar: Sabbath*, II, 88a.

While many maintain that he actually died and was buried in an unknown spot by the Lord himself,[238] the often voiced ancient teaching is that Moses was translated and assumed into heavenly glory without tasting death at that time.[239] So ended the mortal probation of "the great friend of the Most High."[240]

And as some have expressed their view,

Moses was greater than Noah and his sons . . . he was above Abraham and Isaac . . . Moses was greater than Jacob . . . he was above all other prophets.[241]

---

238. *Midrash Tannaim,* 224. See Deutoronomy 34:5-6.
239. Philo, *Vita Mosis,* 2:39; Josephus, *Antiquities,* IV, viii, 48.
240. *Zohar: Bo,* 37a.
241. *Sibylline Oracles,* II, 245; Deutoronomy 34:10.

Jesus Christ

His Family and Relatives

The earthly family of the Savior has received great attention by the early Christians. However, as with most all writings outside the canon of scripture, it is difficult to distinguish tales from the truth. Both are found nicely intermingled among the records left by the ancients. Since various Christian groups emphasized or supported different beliefs and writings, it seems that various documents and stories announce a variety of teachings and traditions about the family in which Jesus grew up.

Joseph, the Savior's foster father, has his genealogies in the Gospels of Matthew and Luke. Both trace the lineage back to David, even though they differ slightly in the names mentioned. Divers opinions were and still are being put forth as to a meaning of this discrepancy. Julius Africanus taught anciently that it was due to the old Jewish law of Deutoronomy 25:5-10, by which the brother of a man, who had died childless, was obliged to marry his brother's wife for the purpose of offspring. He surmised that this might have taken place somewhere in the line since the death of David.[1] He also referred to the belief that King Herod had all the genealogy tables of the Jews burned, which caused great confusion, and was possibly also responsible for the variance in the records.[2] Modern writers think that one list could refer to Joseph's priesthood line while the other perhaps constituted the line of descent of the royal household.[3]

Since Jesus was, however, not Joseph's literal but adopted son, the royal lineage also has to include Mary, the Lord's physical mother. The Gospels are silent on her genealogy and her Davidic descent is only implied in scriptures such as Acts 2:30 and 13:23; Romans 1:33; and 2 Timothy 2:8.[4] In any case, the fact remains that Joseph married her, which made Jesus

---

1. He is cited by Eusebius, *Ecclesiastical History,* I, vii, 2-10.
2. *Ibid.*
3. For a discussion see James E. Talmage, *Jesus the Christ,* p.89, note 5.
4. See also the epistles of Ignatius to the *Ephesians* 18:2, to the *Trallians* 9:1, and to the *Smyrnians* 1:1; the *Protevangelium* by James, 9:2, 4; Justin Martye, *Dialog with Trypho,* 43, 45, 101, 120; Tertullian, *Adversus Marcionem,* III, 17; IV, 1; V, 8.

his adopted and thereby legal son. Since Joseph was a descendant of David and heir to the Jewish throne, then also Jesus, as his legal son, became an heir. Both would have been rulers of the nation, had not the Romans conquered Palestine in 63 B.C. and placed their puppet kings upon the throne.[5] Jesus is therefore rightfully referred to as the "King of the Jews."[6] Even a Jewish source in the Talmud attributed the royal lineage to the Lord:

> Ulla said: "Would you believe that any defense would have been so zealously sought for him? He was a deceiver and the All-Merciful says: 'You should not spare him, neither shall you conceal him.' It was different with Jesus, for he was near to Kingship."[7]

Joseph never seems to have played an important role in the scriptures, even though he was later declared a saint by the Catholics. In the traditions he is always depicted as an older man.[8] He is also credited with having been married before he became the husband of Mary.[9] According to the *History of Joseph the Carpenter,* an Egyptian writing of the fourth century, Joseph was married for some time until his first wife died. He had four sons and two daughters by her. After a year of solitude, he became engaged to Mary for a period of two years before both were married and he died at a high age when Jesus was about eighteen years old.[10]

That Joseph died early during the life of the Savior could be plausible because he is not mentioned in the scriptures after the journey of the family to the temple in Jerusalem when Jesus was twelve years old.[11] Even the bountiful traditions among the early Christians are silent about him, and it would seem that Joseph had died before the Savior took up his ministry. Thus, this inference would give credence to the assertion that he was an older man at the time of the wedding.

The scriptures refer to his occupation as that of carpenter.[12] According to apocryphal literature and tradition, he was a quite mediocre carpenter, who worked mainly on ploughs and yokes and sometimes on the construction of houses.[13] He also manufactured gates, milk pails, sieves, or boxes and Jesus had to help him out of predicaments at times because "he was not very skilled at his carpenter's trade."[14]

5. "Had Judah been a free and independent nation, ruled by a rightful sovereign, Joseph the carpenter would have been her rightful king; and his lawful successor to the throne would have been Jesus of Nazareth the king of the Jews." James E. Talmage, *Jesus the Christ,* p. 87.
6. Such as in Matthew 27:27, Mark 15:26, Luke 23:38, John 19:9.
7. Ulla gives a Rabbinic commentary to a verse in the *Talmud: Sanhedrin,* 43a.
8. *Gospel of the Birth of Mary,* VI, 6; *Protevangelium,* VIII, 13 (Papyrus Bodmer V).
9. Edgar Hennecke and Wilhelm Schneemelcher, *New Testament Apocrypha,* p. 427. Salome was a relative of Mary, perhaps even a sister.
10. *History of Joseph the Carpenter,* II, III, IV, X.
11. Luke 2:42-51.
12. For example, Matthew 13:55.
13. Justin Martyr, *Dialog with Trypho,* 88; *Protevangelium,* X.
14. *I. Infancy Gospel,* XVI, 2-4.

More than on Joseph, the attention is centered on his wife Mary because of the tremendous cult the Catholic Church placed around her. Mary's parents were Anna and Joachim, already well advanced in age but childless. Just as previously in the case of Abraham and Sarah, an angel appeared on day and announced the birth of a daughter, Mary, who was to be dedicated to the temple.[15] Throughout tradition, then, her life is one of service to the temple and to the community of the faithful. In the temple, Mary was later engaged in making a new veil for the holy of holies:

> And the priest said: Cast lots as to who of you shall weave the gold and the white linen and the silk and the hyacinthine, and the scarlet and the purple. And the lot of the purple and the scarlet fell to Mary.[16]

One old text describes her dress while she ministered in the temple service:

> Her tunic came down over her seal and her head-cloth came down over her eyes; she wore a girdle around her tunic, and her tunic was never soiled or torn.[17]

After having served in the temple as one of the many girls who took care of the cleaning and the physical aspects of the rituals, she left this environment at age fourteen to be married. Since she was also of the royal household, Mary could not just wed anyone—only a person of nobility could be her spouse. So a search was conducted for all the eligible bachelors and widowers of the Davidic line. Joseph, who happened to be unmarried at this time, was chosen by divine intervention. An angel told the high priest to gather the staffs of all the candicates and a sign would be given as to which was the chosen person:

> And when they had gathered together they went to the high priest and gave their staffs to him. And he took the staffs of all of them and went into the temple and prayed. And when he had finished the prayer he came outside and gave their staffs back to them and no sign had yet appeared. But Joseph received the staff last and a dove flew down to the staff and then rested upon Joseph's head. And the priest said to him: to you the lot has fallen to take Mary as your wife and to keep her for yourself.[18]

Even though Mary knew very well who her son was, she sometimes seemed not to appreciate his calling and his work, or she misunderstood the real intent of Jesus when he took up his ministry. Perhaps she hoped him to be the type of Messiah whom the Jews in general expected: The great king and strongman who would drive the Romans out of Palestine and restore the country to a great world power. Instead, Jesus led a carpenter's life

---

15. *Protevangelium*, I-IV; *Gospel of the Birth of Mary*, I-III.
16. *Protevangelium*, VIII-IX; *Gospel of the Birth of Mary*, IV-VI.
17. Discourse by Demetrius of Antioch, Fol. 25a, in Wallis Budge, *Miscellanious Coptic Texts*, p. 653ff.
18. *Protevangelium*, VIII-IX; *Gospel of the Birth of Mary*, IV-VI.

until about the age of thirty and then he assumed the role of an itinerant preacher, quite in contrast to the high and worldly hopes of the Jews. We read in the scriptures that Mary called him home from a meeting once where he was preaching (Mark 3:21-22) and he had to renounce her perhaps well-meant chastisement on occasions (Mark 3:33-35; John 2:4; Luke 2:48-49). It also appears that Christ did not spend a great amount of time with her during the years of his public ministry, and there is very little known about Mary's activities during that period. She is not mentioned in the scriptures again until the day of Christ's death, when she stood under the cross and her son asked the apostle John to take care of her (John 19:25-27). Mary seems to have remained with or near the leaders of the Church for a while because she is mentioned in connection with them (Acts 1:14). Some of the apostles and Salome are said to have lived with Mary in Jerusalem,[19] and bishop Cyrill recalled that she lived at the house of John and others for some ten years before her death at about age 57.[20]

There are quite a number of stories about Mary's death.

> And the countenance of the mother of the Lord did shine above the light. She rose up and with her own hand blessed each one of the apostles and all of them praised God. And the Lord spread forth his unstained hands and received her holy and spotless soul.[21]

And also,

> Mary arose from the pavement and laid herself on the bed and, giving thanks to God, she gave up the ghost.[22]

In many narratives, Mary undergoes a quick corporeal change and is taken up into heaven immediately.[23] Other writings refute this idea. Bishop Cyrill of Jerusalem, for instance, makes it quite clear that Mary died normally and that she was not immediately resurrected. He reports Christ as saying on the occasion of his mother's death:

---

19. *The Assumption of the Virgin,* V, in M. R. James, *The Apocryphal New Testament,* p. 194ff.

20. Cyrill of Jerusalem, *Twentieth Discourse,* in Wallis Budge. *Miscellaneous Coptic Texts,* p. 642ff. She died at age 57 (14 years in the temple, 33 during the life of Christ, 10 after his ascension).

21. *The Discourse of St. John the Divine concerning the Falling Asleep of the Holy Mother of God,* 44, in M. R. James, *The Apocryphal New Testament,* p. 201ff.

22. *The Assumption of the Virgin: Latin Narrative of Pseudo-Melito,* VIII, 3, in M. R. James, *The Apocryphal New Testament,* p. 209ff.

23. Such as in the *Discourse of Theodosius* and the *Narrative by Joseph of Arimathea,* in M. R. James, the *Apocryphal New Testament,* p. 198ff. and 216ff. These writings lend the context to the foundation of the assertion of the Catholic Church that Mary was assumed "body and soul into Heavenly glory." (Pope Pius XII: Munificentissimus Deus, on November 2, 1950) in Anne Fremantle, *The Papal Encyclicals,* p. 299.

> I will hide thy body in the earth and no man shall find it until the day when I will raise it incorruptible. . . . Let no man make for himself the trouble of seeking it until the great day of the appearance of Christ.[24]

Another text makes the theory of Mary's bodily assumption into heaven without death quite impossible:

> This is the day wherein the queen, the mother of the king of life, tasted death like every other human being, because she was flesh and blood and, moreover, she was begotten by a human father and brought forth by a human mother.[25]

There are also many stories about the brothers and sisters of the Lord. However, the emphasis placed on them by tradition and early writings was usually neglected because it has long been a repugnant teaching to some Christian faiths that Mary could have had other children besides Jesus. It would undermine the prominent doctrine of many churches that Mary remained the perpetual virgin. Therefore, any references to brothers and sisters in the writings (Mark 6:3; Matthew 27:31; Luke 24:10; Mark 15:40) are quite anxiously interpreted to mean relatives of Jesus, or, at best, children of Joseph by his previous marriage, thus making them step-brothers and sisters of the Savior.[26] Mark 6:3 lists their names as James, Joses (perhaps Joseph), Judas, and Simon.[27] The scriptures do not give the names of the girls, but in the *Story of Joseph the Carpenter* they are referred to as Assia and Lydia. Epiphanius calls them Mary and Salome.[28]

Again it appears that the Savior's family did not take readily to his divinity and joined with other people who thought that Jesus was "beside himself."[29] However, their attitude must have changed later on. Immediately after the resurrection they appear among the apostles (Acts 1:14). James is called the "brother of the Lord" (Galatians 1:19), not to be confused with the James, one of the apostles. His brother James, also called "the Just," is the one Christ appeared to before all the other disciples (1 Corinthians 15:7). A supplementary account of this event is known:

> The Lord . . . went to James and appeared to him. For James had sworn that he would not eat bread from that hour on in which he drank the cup of the Lord until he

---

24. Cyrill of Jerusalem, *Twentieth Discourse,* in Wallis Budge, *Miscellaneous Coptic Texts,* p. 642ff.

25. Cyrill of Jerusalem, *Discourse of Mary Theotokos,* in Wallis Budge, *Miscellaneous Coptic Texts,* p. 642ff.

26. Origin cites the *Protevangelium* by James (8:2-9, 17:1) as the source of the perpetual virginity of Mary:

> But some say, basing it on a tradition in the Gospel according to Peter, as it is entitled, or the Book of James, that the brothers of Jesus were sons of Joseph by a former wife, whom he married before Mary.

27. The *History of Joseph the Carpenter* calls Joses: Joseto or Justus.

28. Epiphanius, *Heresies,* LXXVIII, 8.

29. Mark 3:21. ἐξέστη means to be out of place or out of mind. See also John 7:5.

should see him risen from among tham that sleep. And shortly thereafter the Lord said: "Bring a table and bread." And immediately it was added: And he took the bread, blessed it and brake it and gave it to James the Just and said to him: "My brother, eat thy bread, for the Son of Man is risen from among them that sleep.[30]

According to Eusebius, it was this James who was made bishop of Jerusalem by the apostles:

> For they say that Peter and James and John, after the ascension of the Savior, as if also preferred by our Lord, strove not after honor, but chose James the Just bishop of Jerusalem.[31]

If he, indeed, held this position, he was an important person in the Christian community. Paul and the other apostles met with him often when they were in the city (Galatians 1:19; Acts 15:13ff, 21:18ff). The death of James is recorded in apocryphal literature and tradition. Hegesippus, for example, mentioned that James became a martyr after he refused to deny his testimony:

> A fuller beat out the brains of Justus with a club . . . Thus he suffered martyrdom and they buried him on the spot where his tombstone is still remaining, near the temple.[32]

Josephus reports a similar story:

> The high priest Ananus . . . assembled the sanhedrim of the judges, and brought before them the brother of Jesus, who was called the Christ, whose name was James, and some others . . . and delivered them to be stoned.[33]

Of the other brothers and sisters of the Lord, not too much is known. Paul wrote that some of them were married (1 Corinthians 9:5). Two of the brothers and the two sisters married while Joseph was still alive, and set up their separate households.[34]

A tradition involves the descendants of Christ's brother, Judas. It appears that the Roman emperors were determined to eliminate any trace of the royal house of the Jews after the great rebellion from 66-70 A.D., in order to prevent any resurgence and reoccurrence of the terrible war.[35] But at the time of the emperor Domitian (81-96 A.D.), reports seemed to have reached Rome that some of the descendants of Judas were still alive. Domitian evidently became afraid because of the persistent stories that the

---

30. Reported by Jerome, *Lives of Illustrious Men,* 2.

31. Eusebius, *Ecclesiastical History,* II, i (quoting Clement of Alexandria in his *Hypotyposes,* ch. 6), and IV, v.

32. In *Ibid.,* II, xxiii, 4.

33. Josephus, *Antiquities of the Jews,* XX, ix, 1.

34. *History of Joseph the Carpenter,* XI.

35. See Eusebius, *Ecclesiastical History,* III, xii; III, xixff; III, xxxii, 3.

ruler of the world would one day appear from the lineage of David. He, therefore, ordered the grandchildren of Judas to be brought to Rome for trial and interrogation:

> He put the question to them, whether they were descendants of David and they answered that they were. He then asked them what property they owned and how much money they had. They answered that they possessed between themselves only nine thousand denarii, but not in silver, but in the value of a piece of land of about thirty-nine acres size, by which they supported themselves with their own labor and raised the taxes. Then they showed their hands which testified of their hard labor and the calluses also. When they asked about Christ and his kingdom and of what nature it was and when it was to appear, they responded that it was not an earthly kingdom but a heavenly one and that it would be at the end of the world, when Christ would come in glory to judge the living and the dead according to their works. Domitian did not reply but he despised them and treated them with contempt as fools and dismissed them and he also ordered the persecutions to stop.[36]

Many of the relatives of the Lord became part of the Christian movement either during his lifetime or after the resurrection. It appears that the community of the faithful in the beginning existed predominantly of close relatives: John the Baptist was the son of Mary's cousin, Elizabeth. The apostles James and John were both sons of Mary's sister, Salome. James, Joses, Simon, and Judas were his own brothers, and the apostles Matthew, James (son of Alphaeus) and Judas were sons of cousins or brothers of Joseph.[37] It should not come as a surprise that the Church in its early stages was a family affair which only later grew into a universal movement and brotherhood.

His Youth

There are numerous accounts and stories about the Savior himself. Many of these pertain to his early childhood and youth, about which the scriptures are largely silent, but which were evidently told and circulated within the Christian community.[38]

The strange world of materials begins already with the conception of Jesus by Mary. During the forty-day ministry of Christ among the disciples at Jerusalem after his resurrection (Acts 1:3), he seems to have taught them many hidden and secret doctrines and ordinances. While the apostles were waiting for his appearance one day, the question of how Mary had conceived the Christ occurred to Bartholemew. He therefore approached Peter and implored him to ask Mary, who was also present, how this might have

---

36. *Ibid.*, III, xx.
37. For a discussion see John Wenham, "The Relatives of Jesus," *Evangelical Quarterly*, p. 6-15.
38. Some were not accepted by all the faithful, but by particular groups and sects within the Christian world, who introduced their particular doctrines and views into the legends.

happened: "Thou art the chief, and my teacher, draw near and ask her."
Peter, of course, was quite reluctant, and finally it was up to Bartholemew
to pose the question to the mother of the Lord. So he "came near unto her
with a cheerful countenance and said unto her: Thou art highly favored, the
tabernacle of the Most High, unblemished, we, even all the apostles, ask
thee to tell us how thou didst conceive the incomprehensible . . ." Mary was
reluctant but upon some pleadings she gave in and asked all the men to
stand around her in a circle while she told the story:

> When I abode in the temple of God . . . on a certain day there appeared unto me one
> in the likeness of an angel, but his face was incomprehensible . . . And straightway the
> veil of the temple was rent and there was a very great earthquake, and I fell upon the
> earth, for I was not able to endure the sight of him. But he put his hand beneath me and
> raised me up, and I looked up into heaven and there came a cloud of dew and sprinkled
> me from the head to the feet, and he wiped me with his robe.[39] And he said unto me:
> Hail, thou art highly favored, the chosen vessel, grace inexhaustable . . . And there
> came a very great loaf, and he set it upon the altar of the temple and did eat of it first
> himself, and gave unto me also. . . . And there came a very great cup full of wine, and he
> set it upon the altar of the temple and drank of it first himself, and gave also unto me.[40]
> . . . And he said unto me: Yet three years and I will send my word unto thee and thou
> shalt conceive my son and through him shall the whole creation be saved. Peace be unto
> thee, my beloved . . .[41]

Her account breaks off here because the Savior appeared and told her
to stop "or this day my whole creation will come to an end." The account
agrees with a shorter statement in one of the recently-published documents
from the Nag Hammadi collection:

> If I may speak about a mystery: The Father of all, who came down, united with the
> virgin and a fire was shining for him on that day. He revealed the great marriage room.
> Therefore the body, which came to be on that day, came out of the marriage room.[42]

According to traditions and legends among some early Christians,
Joseph was away on carpenter's business for several months when the angel
came to announce to Mary that the time had come that she was to become
the mother of the Messiah:

> And Joseph said unto Mary: Lo, I have received thee out of the temple of the Lord:
> and now I will leave thee in my house, and I go away to build my buildings and I will
> come again unto thee. The Lord shall watch over thee.[43]

---

39. A cleansing or purification ceremony.
40. The mutual eating of bread (or cake) and drinking of wine constituted the ancient
wedding ceremony, such as among the Jews and the Romans, etc.
41. *The Gospel of Bartholemew,* II, 1-20.
42. *The Gospel of Philip,* 82. The term refers to a holy marriage ordinance or sealing
room or bridal chamber (as translated by R. McL. Wilson, *The Gospel of Philip,* p. 47).
43. *The Protevangelium of James,* IX, 2, in M. R. James, *The Apocryphal New Testament,* p. 42. This could be plausible because Mary would have probably immediately told
Joseph about the annunciation had he been near her, while the scriptures show Joseph quite
surprised about her condition when he found she had been with a child for some time.

Another text mentions that Mary simply returned to her parent's house in Galilee, while Joseph went to Bethlehem.[44] She apparently stayed with her cousin Elizabeth during the early stages of the pregnancy, but moved back to her own home in the sixth month.[45] However, the *Gospel of the Birth of Mary* mentions only a three-month separation period.[46]

> And behold Joseph came from his building and he entered into the house and found her great with child. And he smote his face and cast himself down upon the ground on sackcloth and wept bitterly, saying: With what countenance shall I look unto the Lord my God? And what prayer shall I make concerning this maiden? For I received her out of the temple of the Lord my God a virgin, and have not kept her safe. Who is he that hath ensnared me? Who hath done this evil in mine house and hath defiled the virgin? . . . And Joseph arose from the sackcloth and called Mary and said unto her: O thou that wast cared for by God, why hast thou done this? Thou hast forgotten the Lord thy God. . . . But she wept bitterly, saying: I am pure and I know not a man . . .[47]

The visit of the angel cleared the situation for Joseph, but not for the neighbors and Pharisees. Joseph was in a predicament as far as the towns-people were concerned because he was not yet married to Mary, but only engaged. He was accused by the priests but by some miraculous intervention both he and Mary were shown innocent of the charges.[48] However, the conflict of mind reoccurred to Joseph when he and Mary went to Bethlehem to be recorded as required by the edict of Caesar Augustus:

> And Joseph said: I will record my sons: but this child, what shall I do with her? As my wife? Nay, I am ashamed. Or as my daughter? But all the children of Israel know that she is not my daughter. This day the Lord shall do as the Lord willeth.[49]

When Mary was about to give birth, we are told that Joseph went out to look for a midwife in Bethlehem. He found one and when the two returned to the cave they witnessed the birth:

> And behold a bright cloud overshadowed the cave. . . . And immediately the cloud withdrew itself out of the cave and a great light appeared in the cave so that our eyes could not endure it. And little by little that light withdrew itself until the young child appeared. . . .[50]

---

44. *The Gospel of the Birth of Mary*, VI, 6-7, in *The Lost Books of the Bible and the Forgotten Books of Eden*, p. 22.
45. *The Protevangelium*, XII, 3.
46. *The Gospel of the Birth of Mary*, VIII, 1-2.
47. *The Protevangelium*, XIII, 1-3.
48. *Ibid.*, XV-XVI.
49. *Ibid.*, XVII.
50. *Ibid.*, XIX, 2. The unacceptability of anything material connected with the divine, as espoused by Platonic and Neo-Platonist teachings, evidently prohibited some of the early Christians (the Docetists and others) from believing that the Christ could have been physically "born" by a woman; therefore, the emphasis on the light and the mysteriously miraculous atmosphere.

The childhood of Christ must have held great fascination for the early Christians of the first few centuries. Since the four Gospels are mostly silent about the thirty years up to the Savior's baptism, the gap in knowledge was conveniently filled by stories and legends. As Christianity spread in the Roman Empire, and more and more people joined the ranks of believers, a demand for more information on Christ increased. Many of the converts were less interested in the theological arguments and doctrinal teachings than in the accounts of the miracles. The need was easily met by the circulation of strange Infancy Gospels throughout some of the communities of Christians.[51] In addition, it became necessary to show to the skeptics and ridiculing pagans that Jesus did not just suddenly assume his role at age thirty, but that he was capable of performing miracles even as a boy.

Already in the cradle Jesus spoke to Mary, his mother, and told her that he was the expected Messiah:

> Mary, I am Jesus the Son of God, that word which thou didst bring forth according to the declaration of the angel Gabriel to thee, and my father hath sent me for the salvation of the world.[52]

The *Gospel of Pseudo-Matthew* reports that Christ was born in a cave and only after three days did the family move to a stable.[53] There are also stories of miracles while they resided in Egypt during the Herodian persecutions in Judea: wild animals worshiped Jesus and he commanded trees to provide food for the family, and idols bowed to him in the pagan temples.[54] When the child was three years old, Joseph was told by an angel to return to Palestine, where the miracle stories were multiplied. People were healed by associating with anything Jesus had touched or used. Bartholemew was snatched from death by lying in the Savior's bed:

> And when she had placed him in the bed wherein Christ lay, at the moment when his eyes were just closed to death; as soon as ever the smell of the garments of the Lord Jesus Christ reached the boy, his eyes were opened, and calling with a loud voice to his mother, he asked for bread. . . .[55]

Two sick children were cured by the water in which Jesus had bathed:

> St. Mary said: take a little of the water with which I have washed my son, and sprinkle it upon him. Then she took a little of that water, as St. Mary had commanded, and sprinkled it upon her son, who being wearied with violent pains, had fallen asleep; and after he had slept a little, awaked perfectly well and recovered.[56]

---

51. See J. P. Migne, *Encyclopedie Theologique,* Vol. XXIII, Dictionaire des Apocryphes, Tome 1 (Paris, 1865).

52. *I. Infancy Gospel of Jesus Christ,* I, 3, in *The Lost Books of the Bible and the Forgotten Books of Eden,* p. 38.

53. *The Gospel of Pseudo-Matthew,* 14, in Edgar Hennecke and Wilhelm Schneemelcher, *New Testament Apocrypha,* Vol. I (Philadelphia, 1963).

54. *Ibid.,* 19-20.

55. *I. Infancy Gospel of Jesus Christ,* XI, 6.

56. *Ibid.,* IX, 4-5.

Another boy was healed by the swaddling clothes of Jesus:

> And when the Lady St. Mary had washed the swaddling clothes of the Lord Christ,
> and hanged them out to dry upon a post, the boy possessed with the devil took down one
> of them, and put it upon his head. And presently the devils began to come out of his
> mouth. . . .[57]

It appears that while a little boy, Jesus performed miracles continually.
He not only healed people but he also animated clay figures, killed certain
individuals by the power of his word, and even resurrected others from
the dead:

> And after he made soft clay he modelled twelve sparrows of it but it was the Sabbath
> day when he made them. . . . And a certain Jew, who saw what Jesus did on the Sabbath
> went and told his father Joseph about it: Behold, your child is at the river and has taken
> clay and made twelve little birds and thus defiled the Sabbath day. And Joseph came to
> the place and saw it and said to him: Why do you do these things on the Sabbath which
> is unlawful to do? But Jesus clapped his hands and said to the sparrows: Depart, and the
> sparrows started flying and left chirpingly. And when the Jews saw it they were astonished
> and went and told their leaders what they had seen Jesus do.[58]

> And thereafter he went through the town and a child came and ran against him
> hitting his shoulder and Jesus became angry said to him: you will not finish your course
> of life. And he fell down immediately and died. When they saw what had happened the
> people said to each other: Where was this child born in order that everything he says
> immediately happens? And the parents of the dead child came to Joseph and accused him
> and said: You, who has such a child are not to live with us in this city or you have to
> teach him to bless things and not to curse, because he is killing our children.[59]

> After a while Jesus was playing in the upper floor of a house when one of his play-
> mates fell down from the house and was killed. When the other children, who were
> playing with them, saw this they ran away but Jesus stayed behind. Then the parents
> of the dead child came and accused him of having pushed the boy down. But Jesus
> replied: I did not push him down. However they persisted in blaming him. Then Jesus
> jumped down from the roof and stood next to the child and said with a loud voice:
> Zenon, which was the boy's name, rise and tell me whether I pushed you down? And the
> boy rose and replied: No, Lord, you did not push me down but you raised me up. And
> all who saw this were astonished.[60]

Again, on a different occasion, Jesus helped a clothes dyer to die
various pieces of cloth into any color desired just by the power of his
word.[61] He also helped his foster father, Joseph, with the carpenter's work
whenever there was some need for miracles, such as with the assignment to
Joseph to make a bed for a rich man. When Joseph finally had his task

---

57. *Ibid.,* IV, 15-16.
58. *The Gospel of Thomas,* II, 2-5.
59. *Ibid.,* IV, 1-2.
60. *Ibid.,* IX, 1-3. Other instances of the raising of the dead are in XVII, 1; XVIII, 1.
61. From the *Arabic Infancy Gospel,* 37, in Hennecke-Schneemelcher, *New Testament
Apocrypha,* I, 400.

completed, it was found that one of the beams was shorter than the other. To his amazement, Jesus took hold of one end of the shorter beam and pulled it out to the desired length.[62]

These and numerous other stories and legends, then, filled the gap of the Savior's youth in the scriptures, and seem to have been enjoyed and added upon over the centuries by some of the early Christian groups. A delightful story concerns the attempt of a teacher to make Jesus learn the alphabet in school. Of course, the student was pictured as being far superior in his knowledge to the instructor, and it was the teacher who had to do the learning.

> And Jesus said to him: If you are a real teacher and if you know the letters very well, tell me the real meaning of the Alpha, and I will tell you the same of the Beta . . .[63]

Another time he astonished the spectators by his ability to interpret:

> And he went to the house of schooling and picked up a book which was lying on the desk. But he did not read the things which were written in the book but spoke by the power of the Holy Ghost and taught those who were standing around the law. And all listened attentively, including the teacher, who urged him to continue on.[64]

Later on, when Jesus was brought by his parents to the temple in Jerusalem at age twelve, he astounded the learned men with his knowledge (Luke 2:41-47). The Infancy Gospels tell us what he did with them:

> And everyone was paying attention to him and were astonished, how he, still being a child, was able to silence and quiet the elders and teachers as he expounded the law and the teachings of the prophets to them.[65]

Another text tells that he also taught mathematics, astronomy, physics, philosophy, metaphysics, the faculties of the body, death, resurrection, and the influence of the spirit.[66]

A very interesting description of a spirit moving about is contained in the *Pistis Sophia*, in a passage where Mary tells of an occurrence which she witnessed when Jesus was a little boy:

> When you were little, before the spirit came upon you, and while you were with Joseph in a vineyard, the Spirit came from above into my house. And he looked like you and I did not recognize him because I thought that it were you. And the Spirit said to me: where is Jesus, my brother, that I may meet him? And while he was talking, I became embarrassed because I thought it was an illusion (φάντασμα) to try me. But I

---

62. *The Gospel of Thoman,* XI, 1-3 (or XIII, 1-3); also in the *Gospel of Pseudo-Matthew,* XXXVII.

63. *Ibid.,* XII, 1-2 (or XIV, 1-2).

64. *Ibid.,* XIII, 1-2 (or XV, 1-2).

65. *Ibid.,* XIX, 2.

66. *I. Infancy Gospel of Jesus Christ,* XXI, in *The Lost Books of the Bible and the Forgotten Books of Eden,* p. 58.

bound him to the foot of the bed which is in my house, until I was able to get to you and Joseph out in the vineyard, where Joseph was working. And it happened, that when you heard me tell the story to Joseph, you understood and were happy and said: where is he that I can see him, or I will wait in this place? But it happened that when Joseph heard you say these words he became worried and we left for the house and went inside and found the Spirit tied to the bed. And we looked at you and found both to look alike. We untied the bound one and he embraced you and kissed you, and you kissed him and you two became one.[67]

This quite interesting Gnostic story conveys that spirits were believed to have looked like individuals and were evidently composed of matter or they could not have been physically tied up. In that respect, they had properties like the resurrected Savior later on.

The sinless life of Jesus during the thirty years of preparation for the ministry is attested to by himself in an ancient text. His cousin John had apparently already taken up his calling when the news of him baptizing reached the household of Joseph's family, who seemed interested in the affair:

Behold, the mother of the Lord and his brothers said to him: John the Baptist is baptizing for the remission of sins, let us also go and be baptized by him. But he said to them: In what have I sinned that I should go and be baptized by him?[68]

In this passage Mary is shown to be of the opinion that even Jesus needed baptism, as he seemed to have been an ordinary young man like many others in the village. The special nature of his calling and his personality appeared not to have been impressed upon her until sometime later.

No complete description of what the Lord looked like is available from contemporary sources. Most sketches are from later centuries, such as the famous and widely known version attributed to Lucius Lentulus, who sent the following investigative report to the Roman Senate:

He is a man of lofty stature, handsome, having a venerable countenance. . . . He has wavy hair, rather crisp, of a bluish tinge, and glossy, flowing down from his shoulders, with a parting in the middle of the head after the manner of the Nazarenes. His forehead is even and very serene, and his face without wrinkle or spot, and beautiful with a slight blush. His nose and mouth are without fault; he has a beard, abundant and reddish, of the color of his hair, not long but forked. His eyes are sparkling and bright . . . in stature of body he is tall. . . . In speech he is grave, reserved, and modest, and he is fair among the children of men. . . .[69]

---

67. *Pistis Sophia,* ch. 61, in Carl Schmidt and Walter Till, *Koptisch-Gnostische Schriften,* Vol. I: *Die Pistis Sophia* (Berlin, 1962), p. 78.

68. From the still lost *Gospel according to the Hebrews* or *Gospel of the Nazarenes,* as quoted by Jerome in the fourth century in his writing *Against the Pelagians,* III, 2.

69. This letter, probably of medieval origin, is in B. Harris Cowper, *Apocryphal Gospels* (London, 1881), p. 221. It is interesting that the Savior is normally depicted as a tall and fair-looking person with light to only moderately dark hair, not at all like the typical ancient Jew or Near Eastern person.

Other ancient documents describe his appearance only in general terms as "fair" or "beautiful" or the like.[70] Many of these writings are of Gnostic origins and credit the Savior with being able to adopt any form, or shape, or appearance as he pleases, depending on the circumstances and the understanding of the person who is with him. The *Acts of John* depict the Lord as sometimes being almost bald with a thick and flowing beard and sometimes possessing only the beard of a youth. At times he appeared small in stature, at other times quite tall.[71] Not much emphasis was evidently placed on a preservation of the Lord's semblance for later generations. This would not be unusual, however, as very few of the great men of antiquity were ever fully described in the records.

His Ministry and Teachings

The public ministry of the Savior is generally assumed to have begun with his baptism in the Jordan by his cousin, John. Various accounts of this important event are known in apocryphal literature, even though most are not now extant and have only been preserved in the writings of the prolific theologians of the early Christian centuries. One such version is found in the commentaries of Jerome:

> It happened, when the Lord came out of the water, that the whole spring of the Holy Ghost came down and rested upon him and said to him: My son, in all the prophets I had been waiting for you to come so that I may find my rest in you, because you are my rest. You are my firstborn son, who reigns forever as king.[72]

Another important occurrence at the beginning of his ministry was his calling of the apostles.[73] An ancient text mentions that these men had already been called in the pre-mortal life: "I have chosen you before the world was."[74] It was even claimed that these special witnesses were called by the Lord before his own baptism since they had to be special witnesses to the whole ministry of the Savior.[75] There seems to be no doubt that the apostles themselves were baptized.[76] The accounts of the calling of the Twelve is quite in conformity with the stories in the scriptures such as this one:

---

70. Such as in the *Acts of John*, 73ff; the *Acts of Thomas*, 80 and 149.

71. The *Acts of John*, 89-93.

72. In the *Gospel according to the Hebrews* or *Gospel of the Nazarenes*, as cited by Jerome in his *Commentary of Isaiah*, IV (on Isaiah 11:3).

73. From the Greek ἀπόστολος = sent out (missionary or emissary). The Latin for sent out = *Missa* (missionary).

74. Ephraem, *Commentary of the Diatisseron*, in *Corpus Scriptorum Christianorum Orientalium*, edited by L. Leloir, Vol. CXXXVII, 42-43.

75. See Hennecke-Schneemelcher, *New Testament Apocrypha*, II, 38.

76. Clement of Alexandria, *Hypotyposes*. In *Die Griechischen Schrifsteller der ersten Jahrhunderte*, edited by Carl Schmidt.

There appeared a certain man named Jesus of about thirty years of age who chose us. And when he came to Capernaum he entered into the house of Simon whose surname was Peter and opened his mouth and said: As I passed along the lake of Tiberias, I chose John and James, the sons of Zebedee, and Simon and Andrew and Thaddaeus and Simon the Zealot and Judas Escariot, and thee Matthew, I called as thou didst sit at the receipt of custom, and thou didst follow me. You therefore I will to be twelve apostles for a testimony unto Israel.[77]

Like the master himself, his witnesses also were required to leave all their possessions and their families behind. In some texts we find them talking about it:

We have followed thee with all our heart, have left mother and father, have left vineyards and fields, have left possessions, have left the splendor of a king and have followed Thee, so that thou mayest teach us of the life of Thy father, who has sent Thee.[78]

I [?] came out from [?] the house of my father and my mother; and as my soul liveth [?], I have not [?] again gone into it, and I have not [?] beheld [?] the faces[?] of my [?] father [?] and my mother, neither [?] have [?] I [?] beheld the faces [?] of my [?] children [?] and my wife [?], but I bore my cross every day, following after Thee from morning till night (and I have not) laid it down. Jesus answered and said: I know, Andrew. . . .[79]

That the calling of the apostles was important is attested to by Irenaeus:

. . . [in the church] as in a wealthy treasury the apostles have lodged most copiously all that pertains to the truth so that every man, whosoever will, may draw from it the water of life.[80]

All throughout the old writings we also find the assertion that the apostles knew more than they taught and transmitted to the general membership of the church in their writings and sermons:

The Savior secretly taught these same things not to all but only to some of his disciples who could comprehend them and who were capable of understanding what was indicated by the scenes, enigmas, and parables that he brought forward.[81]

---

77. Epiphanius, *Heresies*, XXX.iv.2.

78. *First Book of Jeu*, 2. In *Koptisch Gnostische Schriften*, edited by Carl Schmidt, Vol. I, 259.

79. J. W. B. Barns, "A Coptic Apocryphal Fragment in the Bodleian Library," *Journal of Theological Studies*, N.S. XI (1960), p. 70-76. Here is also indicated that Andrew was married as were the other apostles (1. Cor. 9:5). Peter was married (Mark 1:29-31) and had children (Mark 10:29). Other apocryphal references to his wife are in Clement, *Stromata* VII.lxiii.3, and in *Recognitions*, VII.25. A daughter, Petronella, is mentioned in the *Acts of Peter* and in the *Acts of Philip*. See also "St. Petronella, the Virgin," in Jacobus de Voragine, *The Golden Legend*, LXXVI. The apostle Philip had children (Eusebius, *History of the Church*, III.xxx.1 and xxxi.3 and xxxix.9), likewise Bartholemew and Thomas (M. R. James, *The Apocryphal New Testament*, p. 182, 185). Paul was also married (Clement, *Stromata*, III.liii.1).

80. In *Contra Haereses*, III.iv.1.

81. Irenaeus, *C. Haereses*, II.xxvii.2.

> The apostles . . . had not revealed everything to everyone. That is to say they had entrusted some things publicly to all, but some in secret to a few.[82]

At times we find the apostles discouraged and in need of reassurance because the world does not receive their message, such as in this text:

> Thomas replied: You have indeed persuaded us, Lord. We realized in our heart and it is obvious that this [is] so, and that your word is sufficient. But these words that you speak to us are laughing-stocks to the world and derided, since they are not understood. So how can we do and preach them since we are reckoned as in the world? The Savior answered and said: Truly I tell you that he who will listen to your word and turn his face or sneer at it or smirk at these things, truly I tell you that he will be handed over to the archon who is above, he who rules over all the powers as their king, and he will turn that one around and will cast him from heaven down to the abyss, and he will be imprisoned in a narrow dark place.[83]

However, they do go out and preach His word, after they receive comfort from the Master:

> Go and preach to the twelve tribes of Israel and to the Gentiles and Israel and to the land of Israel towards East and West, North and South; and many will believe in me, the son of God. . . . Do not be grieved. Truly, I say to you, you are my brothers, companions in the kingdom of heaven with my father, for so has it pleased him. Truly, I say to, also to those whom you shall have taught and who have become believers in me will I give this hope.[84]

Since the discovery of the main bulk of apocryphal literature during the past century, literally thousands of statements and sayings allegedly made by the Savior have come to light. The great majority of this now-available material was written by adherents to the various Christian sects which were spreading throughout the Roman Empire in the first few centuries of the Christian era. Each of these groups, particularly within the ranks of the Gnostics, purportedly claimed some inside knowledge and secret doctrines given to that group alone by a close disciple of the Master. Most of the documents, then, are filled with teachings slanted toward the special understanding of the faction who produced them. Nevertheless, many of the innumerable uncanonical teachings of the Savior are quite interesting and worthy to be introduced here. Some are more specific than

---

82. Tertullian, *De Praescriptione Haereticiorum,* 25. This reaffirms the principle that everyone can receive religious knowledge, but that God will only give men as much as they are ready and worthy to understand. Likewise there are numerous admonitions in apocryphal literature not to pass on knowledge to everyone but only to those who are worthy and willing to receive it. See *Epistula Apostolorum,* 1; *Apocryphon of John,* 79; *Gospel of Bartholemew,* 2:66-67; *Second Book of Jeu,* 43:100-101, etc.).

83. *The Book of Thomas the Contender,* in Codex II of the Nag Hammadi Library, II, 7, p. 142, lines 18-35.

84. *Epistula Apostolorum,* 30 and 32.

the related scriptures in the Bible; others shed a different light onto a well-known version, while some of them are completely new and have no parallel quotations in canonized writing. Indeed we only possess a mere fraction of the acts and teachings of the Savior to the people in Palestine, according to one of the Gospels:

> And there are also many other things which Jesus did, the which, if they should be written every one, I suppose that even the world itself could not contain the books that should be written.[85]

Out of the great number of available sources, these following few will have to suffice for the limited scope of this publication. They will, however, give the reader an insight into the teachings and accepted doctrines within the Christian ranks of the first centuries.

The doctrine that Christ was the God of the Old Testament and of the prophets is made quite clear:

> All that was said by the prophets was thus performed and has taken place and is completed in me, for I spoke through them.

The disciple responded to him saying,

> . . . for in faithfulness and truthfulness you have preached to our fathers and to the prophets, and even to us and to every man.[86]

The doctrine of the Father and the separate entity of Christ is also brought forth in the apocryphal literature:

> The man of heaven, many are his sons, more than the man of earth. If the sons of Adam are many, but nonetheless die, how much more the sons of the perfect man, they who do not die but are begotten at all times.[87]

> . . . the Lord would not have said "My Father which is in heaven" unless he had had another father. . . .[88]

Also, the concept of how the Father and the Son can be "one" is explained by the early Christians:

> And he said to us: "I am wholly in the Father and the Father in me, after his image and after his form and after his power and after his perfection and after his light, and I am his perfect word."[89]

The doctrine of opposition in all things was also taught by some of the early believers:

---

85. John 21:25.

86. *Epistula Apostolorum*, 30, 32.

87. The *Gospel of Philip*, The Nag Hammadi Library, Codex III, Saying 28. This passage is very interesting in that it alludes to the continually begotten offspring of the Father, who is here called a "perfect man."

88. *Ibid.*, Saying 17.

89. *Epistula Apostolorum*, 17.

The light and the darkness, life and death, the right and the left, are brothers one to another. It is not possible to separate them from one another.[90]

Death and resurrection are brought into a clear perspective:

When Salome asked, "How long will death have power?" the Lord answered, "So long as ye women bear children."[91]

Truly I say to you, as the Father awakened me from the dead, in the same manner you also will arise in the flesh. . . . Truly I say to you, the flesh of every man will rise with his soul and his spirit.[92]

The rejection of Christ by the Jews figures prominently in the ancient texts:

Jesus has said: I have stayed in the midst of the world, and I have revealed myself to them in the flesh; I have found them all drunken; I have found none among them who was athirst, and my soul has been grieved for the sons of men, because they are blind in their heart. And they do not see that they have come empty into the world, and empty they seek to go out of the world again.[93]

Jesus has said: Many times have you desired to hear these words of mine which I say to you, and you do not have another from whom you hear them. There will come days when you will seek me and you will not find me.[94]

Jesus said: Seek and you will find, but those things which you asked me in those days, I did not tell you then. Now I desire to tell them, but now you do not inquire after them.[95]

. . . you have become as the Jews, for they love the tree but hate its fruit, or they love the fruit but they hate the tree.[96]

Those who are with me have not understood me.[97]

The well-known passage concerning serving two masters is found slightly expanded in the *Gospel according to Thomas:*

Jesus said: It is impossible for a man to mount two horses and to stretch two bows, and it is impossible for a servant to serve two masters, otherwise he will honor the one and offend the other.[98]

Another saying shows the Master chiding those who rely on their intellect to find out the truth about God:

He said: I want that you all know, that those, who have been born on this earth since the creation, have pondered and tried to find out who God is and of which manner

90. *Gospel of Philip,* Saying 10.
91. From Clement, *Stromata,* III, 45. Here the teaching seems to be that people will still die as long as children are being born.
92. *Epistula Apostolorum,* 21, 24.
93. *Gospel according to Thomas,* Saying 28. It is also found in the Oxyrhynchus Papyrus I.
94. *Ibid.,* Saying 38.
95. *Ibid.,* Saying 92.
96. *Ibid.,* Saying 43.
97. *Actus Vercellanses,* 10; also in *Actus Petri contra Simone,* 10.
98. *Gospel according to Thomas,* Saying 47.

he is. They have not found Him. The wisest among them put forth their conjectures from the rule of the world. However, their suppositions did not come upon the truth.[99]

His admonition to be aware of one's own self is repeated in the texts:

Jesus said: Whoever knows the All but fails to know himself is lacking everything.[100]

A blind man and one who sees do not differ from one another when they are in the darkness. But when the light comes, then the one who sees will see the light but the one who is blind will remain in darkness.[101]

An ass which turns a millstone did a hundred miles walking. When it was loosed, it found that it was still in the same place. There are men who make many journeys, but make no progress anywhere.[102]

Now, if you desire to become perfect, you will observe these things, if not your name is "Ignorant," since it is impossible that a wise man dwells with a fool, for the wise man is perfect in all his wisdom. However, to the fool the good and the bad are all the same. The wise man will be nourished by the truth and will become like a tree growing by the winding stream.[103]

The doctrine that all men are loved and important in the eyes of God, no matter in what condition they are in, is a frequently taught subject in the old writings. Usually the person is equated to a pearl or a diamond, which keeps its value no matter in which surrounding it is found, in the dirt of the road or in the crown of a king:

When the pearl is cast down in the mud it does not become dishonored more, neither does it become more precious when it is anointed with balsam oil. It keeps its value in the eyes of its owner at all times. So it is with the sons of God, wherever they may be. They always keep their value in the eyes of their Father.[104]

Many times in the apocrypha Jesus asked his disciples to follow his admonitions and become a special group of people:

If they say to you; "Who are you?" say: "We are His sons and we are the elect of the living Father."[105]

Jesus said: Whoever drinks from my mouth shall become as I am and I myself will become he and the hidden things shall be revealed to him.[106]

Be alert so that no one can lead you astray saying: Behold, here, or Behold, there. The Son of Man is inside of you. Follow Him. Those who seek Him shall find Him.[107]

And Jesus answered: "Happy are you, that you hunger for the truth, for I will satisfy you with the bread of wisdom. Happy are you that you knock, for I will open to

---

99. *Sophia Jesu Christi,* 80, lines 4-17.
100. *Gospel according to Thomas,* Saying 67.
101. *Gospel of Philip,* Saying 56.
102. *Ibid.,* Saying 52.
103. *Book of Thomas the Contender,* 140, lines 11-18.
104. *Gospel of Philip,* Saying 48. Another great insight is given in the *Acts of Thomas,* where the apostle tells a story of a person coming down from the pre-existence to find its purpose here on earth, which is to bring back with him a pearl (a soul) to the Father.
105. *Gospel according to Thomas,* Saying 50.
106. *Ibid.,* Saying 108.
107. *Evangelium Mariae,* 8, lines 15-21.

you the door of life. Happy are you that you would cast off the power of Satan, for I will lead you into the kingdom of my Mother's angels, where the power of Satan cannot enter.[108]

Jesus said: I will give you what eye has not seen and what ear has not heard and what hand has not touched and what has not arisen in the heart of man.[109]

He said: He who shall not eat my flesh and drink my blood has no life in him.[110]

According to the apocryphal gospels, to follow the Christ means to do more than just have faith in him:

But whoever believes in me and does not do my commandments, receives, although he believes in my name, no benefit from it. He has run a course in vain.[111]

Likewise every man is given the ability to believe in the light. . . . And whosoever has believed in me will live, if he has done the work of light. But if he acknowledges that it is light but does what is darkness, then he has neither anything that he can say in defense nor will he be able to raise his face and look at the Son, which I am. And I will say to him: "You have sought and found, have asked and received. Why do you accuse me? Why did you not withdraw from me and my kingdom? You have acknowledged me and denied me. . . . Whosoever does my commandment and keeps it will be a son of light, which is a son of the Father.[112]

You may escape the laws made by kings, but the laws of your God, these may none of the sons of men escape. And when you come before the face of God, the devils of Satan bear witness against you with your deed, and God sees your sins written in the book of your body and of your spirit and is sad in His heart . . . I tell you truly, no good deed remains unwritten before God, not from the beginning of the world. For from your kings and your governors you may wait in vain for your reward, but never do your good deeds want their reward from God.[113]

An interesting teaching about the Sabbath makes it clear to the faithful of the group who produced the *Gospel of Truth,* that the work which furthers the progress of the kingdom can be enacted on the day of rest:

He labored even on the Sabbath for the lamb which had fallen into a pit. He saved the life of that lamb by having it lifted out of the pit, so that you may know in your heart what the Sabbath is, during which time the work of the redemption must not be dormant.[114]

Admonitions on fasting are also included in the writings:

Go by yourself and fast alone, and show your fasting to no man. The living God shall see it and great shall be your reward. . . . For I tell you truly, except you fast, you

---

108. *Essene Gospel of John,* I.
109. *Gospel according to Thomas,* Saying 17.
110. *Gospel of Philip,* Saying 23.
111. *Epistula Apostolorum,* 27.
112. *Ibid.,* 39. Conventional Protestantism does not favor these texts because they often undermine Protestant doctrine such as the concept of salvation by grace, as the text does in this instance. Yet the tests exist, and should be reported.
113. *Essene Gospel of John,* XVII.
114. *Evangelium Veritas,* f. XVI, p. 32, lines 18-25.

shall never be freed from the power of Satan and from all deseases which come from Satan. Fast and pray fervently, seeking the power of the living God for your healing. . . . Seek the fresh air of the forests and the fields. . . . Then breathe long and deeply. . . . The angel of air shall cast out of your body all uncleanness which defiled it outside and inside.[115]

On six days feed your body with the gifts of the earthly mother, but on the seventh day sanctify your body for your heavenly mother. And on the seventh day eat not any earthly food, but live only upon the words of God. . . . And let no food trouble the work of the angels in your body throughout the seventh day.[116]

A particular aspect of fasting has nothing to do with food and water, but refers to denying oneself the indulgence into worldliness and doing good instead:

Jesus says: If you do not fast as to the world, you will not find the kingdom of God, and if you do not keep the Sabbath as Sabbath you will not see the Father.[117]

His disciples asked him and said: How should we fast and in what way should we pray? Should we give alms, and in regards to food, what should be observed? Jesus said: Lie not and do not what you hate, for everything is known in the heavens.[118]

The principle of love is also a predominant theme throughout the apocryphal literature:

The Lord said to his disciples: And never be joyful, save when ye behold your brother with love. . . .[119]

It is among the greatest sins for a man to trouble his brother's spirit.[120]

Faith receives, love gives. . . . None will be able to give without love. Because of this, that we may receive we believe, but in order that we may give in truth, since if anyone does not give in love he has no profit from what he has given.[121]

The revealed doctrine that men existed before having been born here on earth is quite prevalent in the ancient texts, however, very few of these teachings have been attributed to the Savior himself, such as the following:

The Lord said: Blessed is he who is before he came into being. For he who is, both was and shall be.[122]

But the one who is birthless has no beginning, because everyone who has a beginning, must also have an end.[123]

---

115. *Essene Gospel of John*, VI.

116. *Ibid.*, XXX.

117. *Gospel according to Thomas*, Saying 27. Also in the *Oxyrhynchus Papyrus*, I.

118. *Ibid.*, Saying 6. Also in the *Oxyrhynchus Papyrus*, 654.

119. Jerome in his *Commentary of Ephesians*, 5:4.

120. Jerome in his *Commentary on Ezekiel*, 18:7.

121. *Gospel of Philip*, Saying 45.

122. *Ibid.*, Saying 57. The *Gospel according to Thomas* repeats the saying in number 19, but the texts was changed to "Blessed is he who *was.*

123. *Sophia Jesu Christi*, 84, lines 6-9.

An interesting teaching about the body of men is put forth in the *Essene Gospel of John.* Here the earth is designated as our mother:

> The hardness of your bones is born of the bones of your Earthly Mother, of the rocks and of the stones. . . . The tenderness of your flesh is born of our Earthly Mother. . . . Our bowels are born of the bowels of our Earthly Mother. . . . The light of our eyes, the hearing of our ears, both are born of the colors and the sounds of our Earthly Mother. . . . Man is the son of the Earthly Mother, and from her did the Son of Man receive his whole body. . . . Of her were you born, in her do you live, and to her shall you return again. Keep, therefore, her laws, for none can live long, neither be happy, but he who honors his Earthly Mother and does her laws.[124]

That we are all related to one another and have a common father in heaven who teaches us and wants us to keep his advice follows therefore in the same text:

> No newborn babe can understand the teachings of his father till his mother has suckled him, bathed him, nursed him, put him to sleep and nurtured him. While the child is yet small, his place is with his mother and he must obey his mother. When the child is grown up his father takes him to work at his side in the field, and the child comes back to his mother only when the hour of dinner and supper is come. And now his father teaches him, that he may become skilled in the works of his father. And when the father sees that his son understands his teaching and does the work well, he gives him all his possessions, that they may belong to his beloved son, and that his son may continue in his father's works. . . . Honor your Earthly Mother and keep all her laws, that your days may be long on this earth, and honor your Heavenly Father that eternal life may be yours in heaven. For the Heavenly Father is a hundred times greater than all fathers by seed and by blood, and greater is the Heavenly Mother than all mothers by the body.[125]

The principle of revelation given to living prophets is very vividly put forth in the same writing:

> Seek not the law in your scriptures, for the law is life, whereas the scripture is dead. I tell you truly, Moses received not his laws from God in writing, but through the living word. The law is the living word of the living God to living prophets for living men.[126]

Another teaching sheds an interesting light on the practice of baptism:

> Put off your shoes and your clothing and suffer the angel of water to embrace all your body. . . . I tell you truly, the angel of water shall cast out of your body all uncleanliness which defiled it within and without. . . . No man may come before the face of God, whom the angel of water lets not pass. In very truth, all must be born again of water and of truth. . . . Suffer the angel of water to baptize you also within, that you may become free from all your past sins, and that within likewise you may become pure. . . .

---

124. *Essene Gospel of John,* II.

125. *Ibid.,* IX. This is one of the few places in Christian religious literature where a Heavenly Mother is mentioned.

126. *Ibid.,* IV. These people were using the Old Testament as scripture, which proved quite insufficient in recognizing the truth even when Christ lived upon the earth.

And this holy baptism by the angel of water is: Rebirth unto the new life. For your eyes shall henceforth see, and your ears shall hear. Sin no more, therefore, after your baptism, that the angel of air and of water may eternally abide in you and serve you evermore.[127]

A reoccurring teaching was connected to the nature of our life here on earth and our purpose of existence, which was not to accumulate riches but to become righteous. In the writings the Savior is portrayed as speaking out against the collectors of wealth because it is meant to be a test for those who might fall for it and those who are able to resist its enticings:

Jesus, on whom peace be, has said: The world is a bridge. Go over it, but do not come to rest on it.[128]

Jesus said: The kingdom is like a man who had a treasure hidden in his field without knowing of it. When he died he left it [the field] to his son, who also knew nothing [of the treasure]. When he inherited that field, he sold it, and the man who bought it found the treasure while he was ploughing. Then he began to lend money at interest to whomsoever he wanted.[129]

Jesus said: He who has found the world and acquired riches, let him renounce the world.[130]

A slightly different version to Matthew 19:16-22 is available, where Christ talks to a rich man about what he should do:

He said to him: "Go, sell all that you possess and share it with the poor and then come, and follow me." Then the rich man began to scratch his head: he did not like it. Then the Lord said to him: "How can you say, 'I have kept the law and the prophets?' It is written in the law: 'You shall love your neighbor as yourself." And look, many of your brothers, sons of Abraham, are dressed in filthy rags and are dying of hunger, while your house is filled with many good things, but nothing at all is being given to them. Then he turned to his disciple Simon, who was sitting beside him and said: "Simon, son of John, it is easier for a camel to enter in through a needle's eye than for a rich man to enter into the kingdom of heaven.[131]

Some very interesting statements on diet and the use of meat are also available. Some parts are strongly vegetarian in nature:

From one mother proceeds all that lives upon the earth. Therefore, he who kills, kills his brother. . . . And whosoever eats the flesh of slain beasts, eats of the body of death. . . . Kill not, neither eat of the flesh of your innocent prey, lest you become the

---

127. *Ibid.*, VII. Baptism by immersion is hinted at in the statement "to embrace all your body."

128. The warning that life on earth is a passage and not a home is quoted often in Islamic literature and is attributed first to Christ. An inscription on the South main gate of the mosk in Fathpur-Siki in India gives this particular saying.

129. *Gospel of Thomas,* Saying 109. We often do not know about the real treasures we possess and consequently sell our birthright away to someone who knows the true value and puts it to use.

130. *Ibid.,* Saying 110.

131. Pseudo-Origin (Latin), *Commentary on Matthew,* 15:14.

slaves of Satan. . . . Obey, therefore the words of God: "Behold, I have given you herb bearing seed, which on the face of all the earth, and every tree, in which is the fruit of a tree yielding seed, and to you it shall be for meat. . . . And also the milk of everything that moveth and liveth shall be meat for you, even as I have given the green herb unto them, so I give their milk unto you. . . . But he who kills a beast without cause, though the beast attack him not, through lust for slaughter, or for its flesh, or for its hide, or yet for its tusk, evil is the deed which he does, for he is turned into a beast himself. . . .[132]

Other parts are more general in nature:

Take heed, therefore, and defile not with all kinds of abominations the temple of your bodies. Be content with two or three sorts of food. . . . And when you eat, never eat to fulness. . . . For Satan and his power tempt you always to eat more and more. . . . Trouble not the work of the angels in your body by eating often. . . . Wake not by night, neither sleep by day. . . . And take no delight in any drink, nor in any smoke from Satan. . . . For I tell you truly, all the drinks and smokes of Satan are abominations in the eyes of your God. . . . Shun all that is too hot and too cool . . . that neither heat nor cold should harm your body.[133]

The concept that the Savior is continually near to us becomes quite vivid in this passage:

He is not far from us, my brethren, even as he said in his preaching: I am near to you, like the clothing of your body.[134]

The Master's descriptions of the kingdom and how to enter it are legion. A few examples will have to suffice:

The kingdom of the Father is like a man, a merchant, who possessed merchandise, and found a pearl. That merchant was prudent. He sold the merchandise and bought the one pearl for himself.Do you also seek for the treasure which fails not, which endures, where no moth comes near to devour it and where no worm destroys it.[135]

He said: Verily, I say to you that no one shall ever enter into the kingdom of heaven, because I have commanded him, but only as ye have been perfected in fulness.[136]

No one can attain the kingdom of heaven who has not gone through temptation.[137]

Jesus answered them: Happy are those who endure to the end, for they shall inherit the earth.[138]

The Lord taught about those times and said: The days will come in which vines will grow with 10,000 shoots each, and each shoot will bear 10,000 branches, and each branch 10,000 twigs, and each twig 10,000 clusters, and each cluster 10,000 grapes, and each grape, when pressed, will yield twenty-five measures of wine. When any saint

132. *Essene Gospel of John,* XXIII.
133. *Ibid.,* XXVI, XXVII, XXX, XXXI.
134. *The Manichaean Psalter,* Psalm 239.
135. *Gospel according to Thomas,* Saying 76.
136. *Apocryphon Iacobi.* Codex Jung, p. 2, lines 29-34.
137. As cited by Terullian in *De Baptismo,* xx, 2.
138. *Essene Gospel of John,* XVIII.

takes hold of one such cluster, another cluster will exclaim: I am a better cluster, take me! Bless the Lord through me! Similarly, a grain of wheat will produce 10,000 ears, and each ear will have 10,000 grains, and each grain will yield ten pounds of fine flour, bright and pure; and the other fruit, seeds and herbs, will be proportionally productive according to their nature, while the animals which feed on these products of the soil will live in peace and agreement one with another, yielding complete subjection to men.[139]

As you pray, you will find rest, for you have left behind the suffering and the disgrace., for when you come forth from the sufferings and passions of the body, you will receive rest from the Good One, and you will reign with the King, you joined with Him, and He with you, from now on, forever and forever.[140]

When I lead you to the place of those who have received the inheritance . . . the sun will look like nothing but a tiny speck of cornmeal because of the great distance and because the new world is so much greater.[141]

These, then, are a few selected statements and sayings of the Lord which are available in apocryphal writings. It is difficult to say which, if any, are true, for many disagree with established doctrines. Others, however, harmonize and could therefore be considered worth our attention. If nothing else, the teachings transmit to us an insight into the doctrines which some of the early Christian groups were espousing about the Savior, and give us, therefore, a view into the material circulated during the first centuries after the resurrection.

Another colorful touch is added to the personality of the Savior by the claim of a letter he supposedly directed to a contemporary monarch. The scriptures are silent as to any writings he may have left behind. Indeed, the impression is given that He never did write any letters or compose any treatises during His ministry, unlike his disciples, who found the written word an acceptable medium to circulate their teachings and instructions. That the Savior did know how to read and write, however, is beyond any question.[142] The story of the letter is reported by Eusebius in his *Ecclesiastical History*. According to him, the king of Edessa, Abgar Uchama (perhaps Abgar V) wrote a letter to Jesus asking to be helped from his ailment and also inviting the Christ to live with him in Edessa, since the Jews were not very sympathetic toward the Savior.

Abgarus, prince of Edessa, sends greetings to Jesus, the good Savior, who has appeared in the borders of Jerusalem. I have heard the reports respecting thee and thy cures, as performed by thee without medicines and without any herbs. For as it is said, thou causest the blind to see again, the lame to walk, and thou cleanseth the lepers, and thou castest out impure spirits and demons, and thou healest those that are tormented

139. By Papias, cited by Irenaeus in *Heresies*, V, xxx, 3.
140. *Book of Thomas the Contender*, 145, lines 10-16.
141. *Pistis Sophia*, 186.
142. See above, chapter II, on his encounter with the school teacher and the learning of the alphabet.

by lond disease, and thou raisest the dead. And hearing all these things of thee, I concluded in my mind one of two things: either that thou art God, and having descended
from heaven, doest these things, or else doing them, thou art the son of God. Therefore,
now I have written and besought thee to visit me, and to heal the disease with which I am
afflicted. I have also heard that the Jews murmur against thee, and are plotting to injure
thee; I have, however, a very small but noble state, which is sufficient for both of us.

Jesus supposedly answered this letter of the king by the following
reply:

Blessed art thou, O Abgarus, who, without seeing, has believed in me. For it is
written concerning me, that they who have seen me will not believe, and that they who
have not seen, may believe and live. But in regard to what thou hast written, that I should
come to thee, it is necessary that I should fulfill all things here, for which I have been
sent, and afterwards be received again by him who sent me. And after I have been
received up, I will send to thee certain of my disciples, that he may heal thy affliction,
and give life to thee and to those who are with thee.

Eusebius also added that the apostle Thomas commissioned one of the
seventies, Thaddeus by name, who went to Edessa after the resurrection
of Christ and who healed the monarch and converted him and his household to Christianity.[143]

An even more strange and not well-known event occurred some time
before the arrest of Jesus, when he met with his disciples for some ritual
singing and dancing. A part of this incident is here given from the *Acts of
John:*

He assembled us all and said: "Before I am delivered, let us sing a hymn to the
Father, and thereby go and await what lies ahead." So he told us to form a circle, holding hands while he himself stood in the middle and said: "Answer Amen to me." So he
began to sing the hymn, and said: "Glory be to thee Father." And we, who were in a
circle around him, answered him with Amen.

What follows is a long poetic enumeration of statements, interspersed
with the disciples saying "Amen" after each sentence. Then the groups
seemed to have been dancing, or made shuffling movements while Christ
kept talking to them. The event concluded as it began:

Glory be to thee, Father. Glory be to thee, Word. Glory be to thee, Spirit. Amen.
After the Lord had thusly danced with us, my beloved, he went out.[144]

His Passion

Many stories and teachings about the crucifixion and the resurrection
of the Savior were circulated in the early centuries of Christianity, which

---

143. Eusebius, *Ecclesiastical History,* I, xiii.
144. *Acts of John,* 94-97. The group prayer is reminiscent of the ritual Christian prayer
circle, but dancing is not often associated with this ordinance.

add another interesting insight into the belief of the saints of that period.

The appearance before Pilate is broadly treated in apocryphal literature, particularly in a work called the *Acts of Pilate* wherein the governor is held blameless and the responsibility for the crucifixion was squarely placed on the shoulders of the Jews. It is also in other ways quite fascinating, as can be seen from these excerpts.

> The Jews said to Pilate: "We beseech your excellency to place him before your judgment-seat and to try him." And Pilate called them before him and said: "Tell me, how can I, a governor, examine a king?" They answered: "We do not say that he is a king, but he says he is." And Pilate summoned his messenger and said to him: "Let Jesus be brought with gentleness." So the messenger went out, and when he saw him, he did him reverence, and taking the mantle which was in his hand, he spread it upon the ground and said to him: "Lord, walk on this and go in, for the governor calls you." But when the Jews saw what the messenger had done, they cried out against Pilate and said: "Why did you not order him to come in by a guard, but by a messenger? For as soon as the messenger saw him, he reverenced him and spread out his mantle on the ground and made him walk on it like a king." Then Pilate called for the messenger and said to him: "Why have you done this, and spread your mantle on the ground and made Jesus walk on it?" The messenger answered him: "Lord governor, when you sent me to Jerusalmen to Alexander, I saw him sitting on an ass, and the Jews held branches in their hands and cried out, and others spread their garments before him saying: 'Save us now, thou art in the highest, blessed is he that comes in the name of the Lord.' [145]

The messenger therefore assumed that Jesus was a king or a high dignitary and showed him the respect due to the office. He also embarrassed the Jews, who had cheered the Lord just a few days before and hailed him as their Savior. According to this text, there was nothing more they could respond, particularly, when all the insignia and Roman standards in the palace bowed to Jesus. Interestingly, the Jews accused Christ of several novel stigmas:

> Then the elders of the Jews answered and said to Jesus: "What should we say? Firstly, that you were born of fornication, secondly, that your birth meant the death of the children in Bethlehem, thirdly, that your father Joseph and your mother Mary fled into Egypt, because they counted for nothing among the people." [146]

Pilate can see nothing wrong with the accused:

> And he asked them: "For what cause do they wish to kill him?" They answered Pilate: "They are incensed because he heals on the Sabbath." Pilate said: "For a good work do they wish to kill him?" They answered him: "Yes." And Pilate called to him

---

145. *Acts of Pilate* (also known as the *Gospel of Nicodemus*), I, 2-4.

146. *Ibid.*, II, 3. By saying that Joseph was his father, they dismissed any claims that he could actually be the son of God.

the elders and the priests and the Levites and said to them secretly: "Do not act thus, for nothing of which you have accused him deserves death. For your accusation concerns healing and profanation of the Sabbath." [147]

The Jews therefore had to change to another tactic and accused Jesus of claiming to be the son of God.

> The Jews said to Pilate: "It is contained in our law, that if a man sins against a man, he must receive forty strokes save one, but he who blasphemes against God must be stoned." Pilate said to them: "Take him yourselves and punish him as you wish." The Jews said to Pilate: "We wish him to be crucified." Pilate said: "He does not deserve to be crucified. . . . Why should he die?" The Jews said: "Because he called himself the son of God and a king. . . . You are not Caesar's friend if you release this man, for he called himself the son of God and a king. You wish him therefore to be king and not Caesar." [148]

By this method the Jews made Pilate afraid and he finally consented to the crucifixion, but in general the text tries to vindicate the governor of careless or malicious intent and blames the Jews for the death of Christ.

Just as the later Christians whitewashed the Roman involvement, so the Jews also showed themselves not to be responsible for the death of Christ. A passage in the later Talmud asserts that the Jews did everything possible to defend Jesus before his death:

> Jesus was hanged on Passover Evening. Forty days previously the herald had cried out: "He is being led out for stoning, because he has practised sorcery and led Israel astray and enticed them into apostasy. Whosoever has anything to say in his defense, let him come and declare it." Since nothing was brought forward in his defense, he was hanged on Passover Evening. [149]

Interesting is the tradition which claims that it was from a tree which Joseph, the carpenter, planted that the cross was made upon which the Lord was hung:

> Philip the apostle said: Joseph the carpenter planted a garden because he needed the wood for his trade. It was he who made the cross from the trees which he planted. And his seed hung on that which he planted. His seed was Jesus, but the planting was the cross. [150]

---

147. *Ibid.*, II, 6 and IV, 2.
148. *Ibid.*, IV, 3-4 and IX, 1.
149. *Babylonian Talmud*, Sanhedrin, 43a.
150. *Gospel of Philip*, Saying 91. This passage seems to say that Joseph was still alive at this time when he (unknowingly) made the cross for Jesus. This seems to go against all the traditions. It also refers to Jesus as his seed, which could not be understood in a factual sense.

The cross is at times referred to as a tree in other texts,[151] and a person with outstretched arms is at times compared to the cross, which became the symbol for Christ in later years.

> I stretched out my hands and sanctified my Lord, for the extension of my arms is his sign, and my expansion is the upright tree.[152]

At the moment of the Savior's death there was an earthquake, darkness came upon the land and the veil of the temple was parted, so the Gospels report.[153] Other writers added further information concerning these phenomena. Jerome reports, for instance, that not only was the veil of the temple ripped, but also the great lintel of the temple shattered at that time.[154] The darkness and the earthquake associated with the death are also mentioned in the Pilate literature:

> When the report of Pilate reached Rome and was read to Tiberius Caesar . . . all were amazed that it was because of the lawless conduct of Pilate that the darkness and the earthquake had come upon the whole world.[155]

Many apocryphal writings mention the visit of Christ into the spirit world. In fact, it is almost a stock theme among the ancients.[156] In the *Gospel of Peter* is related an instant where someone, who stood under the cross at the crucifixion, heard a voice from heaven asking Christ: "Hast thou preached unto them who are dead [sleep]?" And the answer from Christ was: "Yes."[157] Likewise the *Gospel of Bartholemew* cites the Lord's visit to the spirits. The apostle evidently saw the spirit of Christ leave the cross after his death. When he met the resurrected Savior later he pursued this event by asking the Master a question as to what was happening:

> Tell me, Lord, where you went from the cross. And Jesus answered: "Blessed are you, Bartholemew, my beloved, because you saw this mystery. And now I will tell you

---

151. For example, the *Gospel of Truth,* 19:26; 20:25.

152. *Odes of Solomon,* 27:1-3; 42:1-3. This work is of Christian origin in spite of the title.

153. Mathew 27:45, 51; Mark 15:33; Luke 23:44,45.

154. Jerome, *Epistles,* (to Hedibia), CXX, 8. Also *Commentary on Matthew,* 27:51.

155. This story comes from the so-called Paradosis to the *Acts of Pilate.* See C. Tischendorf, *Evangelia Apocrypha,* pp. 449-455; and also E. Hennecke and W. Schneemelcher, *New Testament Apocrypha* I, 482. The same event was also mentioned by a writer called Thallus in work written about 52 A.D. It is cited by Julius Africanus and contained in F. Jacoby, *Die Fragmente der Griechischen Schriftsteller,* II, 1157.

156. The visit of the hero in the underworld, which is his lowest point but also his triumph, is a common tradition throughout the great literature of Mesopotamia and Egypt, as well as in Homer and Virgil of the Greek and Roman period. See also Hugo Radau, *Bel, the Christ of Ancient Times.*

157. *Gospel of Peter,* 10.

everything you ask me. When I vanished from the cross I went to the spirit world (under-world) to bring up Adam and all the patriarchs, Abraham, Isaac, and Jacob.[158]

The longest and most colorful description in apocryphal writings of the Christ's visit to the spirit world occurs in the so-called *Gospel of Nicodemus,* where two resurrected persons, who were raised together with many other saints at the time of the death of the Savior,[159] give an account of what happened when Christ appeared among the dead who were waiting for his coming. In this narrative it appears that Satan is engaged in a conversation with a fellow worker, Hades by name. Satan is boasting how he was behind the attempts to have Jesus crucified:

I sharpened the spear for his sufferings; I mixed the gall and vinegar and com-manded that he should drink it; I prepared the cross to crucify him, and the nails to pierce through his hands and his feet, and now his death is near at hand, and I will bring him here, subject to both you and me.[160]

However, Hades is not so jubilant. He fears that this Jesus will not be subject to them, but, in reverse, he will have power over their domain. Therefore he accuses Satan of having acted irrationally:

What inclined you to act thus? For behold, now that Jesus of Nazareth, with the brightness of his glorious divinity puts to flight all the horrid powers of darkness and death. He has broken down our prison from top to bottom, dismissed all the captives, released all who were bound, and all who were formerly groaning under the weight of their torments. . . . Our impious dominions are subdued, and no part of mankind is now left in our subjection, but, on the other hand, they all boldly defy us. . . . Why did you attempt this exploit, seeing that our prisoners were so far always without the least hope of salvation and life? . . . You have acted against your own interest. . . . You should have first inquired into the evil deeds of Jesus of Nazareth, and then you would have found that he was guilty of no fault worthy of death. Why did you undertake, without reason and justice, to crucify him, and did bring down to our region a person innocent and righteous and thereby lost all the sinners, impius and unrighteous persons in the whole world?[161]

And so it was: The powers of Satan could not keep the King of Glory out of the gloomy domain.

The mighty Lord appeared in the form of a man, and enlightened those places which had ever before been in darkness. . . . Then the King of Glory trampled upon death, seized the prince of hell, deprived him of all his power, and took our earthly father Adam with him to his glory. . . . Then Jesus stretched forth his hand and said: "Come

---

158. *Gospel of Bartholemew,* I, 7-9. An ancient text contains a passage which also seems to talk about this doctrine, because it says that Christ went to the spirit world but not to all: "Those who are to accept instruction are taught apart, alone. . ." *Gospel of Truth,* 21:3-6.
    159. See Matthew 27:52.
    160. *Gospel of Bartholemew,* XV, 10. At times this gospel is still counted as part of the *Acts of Pilate: The Descent into Hell.*
    161. *Ibid.,* IVIII, 1-5, 7, 11, 12, 13.

to me, all you my saints, who were created in my image. . . . And taking hold of Adam's right hand, he ascended from hell, and all the saints of God followed him.[162]

Additional testimonies of the literal resurrection of the Lord are also available in the apocryphal literature. A favorite theme is the visit of the women to the tomb early on the day following the Jewish sabbath.

> And they feared lest the Jews should see them, and said, "Although we could not weep and lament on the day he was crucified, yet let us now do so at his sepulchre. . . . So they went and found the supulchre opened. And they came near, stooped down and saw there a young man sitting in the midst of the sepulchre, comely and clothed with a brightly shining robe, who said unto them: "Wherefore are ye come? Whom seek ye? Not him who was crucified? He is risen and gone. But if ye believe not, stoop this way and see the place where he lay, for he is not here. For he is risen and is gone thither whence he was sent.[163]

The women were quite brave to go to the tomb so soon, considering that the apostles and other friends were still hiding and did not dare to be seen in the city. As Peter supposedly wrote later on:

> But I, with my companions, was grief stricken. Wounded in our hearts we were hiding, because they were searching for us as if we were criminals, who had planned to set fire to a temple. Since all this happened we fasted and sat mourning and weeping night and day until the Sabbath.[164]

An account of the meeting between the resurrected Lord and Mary Magdalene is preserved in a Manichaean source:

> Mariam, Mariam, recognize me but do not touch me. Hold the tears of your eyes and know that I am your master. But touch me not for I have not yet seen the face of my father. Your God was not stolen away. . . . Your God did not die, but he mastered death. I am not the gardener. . . . Be a messenger for me unto those wandering orphans. Hurry, and go to the eleven, rejoicing.[165]

The hidden apostles, nevertheless, found it difficult to believe Mary's message that Jesus had risen from the dead. They doubted the news until the Christ actually appeared before them:

> And we doubted and did not believe. He came before us like a ghost and we did not believe that it was he. But it was he. And thus he said: "Come and do not be afraid. I am your master whom you, Peter, denied three times, and now do you deny me again?"[166]

---

162. *Ibid.*, XVI, 18; XVII, 13; XIX, 1, 12.

163. *Gospel of Peter,* 12.

164. *Ibid.,* 7.

165. *Coptic Psalmbook,* II, 187, as cited in E. Hennecke and W. Schmeemelcher, *New Testament Apocrypha,* I, 354.

166. *Epistula Apostolorum,* 11.

It was not until the disciples actually felt his body that they realized that it was indeed their beloved Lord who stood before them in a resurrected state:

> See whether my foot steps on the ground and leaves a footprint. For it is written in the prophets: But a ghost, a demon, leaves no footprint on the ground. But now we felt him, that he truly is risen in the flesh. And then we fell on our faces before him, asked him for forgiveness and entreated him because we had not believed him.[167]

Other testimonies of the apostles are found in different texts:

> But I both saw him in the flesh after the resurrection and I believe that he is in the flesh.[168]

> And when the Lord came to those about Peter, he said to them: "Take, handle me and see that I am not a disembodied spirit. And straightway they touched him and believed, being convinced by his flesh and by his blood.[169]

The literature on the death and resurrection of Christ is not quite as abundant as that on his teachings. Apparently there are only so many different ways the same story can be expressed before it is too evident that some tampering has occurred, while the teachings of the Lord could be expanded and multiplied to suit everyone's taste and understanding without a check being applied to ascertain that particular statements were true or false.

His Hidden Teachings

A great amount of material has also been collected and circulated about the Savior as a resurrected being who instructs and guides the apostles before his permanent ascension into heaven. Many of the writings were composed by particular groups of Christians who began to divide and espouse different doctrines, as soon as the last original witnesses for the truth were no longer able to supervise the correctness of the teachings within the ranks of the adherants. People stepped forward who claimed to have received special instructions and more complete insight and knowledge into the doctrines, while others counterclaimed the assertions or even produced secret ordinances and initiations which they had received in secret by some leader of the church. With none of the original leaders of the church still alive, there was no longer a built-in check system and the claimants of strange doctrines went about unchallenged. To substantiate their assertions these men and their followers produced certain books,

---

167. *Ibid.*
168. As cited by Jerome in *De Viris Illustribus,* 16.
169. Ignatius, *Smyrnaeans,* III, 1, 2. This statement in its wording is close to the canonical Luke 24:39.

which were purportedly written by an apostle who, in turn, had received his special insight through a private revelation from the Savior himself.[170] Many of the writings, therefore, have to be read with scrutiny. It is beyond the intent of this publication to investigate this material fully, but a few quotations will be interesting as they portray an insight into the mind of the Christian world during the post apostolic period.

Many of the texts contain phrases which identify the writer and the fact that he received some secret knowledge, thus giving credence to the teachings therein contained:

> These are the secret words which the living Jesus spoke and Didymos Judas Thomas wrote . . .[171]

> The [secret] teachings [which Jesus revealed with] secret [words] in silence. [And the Savior] taught them to John [and John wrote them down].[172]

> The secret [book] according to John.[173]

> These are the secret words which the Savior spoke to Judas Thomas, which I wrote down, I, Mathias, as I was walking and listening to them when they talked to one another.[174]

> This is the book of the knowledge of the invisible God concerning the secret mysteries which show the way to the chosen race . . .[175]

In these writings, the Savior usually appears to an apostle or to the whole group and instructs them concerning some hidden principle of the kingdom, or they may ask him questions which he answers in an elaborate way. He appears most often in glorious light as a divine personage:

> I am sent to you by the father that I may make the light of life shine before you. The light lightens itself and the darkness, but the darkness knows only itself and not the light. I have still many things to say to you, but [you] cannot bear them now. For your eyes are used to the darkness and the full light of the heavenly father would make you blind. . . . When you can gaze on the brightness of the noonday sun with unflinching eyes, you can then look upon the blinding light of your heavenly father, which is a thousand times brighter than the brightness of a thousand suns. . . . Believe me, the sun is as the flame of a candle beside the sun of the truth of the heavenly father.[176]

> The power of the light came down upon Jesus and surrounded him completely while he sat apart from the disciples. And he shined brightly and there was no measure

---

170. Many such sects were grouped together as the Gnostics, from the Greek term γνωσις = knowledge. It was used to denote a special and secret knowledge. The English word "to know" still carries the silent "k" as a remnant of the Greek "γ" (gamma). Many of these Gnostic writings refer to the forty-day teaching period of the Savior, mentioned in Acts 1:3.

171. The opening statement of the *Gospel according to Thomas.*

172. The opening statement of the *Apocryphon of John* as translated by Soren Giberson.

173. *Ibid.,* The closing lines.

174. The opening lines of the *Book of Thomas the Contender.*

175. The opening lines of *I. Jeu* (Codex Bracianus) by Carl Schmidt.

176. *The Essene Gospel of John,* XI.

for the light which was on him. And the disciples could not look upon him because of the great light in which he was. . . . And his light was not the same everywhere, but it was different and of different form, in that some rays were different from others, and the whole light was of three degrees. . . . And the disciples said to him: "O Lord, withdraw this brightness so that we may see you, or our eyes are darkened and we are excited and the whole world is excited because of the great light which is upon you.[177]

His appearance, however, was the appearance of a great angel of light. His form I cannot describe. No mortal flesh would be able to bear it, but only a pure and perfect flesh the way he had when he showed himself to us on the mountain which is called Olivet in Galilee.[178]

Then Christ, in his glorious condition, asks the disciples to pay attention to the things he will teach them:

Then spoke Jesus, the merciful, to them: "Rejoice and be happy from now on, because I went to the place from which I came. From this time on I will speak openly and frankly with you from the beginning to the end of the truth, and also face to face without any parables. I will not hide from you from henceforth anything pertaining to the height and all things of the place of truth. . . . Hear now so that I can tell you all these things.[179]

The Savior said: Brother Thomas, while you still have time in the world, listen to me so that I can reveal to you those things which you have pondered in your mind. It has been said that you are my twin and my true companion, therefore ask, so that you may understand who you are, how you will exist, and how you will come to be. Since you are my brother it should not be that you are ignorant of yourself.[180]

The doctrines and the behavior of the Savior after his resurrection are of quite a different nature than the activities and preachings before that event. Following then are samples of the type of exhortation and conduct encountered in the post-resurrection literature:

Jesus answered and said to Mary: "One day of light equals one thousand years of the world, so that 365,000 years of the world are one year of light. I will spend 1,000 years of light as a king among the last helpers and as king over all emanations of light and over the whole number of perfect souls who have received the ordinances of light.[181]

The teaching that ordinances are important for the entrance into the kingdom is a prominent feature, particularly in a Gnostic work called Pistis Sophia:[182]

---

177. *Pistis Sophia*, chapters 2 and 4.
178. *Sophia Christi*, p. 78, lines 15-17 to p.79, lines 1-9 of Papyrus Berolinensis 8502.
179. *Pistis Sophia*, ch. 6.
180. *Book of Thomas the Contender*, Nag Hammadi Library, Codex II, p. 138, lines 4-12. 'Toma' means 'Twin' in Aramaic. It is interesting that Thomas also was a carpenter by profession, see *Acts of Thomas*, I, 3.
181. *Pistis Sophia*, ch. 99.
182. The reoccurring word μυστήριον should probably be translated as "ordinance" and not as done by most translators, as "mystery." This should also be the case in the New Testament.

Verily, verily, I say unto you: Before I came into the world, has no soul entered into the light, and only now, when I came, have I opened the gates and the ways which lead to the light. And now may he, who will do that which is worthy, receive the ordinances and enter into the light.[183]

Therefore I have brought the key of the ordinances of the kingdom of heaven, else no flesh on the earth would be saved, because no one will enter into the kingdom of light without the ordinances, may he be righteous or a sinner.[184]

But verily, verily, I say unto you: even if a righteous man has never committed any sins, he cannot be brought into the kingdom of light at all, because he does not have with him the token of the kingdom of ordinances. In one word, therefore, it is impossible to bring souls to the light without the ordinances of the kingdom of light.[185]

Even possession of some ordinances will not be enough, according to this text; one has to have obtained the right kind and right degree of ordinance:

But the Savior answered and said to Mary: Surely, everyone who will receive the ordinance of the kingdom of light, will enter and inherit up to the place to which he has received the ordinance, but he will not know the knowledge of the universe, why everything has come about, except if he knows the single word of the ineffable. . . .

He will go to the place up to which he has received the ordinances. Whosoever receives something less, will receive the lesser ordinance, and whosoever will receive a higher ordinance will inherit the higher places. And everyone will remain in his place of light in my kingdom, and everyone will have power over the orders below him, but he will not have the power to go to the orders which are above, but he will remain in the place of inheritance of light in my kingdom.[186]

Not only seem many of these teachings out of touch with most of the ideas of conventional Christianity about the life and the purpose of Christ, because they find only little resemblance to the doctrines presented in the canonical writings, but other apocryphal texts from the Gnostics probably appear even more fantastic and questionable. The concept that Christ could have introduced other teachings and more ordinances which were necessary for entrance into the kingdom has always been received with great caution, if not outright rejection, by the Catholics and Protestants, but they are not strange among the early Christian sectaries, who seem to have felt comfortable with these views. Some Gnostic texts refer with almost natural regularity to certain passwords, symbols, signs, and names, which had to be taught and known by the candidate for the heavenly kingdom. Christ instructed his disciples into the attainment of heavenly degrees and stages, and the symbols and words necessary to pass by the guards, before they would be allowed to pass on to the next state:

183. *Pistis Sophia*, ch. 135.
184. *Ibid.*, ch. 133.
185. *Ibid.*, ch. 103.
186. *Ibid.*, ch. 97.

Hear now the position of this treasure. When you arrive at that treasure seal your-self with the following seal:

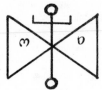

This is its name: $\zeta\omega\xi\varepsilon\sigma\zeta\omega\zeta$

Say it once while the following number is in your hand: 600525

And say this name three times: $\omega\omega\,\iota\,\varepsilon\eta\zeta\alpha\zeta\alpha\mu\alpha\zeta\alpha$

Then the guards and the orders and the veils will be removed, until you arrive at the place of the father who will give you his name and his seal, until you arrive at the gate of his treasure.[187]

These types of instructions are typical of the secret codes one had to have knowledge of in order to gain the highest reward. One more example will suffice to show the ritual nature of these perhaps strange and misunder-stood teachings.

And Jesus sealed the disciples with this seal:

This is its name: $\zeta\alpha\chi\zeta\omega\zeta\alpha$

And this is its meaning: $\vartheta\omega\zeta\omega\nu\omega\zeta$

And it happened, when Jesus had sealed them with this seal, he stood by the incense which he had placed upon it [probably an altar], and placed his disciples before the incense and dressed them in linen garments, in which was the number of the seven voices in their hands, namely 9879.[188]

That these teachings and ordinances were secret and not to be spread about or divulged to others is also made plain in the writings:

Hear now the things which are told to you in the ordinance and guard them. Do not pass them on to the children of this generation because you yourselves will be spoken evil of during this aeon, because they do not know you.[189]

He spoke to them again: These ordinances, which I will give to you, keep them and give them to no one, only if they are worthy of them. Do not give them to father or mother, or brother or sister or relatives, not for food or drink, not for women, not for gold or silver, nor for anything of this world.[190]

---

187. The *First Book of Jeu,* ch. 33, in Carl Schmidt, *Koptisch-Gnostische Schriften.*
188. The *Second Book of Jeu,* ch. 47. The use of secret names and seals was quite common among the mystery religions of the Near East. Catholics and Protestants find it difficult to believe that Christ and his disciples practiced these things—they were assumed to be ordinances which crept into Christianity from the pagans.
189. *Gospel of Peter,* Nag Hammadi Library, Codex VII, p. 73.
190. *II. Jeu,* ch. 43.

Another very common topic in the apocryphal literature, particularly that of Gnostic origin, is the creation of the earth and of man. A lively preoccupation with this event must have captured the early Christian mind. Again, Platonic philosophy prohibited divine association with matter, and therefore it was difficult for them to understand why God should have created this obviously material universe. Their writings contain many different solutions and hypotheses why and how this came to be, too numerous to be included in this limited study on apocryphal documents connected to the Savior. Suffice it to say that the fascination with the creation is reflected in many texts where Christ is reported to have been requested by his disciples to explain to them the mystery of that important event.[191] Following are a few of the more interesting statements attributed to the Lord:

And He took the clay from the hand of an angel and made Adam according to our image and likeness, and He left him lying for forty days and forty nights without putting breath into him. And he heaved sighs over him daily, saying: "If I put breath into this man, he must suffer many pains." And I said unto my Father: "Put breath into him. I will be an advocate for him." And my Father said unto me: "If I put breath into him, my beloved son, you will be obliged to go down into the world and to suffer many pains for him before you will have redeemed him, and made him to come back to his primal state." And I said unto my Father: "Put breath into him. I will be his advocate, and I will go down into the world, and I will fulfill thy commandment.[192]

And I called down Gabriel and Michael out of the eternal world, as I had been commanded by my father, to do the first ordinance which is to observe things, and I gave them the power of the flow of light and let them go into matter unorganized . . .[193]

And this is the firstborn to whom the one inside and the one outside have promised everything that he would desire. And it is he who parted and separated all matter and he placed himself over it like a bird who spreads his wings over his offspring. So has the firstborn done it with matter and has assembled myriads upon myriads of species and kinds. . . . And he gave them a law to love one another and to honor God and to praise him and to search for him, who he is, and what kind he is and that they admire the place they have come from . . .[194]

And the Lord of glory came down and separated the matter and parted into two groups and two places and he gave each a boundary and taught them that they descended from one father and one mother. . . . And he set up veils between the boundaries so that they would not see each other and put up guards at the veils. And he gave those who had prayed to him many privileges and made them superior over them who had opposed him. . . . And he separated the parts on his right into many areas and degrees, and heavens, and firmaments, and places and rooms. . . . And he said: Remain in my word

---

191. For instance, parts of *Pistis Sophia, Discourse on the Abbaton, Apocryphon of John, Hypostasis of the Archons,* etc., dwell on the creation theme.

192. *Discourse on the Abbaton* by Timothy, Bishop of Alexandria. Fol. 11b-12-a.

193. From *Pistis Sophia,* ch. 64.

194. Carl Schmidt, *Unbekanntes Altgnostisches Werk,* in *Koptisch-Gnostische Schriften,* pp. 357, 358. (ch. 16).

and I will give you eternal life and powers . . . and you will create aeons and worlds
and heavens so that the intelligent spirits can come and live on them and you will become
gods and will know that you descended from God . . . [195]

The doctrine that all men will resurrect in the flesh, as the Master himself had done, is also taught in some of the works:

For truly I say unto you: As my Father awakened me from the dead, in the same
manner shall you also rise in the flesh. . . . Truly I say unto you: the flesh of every man
will rise with his soul and his spirit. . . . Truly I say unto you: The flesh will arise with
the soul, that they may confess and be judged with the work. [196]

Concerning the end of the world and the sending out and preaching of
the disciples unto those who have not heard the Gospel, there are some
worthwhile passages:

And Christ addressed them this way: The end of Satan's authority on the earth
has been reached, but some other terrible things are approaching to those sinners on
whose account I went down to death so that they might repent and sin no more. In
order that they might inherit the spiritual and never ending glory of righteousness, go
out into all the world and preach the gospel to all the creation. [197]

And Jesus rebuked them and said: Why this small faith of yours? Behold, I have
given you my promises and have fulfilled your questions to me, and you shall speak
in many tongues and nothing shall be kept from you. I have placed the Holy Ghost in
you, and have put my truth into your hearts for your benefit and for the sake of
salvation and for the entrance into the kingdom of heaven for all those who hear and
read your words. It is not the same with the other gospel preachers, who only repeat
what others have seen and heard, but you shall speak with the power and spirit of my
father about the things which are and which come to pass. And all those who believe
and do the work shall see a renewed life in the kingdom of my Father in heaven. [198]

An interesting promise is given to the apostle John, who was translated
without tasting death. According to one manuscript, he is to be the one who
will be killed in Jerusalem during the wars preceding the Second Coming
(Revelations 11:8):

O my beloved John, you shall not die until the thrones have been prepared on the
day of resurrection. . . . You shall be dead for the space of three and one half hours, lying
upon your throne, and all creation will see you. I will have your spirit return to the body
and you rise and stand there in your garment of glory, as someone who had been in the
marriage room. You shall judge the world as I have it set for you. You shall sit upon
thrones and you shall judge the twelve tribes of Israel. [199]

---

195. *Ibid.,* ch. 19, pp. 359-360.
196. *Epistula Apostolorum,* 20, 24, 26.
197. Jerome reports it in *Against the Pelagians,* II, 15, and it is also found in the Wash-
ington Codex.
198. *Gospel of the Twelve Apostles,* by J. Rendel Harris, p. 28.
199. *Discourse on the Abbaton,* Fol. 27b-28a.

A great number of apocryphal references refer to women in the company of the Savior. This is surprising since the early Gnostics and the Catholics thought it unworthy of him. To be tied down to material possessions and passions was not part of the divine nature, according to Platonic philosophy, which was so readily adopted by the sects. Nevertheless, we find many women among the disciples of Christ during the forty days of ministry after the resurrection.

> And Jesus spoke to his disciples which were around him, the Twelve and the female disciples: "Stand round about me, my twelve and the women, so that I can tell you about the great ordinances of the treasure of light.[200]

> When they came after he had risen from the dead, namely his twelve disciples and the seven women, who had followed him, up to the mountan which is called the place of the time of ripeness and joy. . . .

> But while Jesus was saying this, Thomas, Andrew, James and Simon the Canaanite were to the West with their faces turned toward the East, but Philip and Bartholemew were in the South, turned toward the North, but the other disciples and the women stood behind Jesus. However, Jesus stood next to the altar.[202]

Some of them are mentioned by name, such as Martha;[203] and Salome; and quite commonly, Mary, the mother of the Lord, and Mary Magdalene. Surprisingly enough, in the *Pistis Sophia*, it is Mary Magdalene who is mentioned more often than all other disciples, including the apostles themselves. That old Gnostic work is a question and answer session between the disciples and the resurrected Master. Not only does she ask and answer more questions than any other of the persons in attendance, but she talks more than all of them combined! A breakdown of the number of responses given by the participants reveals approximately the following:

All as a group	: 8
Mary Magdalene	: 52
John	: 10
Peter	: 5
Andrew	: 5
Philip	: 4
Thomas	: 4
Martha	: 4
Salome	: 4
James	: 3
Mary (mother)	: 3
Matthew	: 2
Bartholomew	: 1

---

200. *II. Jeu,* ch. 42. The Greek says μαϑηταί (male disciples) versus μαϑήτριοι (female disciples).

201. *Sophia Christi,* in Papyrus Berolinensis 8502, pp. 77, 78.

202. *Pistis Sophia,* ch. 136.

203. Martha in *Pistis Sophia,* ch. 38, for example, and Salome in ch. 52 as well as in the *Gospel according to Thomas,* saying 61.

In fact, the women, particularly Mary Magdalene, are dominating the meeting so much that Peter gets quite irritated and asks the Savior to restrict them in their talking so that others may have a better chance to participate:

> Peter fell forward and spoke to Jesus: "Lord, we will not be able to bear this woman any longer since she always takes up the time and lets none of us talk but talks much herself." [204]

> And Peter spoke: "Lord, may the women cease to ask questions so that we may ask also." And Jesus said to Mary and the women: "Let your brothers have the opportunity that they may ask also." [205]

The same occurs in other writings where Peter speaks out against the women and even battles it out with them: After all, is he not the chief apostle and does he not deserve the respect?

> Simon Peter said to them: "Let Mary go away from among us, because women are not worthy of the Life. [206]

In another text Mary reports to the apostle about a visit of the resurrected Savior to her and what he told her during this private vision. But two of the apostles doubt that this happened:

> But Andrew responded and said: "Brethren, what do you think about that what she just said? I, for my part, do not believe that the Savior has said this, for surely these teachings are not his thoughts. Peter responded and questioned her: "Did he talk secretly to a woman before he would talk to us? Shall we all turn around and listen to her? Did he prefer her over us?" Thereupon Mary wept and said to Peter: "My brother Peter, what do you believe? Do you believe I that imagined all this myself in my heart or that I would lie about the Savior?" Levi responded and said to Peter:
> "Peter, you have always been of quick temper, and now you argue against the woman like an adversary. If the Savior has made her worthy, who are you to reject her?" [207]

It is not accidental that Mary Magdalene figures in so prominently in some of the apocryphal literature. A few of these sources claim that Jesus was very intimately acquainted with her, even that she was his wife. That assumption could explain the animosity between Peter and Mary, because in her position as wife or consort of the Lord, she would naturally attract a great amount of attention and reverence away from the chief of the disciples. The papyrus just quoted continues with Andrew reminding Peter:

> For the Savior has known her thoroughly enough and loved her more than us.

---

204. *Pistis Sophia*, ch. 36.
205. *Ibid.*, ch. 149.
206. *Gospel according to Thomas*, Saying 114.
207. *Evangelium Mariae*, p. 18. It is part of the famous Papyrus Berolinensis 8502. The same parts can also be found partially in the Rylands Payrus 463.

And even Peter has to admit:

> Sister, we know that the Savior loved you more than other women. Tell us the words of the Savior which you remember and which you know, but which we do not know and have never heard.[208]

There is no problem in attributing a wife to the Savior while he was on the earth, except that many groups, and later the Catholic Church, were opposed to such a concept because of Platonic philosophies that matter was evil and that earthly desires and actions are best to be avoided. The real life, to them, was a spiritual and contemplative existence which culminated in association with the divine only when one's spirit became one with the one God, who was also a spirit. It was therefore unthinkable that God or the son of God could have any connection to material possessions, which would include a wife. If Jesus did have a spouse here on earth, any references would have been carefully excluded from the official text and doctrines, and would only have survived in apocryphal writings which were usually condemned by the dominant church and which had to be handled and circulated secretly. Whether Jesus was married or not can therefore not easily be ascertained by canonical or uncanonical literature. However, the fact remains that Mary seems to be treated in a special manner by the Savior:

—He often stayed at the house where she and her brother Lazarus lived.
—She once annointed his feet with oil and wiped them with her hair (John 12:3).
—He loved her (John 11:5).
—He called for her to come to him (John 11:28-29).
—She stood under the cross at the crucifixion, while most of the other disciples were hiding in fear (Matthew 27:56).
—She was named first, before his mother Mary (Matthew 27:56).
—She was the first to come with spices and oils to the sepulchre in the morning (John 20:1).
—Christ appeared to her first (Mark 16:9).
—She brought the news of the resurrection to the apostles (John 20:18).

It seems that Mary was always there where one would expect a wife to be. She was also the one who wanted to go to Rome to complain to Caesar about the injustice of the crucifixion:

---

208. *Ibid.,* p. 10.

Who shall make this known to all the world? I will go to Rome to Caesar. I will show him what evil Pilate has done by consenting to the wicked Jews![209]

Christ praised her very often, and in much stronger terms than the apostles, whom he at times even chided or rebuked for their little fatih:

Then answered Jesus the merciful one and said to Mary: "Mary, you blessed one, who shall be inducted into all the ordinances from on high. Speak openly, you, whose heart is more directed toward the kingdom of heaven than that of your brethren.[210]

And it happened when Mary had ended her words, he said: "Excellent, Mary, for you are blessed above all women on the earth, because you will be the fulness of all fulness, and the completion of all completion."[211]

And it happened when Jesus had heard these words, that he said: "Excellent, Mary, you blessed one, will inherit the kingdom of light."[212]

Some passages in the apocrypha are quite blunt as to the involvement of Jesus with Mary, even to the point of overstatement:[213]

There were three who walked with the Lord at all times; Mary, his mother, and her sister, and Magdalene, whom they call his wife, for Mary was his sister and his mother and his wife.[214]

And the wife of Christ is Mary Magdalene. The Lord loved Mary more than all the disciples, and kissed her on her mouth often. . . . And they said to him: "Why do you love her more than all of us?" And the Savior answered and said to them: "Why do I not love you more than her?[215]

The *Pistis Sophia* sums it all up:

But Mary Magdalene and John, the virgin disciple, shall surpass all my disciples and all men who will receive the ordinances of the unspeakable. They will be on my right hand and on my left, and I am they and they are I. . . .[216]

The question as to a marriage of Christ here on the earth is a very touchy subject and few statements have been made by responsible authorities. It is only by inference that the assumptions can be made because the only passages of affirmation can be found are in apocryphal literature, which has to be subjected to close scrutiny.

---

209. *Acts of Peter,* part I, Recession B of the Greek, ch. XI, in M. R. James, *The Apocryphal New Testament,* p. 117.

210. *Pistis Sophia,* ch. 17.

211. *Ibid.,* ch. 19.

212. *Ibid.,* ch. 61.

213. There were some Gnostic sects who attributed some almost obscene practices to Jesus and taught of his sexual relations with a woman. For example, Epiphanius, *Panarion,* 26:8, 2-3.

214. *Gospel of Philip,* Saying 32. κοινωνός can mean consort, companion, partner, or also wife. Three of the important women in Christ's life were named Mary: his mother, his sister, his wife.

215. *Ibid.,* Saying 55.

216. *Pistis Sophia,* ch. 96.

Conclusion

From the few passages cited, it can be readily seen that there are many interesting aspects to the apocrypha—aspects which can give us new insight into the early Christian writings and into the lives of the early prophets and the Savior himself. All these works are worth our attention, even though all apocryphal writings have to be approached with caution, for there is the constant possibility that they contain erroneous teachings that have been interpolated by the hands of men. The truth of non-canonical writings can be discerned, to a great degree, through the promptings of the Spirit, by those who have the ability to receive such assistance.

Many passages which were obviously false have been omitted from this writing, while others with doctrinal problems have still been included. They deserve our interest because they exhibit some colorful elements or because they have interesting parallels to the revealed words of scripture. Every reader must ascertain for himself which quotations he chooses to accept as genuine and which he feels are not.

Two more passages are cited in conclusion because they sum up the meaning of the life and ministry of the Savior and of the high position he holds:

> But he is called Christ by a certain excellent rite of religion; for as there are certain names common to kings, as Arsaces among the Persians, Caesar among the Romans, Pharaoh among the Egyptians, so among the Jews a king is called Christ.[217]

And also:

> Therefore he rose from his throne, just as a father did not hold back his own blood for the sake of his children . . . to even present mercy unto the heathen and to have compassion toward all the souls of men. As an elected king for the realm to come, he fought against the one who rules over the present world according to set laws. The thing which saddened him most of all is, that he was rejected by ignorance of those same people for which he carried on the fight. But he loved even those who hated him, and mourned for those who did not believe in him; he blessed those who despised him, and prayed for those who were his enemies. He not only acted as a father to all but also taught his disciples to act with one another as brothers. Thereby was he a father and thereby was he also a prophet. And by cautious hope will he also be a king over all his children, so that eternal peace can rise forth by his fatherly love for his children and by the virtue of the simple reverence the children will have for him as their father.[218]

---

217. Clemment, *Recognitions,* ch. 45.
218. As given in Pseudo-Clement, *Homilies,* III, 19.

Index

A

Aaron, receives his brother Moses, 125; makes the golden calf, 140.

Abel, born, 31; name, 33; righteous, 34; at the altar, 36; killed by Cain, 36; burial, 38.

Abgarus, king, writes a letter to Christ, 177.

Abiram, rebelled against Moses, 148.

Abraham, born as Abram, 66; stars at birth, 66; prophecy about his mission, 66; saved from Nimrod as a baby, 66; cultivates the ground, 68; invents a ploughing instrument, 69; refuses to build the Tower of Babel, 69; questions the use of idols, 70ff; before Nimrod, 74; in jail to be killed, 77; miraculously saved, 78; leaves Ur, 79; marries Sarai, 80; receives the priesthood, 80; practices astrology, 80, 93; missionary, 81; dedicates place for the temple, 82; moves to Egypt, 82; wife taken by Pharaoh, 85; returns to Canaan, 86; trouble with Lot, 86; hospitable, 87, 90ff; pleads for the Sodomites, 89; son promised 92, 93; Ishmael born, 93; dismisses Ishmael and Hagar, 94; Isaac born, 94; accused by Satan, 95; sacrifice of Isaac, 96ff; buries Sarah, 101; white hair, 101; marries again, 102; instructs Isaac, 102; visited by Michael, 103; death, 104.

Adam, creation, 13; viceroy of God, 15; names the animals, 15; meaning of his name, 16; marriage to Eve, 17; fall, 21; punishment by the Lord, 23; driven out of the garden, 24; receives his garments, 25; loss of glory in the mortal existence, 25; in the lone and dreary world, 26ff; learns about the redemption, 28; baptized, 29; a gentleman, 31; had a beard, 31; children, 31; prophecy of the future, 39; problems of old age, 40; seeks the oil from the tree in the garden, 42; meets with his descendants, 42; death, 42; his body on the ark, 54.

Adikam, pharaoh of Egypt, 121ff; permits Israel to leave, 131; persues Israel, 133.

Adoniah, queen of Cush, wife of Moses, 117.

Amram, father of Moses, 110.

Angels, turned wicked on earth, 47.

Animals, named by Adam, 15; disrespectful toward men, 39; became wicked and perverted, 46; gathered before the flood, 54; on the ark, 55ff.

Apostasy, at the time of Adam, 39; at the time of Noah, 45; at the time of Abraham, 62.

Apostles, called by Christ, 166; rejected by the people, 167ff; in hiding at the crucifixion, 183; see the Christ, 184; with Christ before the ascension, 185ff.

Ark, trees for it planted, 52; construction, 53; specifications, 53; light on the ark, 53; first ark burned, 53; on the water, 56; lands on Mt. Ararat, 58.

B

Balaam, astrologer of Pharaoh, 109, 113.

Baptism, of Adam and Eve, 29; of Christ, 166; teaching of Christ, 174.

Benetos, mother of Noah, 48.

Bithia, daughter of Pharaoh, finds Noah, 112; names him, 113.

Body, teaching of Christ, 174.

C

Cain, born, 31; name, 32; listens to Satan, 33; is after gain, 34; at the altar, 36; kills Abel, 36; receives a mark, 38; death, 43.

Canaan, son of Ham, violates Noah, 61; does not go to the assigned area, 81.

Christ, his foster father, 153; his mother, 155; his brothers and sisters, 157; his conception, 159; his birth, 161; as a boy, 162; performs miracles, 162ff; education, 164; his appearance, 165; his baptism, 166; call of the Twelve, 168; his teachings on the Godhead, 169; opposition in all things, 169; teachings on death and resurrection, 170; his rejection by the Israelites, 170; serving Christ, 170; teachings on knowing oneself, 171; to follow Christ, 171; teachings on the Sabbath, 172; teachings on fasting, 172; teachings on love, 173; teachings on the pre-existence, 173; concerning the physical body, 174; about prophets, 174; teachings on baptism, 174; concerning riches and wealth, 175; teachings about the word of wisdom, 175; about the hereafter, 176; a letter to and from Christ, 177; his ritual dance and song, 178; before Pilate, 179; his death, 181; in the spirit world, 181; his "secret" teachings after the resurrection, 184ff; glorified, 185;

197

NOTES

NOTES